# *CAPTAIN AMERICA*

## *and the **NATIONALIST SUPERHERO***

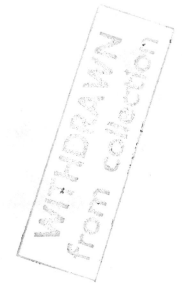

*Massacre in Haditha*, by Tanya Tier. (Used with permission from the artist.)

Jason Dittmer

# CAPTAIN AMERICA

### and the

# NATIONALIST
# SUPERHERO

## METAPHORS, NARRATIVES,
## AND GEOPOLITICS

TEMPLE UNIVERSITY PRESS
PHILADELPHIA

TEMPLE UNIVERSITY PRESS
Philadelphia, Pennsylvania 19122
www.temple.edu/tempress

Library of Congress Cataloging-in-Publication Data

Dittmer, Jason.
  Captain America and the nationalist superhero : metaphors,
narratives, and geopolitics / Jason Dittmer.
    p. cm.
  Includes bibliographical references and index.
  ISBN 978-1-4399-0976-8 (cloth : alk. paper) —
ISBN 978-1-4399-0977-5 (pbk. : alk. paper) —
ISBN 978-1-4399-0978-2 (e-book)   1.  Comic books, strips, etc.—
History and criticism.   2.  Superheroes in literature.
3.  Nationalism and literature.   4.  Geopolitics—Social aspects.
5.  Popular culture—Political aspects.   6.  America, Captain
(Fictitious character)   I.  Title.
  PN6714.D58 2013
  741.5'3581—dc23
                                                        2012015512

Printed in the United States of America

2  4  6  8  9  7  5  3  1

*For Stephanie, my everything*

# Contents

# Acknowledgments

I owe special thanks to Paul Adams, Caroline Bressey, Michael Brown, Sean Carter, Simon Dalby, Klaus Dodds, Dan Hassler-Forest, James Kneale, and Alec Murphy for providing feedback on draft chapters. Many of the insights about Canada and Canadian superheroes belong to my friend and collaborator Soren Larsen, who partnered with me to conduct the Canadian portion of this research. He graciously allowed me to use our findings in this book.

I am also indebted to Randy Scott and the Special Collections staff at Michigan State University, to Steven Hensen and the Special Collections staff at Duke University, and to the very helpful staff at the Canadian Library and Archives. More generally, I am grateful to the faculties at Georgia Southern University and University College London for their support during this project. I completed the first draft of this book while I was on a visiting fellowship at the London School of Economics, to which I am grateful as well.

The research findings herein were tested and refined through innumerable conference presentations and at seminars and colloquia at the University of Georgia, Ohio University, the University of Sussex, the University of Amsterdam, and Johannes Gutenberg University. I am grateful to all participants for their thoughts and criticisms. Research funding was provided by the British Academy, a Canadian High Commission Faculty Research Grant, and a Georgia Southern University Faculty Research Grant.

I owe the greatest debt of gratitude to my supportive friends and family—especially Stephanie Dittmer, who, from the very beginning of this project, was my unceasing advocate.

# CAPTAIN AMERICA
## and the NATIONALIST SUPERHERO

*1*

# Introducing Nationalist Superheroes

The painting in this book's frontispiece (and on the cover of the paperback edition), *Massacre in Haditha*, by British Jordanian artist Tanya Tier, is a revisioning of Pablo Picasso's *Massacre in Korea* (1951—see Figure 1.1). In this painting Picasso expressed his horror at the American machine-gunning of civilian refugees during the Korean War (at No Gun Ri, 1950).[1] These refugees had been trying to get behind American lines during the early stages of the war to avoid being caught between the two armies; however, the Americans, concerned about North Korean infiltrators, massacred the whole group. Picasso's painting can be understood as representing a violent, geographic concern about shoring up the barrier between "our" territory (behind the lines) and its constitutive outside.[2] Moved to rework the painting for a more contemporary audience when she saw the mirror image of Picasso's vulnerable civilians in the twenty-four Iraqis murdered by American Marines at Haditha in November 2005, Tier used the visual language of superheroes:

> [With the figures] dressed as the iconic fictitious characters which are so entrenched in American culture, the powerful imagery of the super-hero is a reference to the jingoism and propaganda deployed by governments and western media commentators when reporting the conflict. The US government in particular needed to establish and convince the public—in the most simplistic of terms—that their soldiers are the "good guys." Donning the superhero uniform gave the troops permission to become defenders of the faith, protectors of the American people and safe-guarders of American interests. The way the conflict was being portrayed in the US media reduced it to the level of comic book fantasy or video game, an imaginary world where the good guys ("us") always triumph over the bad guys ("them").[3]

Tier understands superheroes as more than propaganda for U.S. foreign policy; she sees the superhero genre as contributing to public discourse around the

Figure 1.1: *Massacre in Korea*, by Pablo Picasso (1951). (Copyright © Succession Picasso/ DACS, London, 2011. Used with permission.)

invasion of Iraq. To Tier's own commentary I would add only that the garish colors that she uses for the superheroes in her painting add a sense of absurdity—how can people who look so silly be doing something so serious?

The combination of power and silliness embedded in *Massacre in Haditha* is central to the politics of superheroes—they are both bluntly obvious and seemingly innocuous. Superheroes suffuse our everyday existence via TV cartoons, big-budget cinema, and everyday objects such as T-shirts and Pez dispensers, occupying narratives in which Manichean categories of good and evil are embodied by heroes and villains, usually marked as such by their name and costume for all to see. Tier's superheroes juxtapose America's simplistic moralistic framing of its foreign policy with its near-limitless capacity to inflict violence on others in a way that simultaneously illustrates the enormity of this power and belittles it.

This understanding of superheroes as simplistic, brawny, and reflecting a uniquely American understanding of power and morality is widespread and seemingly "commonsense," for both their fans and their critics.[4] In fact, this ability to serve as a proxy for American geopolitical identity has made the superhero genre the subject of critical debate for many decades. However, one of the goals of this book is to reposition the role of superheroes within popular understandings of geopolitics and international relations from being understood as a "reflection" of preexisting and seemingly innate American values to being recognized as a discourse *through which* the world becomes understandable. In this view, the pop-cultural dimensions of politics (e.g., superheroes) are neither the result of political meta-beliefs (such as American exceptionalism) nor the condensation of economic ideology.[5] Rather, superheroes are *co-constitutive* elements of both American identity and the U.S. government's foreign policy practices. Obviously, superheroes are not the only, or even the most important, elements of the muscular geopolitical discourse identified as Americanism. Nevertheless superheroes serve as a crucial resource for legitimating, contesting, and reworking states' foreign policies, and as such have arguably grown in importance over the past several decades.

The nationalist superhero subgenre is the focus of this book because this subgenre speaks most clearly to a phenomenon that has been at the center of work in the field of critical geopolitics: the state-centrism that has become the focus of political thought over the past century.[6] While there has been a lot of emphasis on state actors positioning the state as the only legitimate venue for politics, scant research considers the processes by which geographical imaginations of everyday people come to have the nation-state centrally embedded within them.[7] The fusion of the nation (an identity through which people define themselves) and the state (a sovereign governmental apparatus) into the nation-state is accomplished precisely through the banalization of elision. The terms *nation* and *state* are thrown around with imprecision, and the same adjectives (e.g., *British, Brazilian, Belarussian*) are used to identify both the nation and the state. As Matthew Sparke argues, it is the hyphen in *nation-state* that

> came to represent two mutually reinforcing geographic processes. On the one side were the diverse state practices such as border policing, migration control, and planning that regulated territorial belonging. On the other side were the modern space-producing social and cultural dynamics that, in generating taken-for-granted national landscapes, national monuments, national maps, and so on, gave state regulation its space and place of legitimacy.[8]

The purpose of this book is then to describe not just what nationalist superhero narratives *say*, but also what kind of work they *do* in setting the political stage. This introductory chapter contributes to the book's overarching goal by introducing the subgenre of nationalist superheroes, tracing the influence of the subgenre's origins on its politics, and illustrating the diffusion/adaptation of the subgenre from the United States into the British and Canadian contexts.

Methodologically the remaining chapters of the book proceed largely using discourse analysis of comic books to examine how the territorial nation-state is produced as a dominant scale of identity and politics, supplemented when possible with reference to interviews with writers as well as readers' letters to the editor. This is done to show both groups' understandings of the nationalist superhero discourse and to trace the active negotiation between the two groups. Ultimately it is not writers and artists who construct meaning from comic books, but readers. Nevertheless the permeability of the barrier between these two groups makes it difficult to envision the production of nationalist superhero discourse as anything but a collaborative effort; not only do the groups mix in regular conventions and via social media, but also many of the names on letters to the editor make their way to the bylines of the title page.[9] These interactions might be understood as Charles Tilly's "creative interaction," which he exemplifies with jazz or soccer: "participants work within rough agreements on procedures and outcomes [e.g., genre conventions]; arbiters [market capitalism] set limits on performances; individual dexterity, knowledge, and disciplined preparation [cultural capital among writers, artists, and readers] generally yield superior play; yet the rigid equivalent of military drill destroys the enterprise."[10]

This understanding of narrative as emergent highlights the complex question of authorship;[11] while literary scholars have questioned the idea of the author for several decades now, the question is particularly vexed in regard to mainstream, commercial superhero comics. Even the question of authorship at its most basic is problematic: who is the "author," the writer or the artist? This question can be answered only in more specific contexts, as the relative power relations between these two roles have ebbed and flowed in recent decades. Further, how much agency can be exercised by either of these roles in the face of editorial or corporate opposition to a plot or specific image? How does even the tacit *potential* for editorial intervention shape the creative process? Interviews with writers, conducted for this project, can call attention to the behind-the-scenes negotiation between writers, artists, and editors, but by definition they are partial accounts that tend to emphasize the writers' agency. The preceding questions become all the more interesting given the transnational basis of some of these relationships. Many of the examples traced in this book are of British or Canadian writers and artists creating nationalist superhero tales while working for American editors at an American company (Marvel Comics). Are these "indigenously" produced comics, or are they forms of cultural imperialism? Or are both of these terms inadequate for this form of cultural production?

The question of authorship becomes even more complicated when the audience is considered. While all commercial popular culture is in some way a prisoner of its audience, comic books in particular have always lived close to the edge, trying to track the latest trends in broader culture. Comics that sell poorly rarely last more than an issue or two after they become unprofitable. This relentless exposure to market forces means that the audience, or at least the specter of the audience, looms increasingly large in the production process and therefore shares in the author-ity of narrative.

So who is this audience? Stereotypes abound, some with connection to truth and some outdated exaggerations. The popular image of comics as children's fare dates from the medium's earliest days, when they were included as inserts in other periodicals or used as giveaways in products sold to mothers. Certainly the average reader of a superhero comic during World War II was a preadolescent male, although millions of comics were also sent overseas as entertainment for the troops (Figure 1.2). However, as the medium has aged, so has its readership. In the 1960s and 1970s comics become popular fare on college campuses, and the introduction of direct distribution (skipping news-

Figure 1.2: A small boy, approximately six years of age, sitting and reading a *Captain America* comic at a newsstand, circa 1942. (North Carolina Collection, University of North Carolina Library at Chapel Hill. Photo by Hugh Morton. Used with permission.)

stands entirely and instead going only to specialist stores) in the 1980s eroded the younger casual fan base in favor of older fans who had been collecting for their adult lives. While the audience of superhero comics certainly skews male, it is not as overwhelmingly male as stereotyped in popular culture.[12] Letters to the editor are not, of course, necessarily accurate representations of audience opinion, as those who write are, of course, both self-selecting (requiring time, enthusiasm, and so on) and editorially selected. Letters-to-the-editor columns are typically full of praise for the creative staff, but this makes the eruption of controversy all the more notable and interesting. Often editors cultivate controversy and let debates unfold for months at a time to show the cultural relevance of their product and give the impression of their comics as part of the public sphere. For these reasons and more (most especially the lack of alternative archives), analysis of letters to the editor has become common in comics studies as a way into comics' reception at the time of publication.[13]

In the United States the superhero genre has become nearly synonymous with comic books (many other genres exist, but they are commercially dwarfed by superheroes). Even if the superhero genre is primarily associated with the United States and carries the trace of its origins, it is nevertheless a resolutely transnational phenomenon whose appeal exceeds national borders. This book's engagement follows the primary genealogy of nationalist superheroes from their original American context into Canada and the United Kingdom. Nationalist superheroes have been used in the past as a way of "localizing" the comic book as a commodity and trying to subvert nationalistic pride to sell American-style comic books in countries with their own publishing tradition.[14] Comic books in Japan and the Francophone world (the two main centers of comic book production outside the Anglophone world) tend to emphasize genres other than superheroes, although both have their own superhero or superhero-esque traditions. In Japan, for example, there are long traditions of both super-robots (such as Astro Boy), collective teams (such as the Mighty Morphin Power Rangers, in which each member is fairly similar to all the others and teamwork is key; these are different from U.S. superhero teams, which are always groups of distinct individuals), and occasionally combinations of both (such as Voltron).[15] To the French the notion of the superhero is not so foreign, but nevertheless it is marked as a distinctly American phenomenon. For instance, Fantax, arguably the first French superhero (first published in 1946), is actually Lord Horace Neighbour, a diplomat at the British embassy in Washington, D.C. This externalization of the superhero to the Anglo-American context indicates its identification as exotic to the French milieu.

This chapter now turns to an examination of the nationalist superhero as a particular subgenre, initially by examining the origins of the subgenre, as this starting point provides the array of cultural resources with which subsequent practices of production and consumption play. This focus on the generic conventions continues with a critique of the nationalist superhero subgenre as crystallizing a relationship between power, authority, and violence that contributes to both traditions of American exceptionalism and exclusivist state-centrism. The chapter concludes by tracing the diffusion of the subgenre to Canada and the United Kingdom, where it was transformed both by the exigencies of the publishing industry and by the local contexts of nationalism.

## Definitions and Conventions

So what is a superhero? Peter Coogan argues that the superhero genre is linked to the characteristics of the protagonist in ways that other genres are not—murder mysteries need not be about detectives, for instance, but are instead defined by the kind of narrative that unfolds.[16] Coogan identifies the hero's altruistic mission, special powers, and secret identity (i.e., costume and code name) as the core elements of the superhero genre but concedes that not every superhero meets all three criteria and that some elements are common to other genres. This somewhat tortured attempt to focus on the protagonist in order to shore up an exclusivist notion of the superhero genre as distinct from science fiction or fantasy leads to some pretty arbitrary boundary marking on Coogan's part: "If a character to some degree fits the mission-powers-identity qualifications of the definition but can be firmly and sensibly placed within another genre, then the character is not a superhero."[17]

Rather than obsess about who is a superhero and who is not, I see it perhaps more useful to consider genres as continually in interaction with one other, each a hybrid form, continually in process, with influences from a wide array of antecedents. The naming and delineating of what is, or is not, within a genre is itself an act of power and control. Richard Reynolds argues that "the superhero genre is tightly defined and defended by its committed readership—often to the exasperation of writers and artists, many of whom have proclaimed it to be a worn-out formula from as long ago as the 1970s."[18] Coogan's protagonist-focused genre definition is drawn from Judge Learned Hand's definition of the superhero in a 1952 copyright infringement ruling—a legal context that values exclusivity and intellectual originality rather than hybridity and intellectual borrowing, and which explains the Coogan definition's focus on the protagonist (the case was about whether Captain Marvel was a copy of Superman) rather than on narrative elements of the superhero genre (which are not copyrightable).[19] Following from this, it is correct to assume that *this* book attempts no final definition of superheroes, nationalist or otherwise.

This book's empirical focus is not on superheroes generally, but instead on a subgenre identified as that of the *nationalist superhero*. To be clear, my calling forth of this subgenre is just as much an act of power as Coogan's attempt to define the larger superhero genre. The term *nationalist superhero* is not in wide usage, and above all it reflects my interests in geopolitics and nationalism. My intention is not, however, to produce a once-and-for-all delineation of the subgenre; rather, it is to conjure up a working definition of *nationalist superhero* that is both flexible and useful for my purposes. These are superhero narratives in which the hero (or very rarely, the heroine) explicitly identifies himself or herself as representative and defender of a specific nation-state, often through his or her name, uniform, and mission. It is, admittedly, a thin line that separates Captain America from Superman: the latter fights for "truth, justice, and the American way" and has his origins in an American immigrant narrative.[20] Still, Superman is generally a prosocial hero, fighting for the American people (among others) rather than for America as an abstract idea.[21] Captain America, on the other hand, was written as a super-soldier created by the U.S. government and later sees himself as the living embodiment of the American Dream (rather than a tool of the state). When you add in the star-spangled uniform and the name, the comparison is not even close anymore. The World War II American newsstand would have been covered in nationalist superheroes, but in the post–World War II era, nationalist superheroes such as Captain America are a tiny proportion of the superheroes in publication; there are many more generally prosocial heroes such as Spider-Man and Batman than there are nationalist superheroes such as Union Jack or Captain Canuck. Because of this extreme minority status, many of the arguments that follow in this book can also be made about superheroes in general, and indeed my research draws on the insights of the broader literature on superheroes.

Nevertheless, the nationalist superhero bears an additional burden that other superheroes do not—embodying the nation-state. This embodiment has implications for the kind of stories that are likely to be told and the ways they are likely to be read. Larry Porter wrote a fan letter to *Captain America* to express his vision of the hero as distinct from other superheroes:

> Captain America should be a globetrotting adventurer who is heavily involved with [U.S. spy agency] SHIELD. He should be fighting against the things that threaten the freedoms and liberties that he has sworn to protect. [. . .] Too many times, it seemed like Cap was really only interested in protecting New York City from the latest spandex-clad bad guy.[22]

Comics writer Rob Williams puts it this way: "There's just so much inherent subtext, metaphor and gravitas the moment you dress a character in a flag and make him the symbol of a nation. You can't help but carry issues and a certain depth into such a story, even if you're ostensibly telling a knockabout action narrative."[23] Thus, while superheroes like Iron Man and Spider-Man can be seen as rooted in U.S. foreign policy, they are not freighted in the same way as Captain America and his ilk.[24]

## Origins and Politics of the Nationalist Superhero Genre

The superhero genre and its conventions emerged out of the pulp heroes and masked crime fighters of the Depression, with the locus of publishing centered in New York City. Because of this, the genre crystallized in a particular spatio-temporal context that has implications for understanding the superhero genre today.[25] Equally, the beginning of World War II in Europe soon thereafter and the eventual entry of the United States into that war sparked the emergence of a subgenre: nationalist superheroes. Nationalist superheroes, while ultimately produced and consumed through an open and flexible set of cultural resources, owe the fundamentals of their genre to this point of emergence. Mikhail Bakhtin describes genres as "organs of memory" that carry their origins into the present; through them cultural artifacts "remember the past [. . .] and redefine present experience in an additional way," which Bakhtin refers to as "double-voicing."[26] Because tracing this double-voicing as the nationalist superhero genre localizes in new contexts is, in many ways, the task of this book, we now turn to the creation of the subgenre.

### New York Origins

The archetype of the nationalist superhero is undoubtedly Captain America, although he was not the first. Captain America first saw print after the start of the war in Europe but still ten months before Pearl Harbor and America's first bloodying.[27] That Captain America was fighting Nazis well before the U.S. armed forces were (he appears on the cover of *Captain America Comics #1* punching Hitler in the face) is an intriguing historical oddity, the explanation of which helps to explain the emergence of the subgenre itself.

Most superheroes avoided the war in Europe for reasons both creative and commercial. First, it was difficult to imagine a scenario in which a super-empowered hero like Superman could intervene in Europe and not fundamentally alter the balance of combat.[28] More crassly, comic book publishers were in no hurry to alienate isolationists in the United States. Crucial to breaking the hold of this studious fence-sitting was the news of *Kristallnacht*, rumors of which swept through the Jewish American communities of New York. Given the heavy Jewish presence in the comic book industry among writers, artists, and publishers, it is perhaps then not surprising that superheroes soon began to turn their attention to purported German plots to strike at the United States. Jews had congregated in the comic book industry in part because of exclusion from higher-end illustration jobs, and their ethnicity inflected many of their products. Michael Chabon, in his novel *The Adventures of Kavalier and Clay*, highlights the historical links between early superheroes and the Jewish tradition of the golem, an enchanted man made from clay to protect the Jewish community from oppressors. Writer-artist Will Eisner, who directly participated in this early Golden Age of comics, saw Jewish mythology as directly inspiring superheroes: "*We have this history of impossible solutions for insoluble problems.*"[29]

Joe Simon and Jack Kirby, the creators of Captain America, had teamed up as a freelance writer/artist (respectively) collaboration to sell ideas to the publishers. They saw in Adolf Hitler a believable "supervillain" making a bid for global domination: "There never had been a truly believable villain in comics. But Adolf was alive, hated by more than half of the world."[30] They imagined Hitler's antithesis to be a member of the U.S. armed forces, clad in a star-spangled uniform with a shield shaped like a police badge to connote impartiality and justice, and aided by his teen sidekick, Bucky. Here, however, they ran aground on the commercial circumstances of the early comic book industry—their badge-like shield too closely resembled that of an already existing nationalist superhero—the somewhat unimaginatively named hero "the Shield." With the threat of a lawsuit Simon and Kirby were forced to change the design to a round shield, which as it happens was much better as it allowed Captain America to hurl his shield as an offensive weapon and have it (rather implausibly) bounce right back to him.

Jack Kirby's art went on to be legendary within the comic book industry, and his career lasted for more than fifty years. At this early stage in his career, however, his artistic style was not yet developed into his distinctive later style. *Captain America Comics* provided a forum through which Kirby could express his view of America from an immigrant neighborhood in New York City (Kirby was the son of an Austrian immigrant and grew up in the Lower East Side of Manhattan in a Jewish neighborhood).

He [Kirby . . .] cited his experiences growing up in a tough neighborhood where good boys learned to survive by acting tough and standing
up to bullies as a primary inspiration for his comic book work and his
politics[.] Kirby later recalled that he had been drawn to comic art because of its simplicity and directness, which he equated with the American way. "I thought comics were a common form of art and strictly
American," he said. "America was the home of the common man, and
show me the common man that can't do a comic."[31]

The comic's first issue (marked by the aforementioned Hitler-bashing cover art)
sold more than one million copies and sparked a flurry of imitation not seen
since Superman's appearance in *Action Comics* two years earlier. The fan club
for Captain America that was started in response to this outpouring was called
the Sentinels of Liberty and encouraged fans of Captain America to partake in
his mission of protecting the United States from extraterritorial incursions by
being aware of activities in their hometowns and reporting suspicious behavior
to adults. The Sentinels of Liberty would even appear in the comic's narratives
as allies of Captain America, further blurring the relationship between vigilance in the comic book and the vigilance to be exercised by readers.

Simon and Kirby would not last on the comic book, their tenure being
short as were many in the industry at this time. They accepted a better offer from another publisher, but their hero carried on in others' hands (Kirby
would return to the title in the 1960s). The success of *Captain America Comics* and Hitler's public criticism of Superman as a Jew (Superman comics were
banned in Nazi-occupied Europe) pushed all the comics publishers into the
interventionist column well before the United States became actively involved
in the war. Captain America and his various clones (as well as those few nationalist heroes who preceded him, such as the Shield), while resulting from
a particular ethnic and commercial context, had managed to break out and
enter the national consciousness. The conventions of the nationalist superhero
were now well enough known that even those who never read comics understood the idea of a superhero explicitly connected to a state through name,
costume, and values.

## The Politics of American Exceptionalism

Captain America's small role in the shifting of the United States toward an
interventionist attitude is but one manifestation of how superheroes, and especially their nationalist variant, can be understood as geopolitical. Superheroes are not reflections of, but are instead (along with many other elements)
co-constitutive of, the discourse popularly known as American exceptionalism.
American exceptionalism refers to the idea that the United States is distinct
from other countries as a result of its historical development, its frontier experience, or simply its function within the international order.[32] A wide array of

arguments has historically been brought to bear in the effort to represent the United States as fundamentally unlike other countries. The discourse of American exceptionalism is not only produced through the arguments of political and academic elites; it is also co-constituted through popular culture.

Robert Jewett and John Shelton Lawrence argue that in the 1930s an "American monomyth" emerged that became the basis for a whole range of narrative storytelling.[33] In this myth, a feminized community is endangered or exploited by a rogue masculine force. A nomadic hero arrives on the scene and, noting the exploitation, remedies the situation through equally masculine intervention.[34] This hero, however, never remains to partake in the domestic tranquillity that he (indeed, the hero is almost always male) has produced but instead moves on, presumably to save more communities. This is most obviously apparent in the western genre of movies, which emerged during this time to narrate the American experience on the frontier, a site simultaneously understood as being beyond the reach of the state's judicial apparatus and yet also the mythic locus of freewheeling American entrepreneurialism and individual responsibility. A gunman (usually wearing a white hat) rises up organically from civil society to impose order but then fades away, neither retaining the political power he has temporarily taken up nor even remaining in the town—but instead riding off into the sunset.

Jewett and Lawrence's American monomyth can be compared to Joseph Campbell's "classical monomyth,"[35] to which Campbell mistakenly attributed universality. Nevertheless, it is a common narrative structure that certainly has pride of place in popular culture (famously influencing George Lucas in his production of the *Star Wars* trilogy).[36] In the classical monomyth, a male youth comes of age by leaving the community, facing adversity and being transformed by it in a foreign land, and then returning home to take on a leadership role within the community. Jewett and Lawrence argue that the spatial elements of these narratives are central; indeed they highlight the hero's lack of reintegration into sociopolitical structures within the American monomyth. "We suggest that this new myth system, which crystallized its conventions of plot and character in the axial decade of the 1930s, shows a democratic face in that the protagonist is an Everyman, yet has a pop-fascist dimension in that these unelected, law-transcending figures exercise superpowers to overcome foes."[37] This quotation highlights Jewett and Lawrence's belief that the superhero genre clearly adopts the narrative of the American monomyth, with superheroes not physically moving from community to community but instead refusing to be bound by societal authorities, as evidenced by the secret identities and the occasional cooperation with, but not subordination to, legally constituted authorities.

This lack of integration, and the desire for liberation from society's shackles that it enunciates, has clear links to American exceptionalism. Donald Pease argues that the creation of the National Security State in the 1950s marked the beginning of a new spatiality:

In conducting the cold war, the state was neither within the order nor outside the order. The state situated itself within the order that it protected but it occupied the position of internal externality of the exception. For in order to defend the order it also represented, the state was first required to declare itself an exception to the order it regulated. The State of the Exception is marked by absolute independence from any juridical control and any reference to the normal political order.[38]

Pease's notion of the U.S. state as an "internal externality" hints at the complex topology at work here; the United States is both exemplar and exempted. This ambiguity is found embedded in Scot Myers's letter to the editor published in *Captain America* in 1998: "The Japan backdrop was fabulous and really served to show how truly international Captain 'America' can really be. I hope you take advantage of this while, at the same time, keeping him the symbol of the best our nation has to offer."[39]

Copious amounts of ink have been spilled arguing for the freedom of American action from the very liberal international order that the United States has fought to produce since President Woodrow Wilson's Fourteen Points.[40] This liberal international order includes the restrictions on the use of force found within the UN Charter, the legal requirements for the treatment of prisoners found in the Geneva Conventions, and the International Criminal Court (ICC).[41] Each of these institutions or legal frameworks has been in the news over the past decade as the U.S. government has variously pretended to follow the first, subverted the second, and outright opposed the third. Pierre-Robert Prosper, a diplomat in the George W. Bush administration, argued against the establishment of the ICC in 2002 in this manner: "What we've learnt from the war on terror is that rather than creating an international mechanism to deal with these issues it is better to organize an international mandate that authorizes states to use their unilateral tools to tackle the problems we have."[42]

By shifting the scale from the "real" international to the fictive national, it is possible to find arguments made within superhero comics that mirror those made by Prosper. For instance, the *Civil War* crossover spectacular found within Marvel Comics in 2006–2007 told the story of a schism within the superhero community over a proposed law that would require superheroes to register their true identities with the government and work as civil servants under properly constituted authority. This story line was widely seen by critics as an analogue for debates over the USA PATRIOT Act and related Bush administration policies that seemed to promise security in exchange for civil liberties, but this interpretation relied on the assumption that readers would identify with the anti-registration superheroes rather than with the vulnerable humans forced to scatter in terror whenever superhero and supervillain meet in their highly destructive melees. An alternative (but rarely voiced) reading would take the perspective of these usually unnamed members of the public and might see the *anti*-registration superheroes as analogues for the Bush administration, which denied the claim on it made by other branches of the U.S. government as well as international actors such as the United Nations and its member states.

It is impossible to say why the most popular reading of this story line, with rebel heroes analogous to everyday Americans and pro-registration heroes seen as proxies for the Bush administration, became hegemonic in the media, but it certainly has something to do with the positioning of readers' subjectivities via generic conventions. Superheroes almost always serve as the moral center of their own story line, and the desire bubbling beneath the surface of many readers' engagements with superhero comic books—the desire to leap, fly, hurl, pound—further encourages identification with the superpowered. Geopolitics scholar Gearoid Ó Tuathail identifies a similar phenomenon in his exegesis of the film *Behind Enemy Lines* (2001): "*Behind Enemy Lines* articulates an [American] 'everyman' frustration with the confusion of the post–Cold War era and then delivers on the desire for a Manichean world of clarity and moral certainty. Action and righteous violence are made possible by a clarified world where there are recognizably othered enemies and adversaries."[43] The desire for this kind of cathartic violence in the face of frustration, whether the frustration over the inability of the United States to truly tee off on an enemy in the wake of the September 11, 2001, attacks or the more mundane frustration of a comic book reader with his or her banal existence within a society full of norms and requirements, speaks to the strong forces seeking to align the perspective of the reader with that of the superhero.

Another factor central to this interpretation of the *Civil War* story line is the emplotment of Captain America as the leader of the rebellion against the Superhero Registration Act.[44] This aspect is highly pertinent, given the historical use of Captain America as a self-proclaimed representative of the American Dream or American ideals (often as a mirror to hold up to the U.S. government's activities, which is more fully detailed in the chapters to come). Captain America's views on the Superhero Registration Act can be usefully juxtaposed with those of Pierre-Robert Prosper on the ICC, quoted previously. The following exchange is between Captain America and his girlfriend, Sharon Carter:

> **Captain America:** Should [superheroes] be denied the right to make that choice [exposing their secret identities]?
> **Sharon Carter:** Maybe . . . yes. Because they're risking other people's lives every time they jump into a firefight. And because it's against the law. And the rule of law is what this country is founded on.
> **Captain America:** No . . . it was founded on breaking the law. Because the law was wrong.
> **Sharon Carter:** That's semantics, Steve. You know what I mean . . .
> **Captain America:** It's not semantics, Sharon. It's the heart of the issue. The Registration Act is another step toward government control.[45]

Thus, Captain America discursively frames the Superhero Registration Act in terms of government control and individual liberty—the same terms that the U.S. government uses to describe its own need to escape the bounds of international society. The need for independent action is claimed in both cases by the strong, *ostensibly* to protect the weak. Both "superpowers" serve as American exceptions from the legal orders that they purport to protect. Therefore, the generic conventions of the nationalist superhero speak to the era of American hegemony in which the genre emerged and justify exactly the kind of superheroic interventions valorized in the comics.

## Bolstering State-Centrism and the Weberian State

While generically it can be said that superheroes make an argument for American exceptionalism, as stated earlier nationalist superheroes such as Captain America overtly introduce the nation-state into the equation. These heroes have a somewhat complicated position vis-à-vis the states from which they draw their names. On the one hand, it is clear that nationalist superheroes play a part in the discursive formation of the state-centric politics that define our contemporary world. It has been noted by many that the discourse of politics has long been colonized by the state.[46] For example, politics is defined as either *within* formal state institutions (domestic politics) or *between* states (international politics). Feminist scholars have in particular noted that this categorization limits politics to that which is addressed by state institutions, which have historically had an ambivalent relationship to women and women's issues.[47] The divide between a public sphere of manly politics and a private sphere of feminine domesticity erases other types of politics, such as that within households.[48]

Max Weber famously, and influentially, argued that the ideal state claims a monopoly on the legitimate use of violence in a specific territory, although in practice this is never a complete closure and violence is used in many circumstances that are socially acceptable, such as in self-defense or the protection of others.[49] It is in this sense that nationalist superheroes remain "rogue" actors, whose personal vision of justice supersedes purportedly inept legal bureaucracies. Jason Bainbridge argues for the longer roots of this aspect of superheroism: "Invoking the idea of justice in the absence of law is hardly surprising as it ties back into most mythologies' notion of justice being *embodied*, from the blindfolded figure of Justice herself to Greek ideas of the Furies and the Nemesis."[50] Just as many scholars argue that the difference between "rogue states" and the hegemonic state is the hegemon's ability to script its actions as innately legitimate,[51] superheroes, by dint of their emplotment and alignment with the status quo, can be understood as distinguishable from their opponents not through the nature of their violence (although this attempt is often made through narrative, both in comics and in international relations) but through their political objectives.

With this in mind, the existence of nationalist superheroes, and their use of vigilante violence, can paradoxically be understood to buttress the state's claims to a monopoly of legitimate violence by taking the nationalist super-hero's "necessary" violence and linking it through name and visual motif to the state. Indeed, at varying times superheroes are brought under the umbrella of the Weberian ideal state's monopoly on power by being "deputized" or otherwise authorized by the government. Consider this letter to the editor from reader Shon, who regrets Captain America's association with the superhero/ vigilante tradition:

> I think it's about time Cap discarded his mask. I know the "A" and "Ol' Winghead" are part of the legend and Cap's tradition, but masks are still considered by law agencies as the tools of vigilantes, no matter how well-respected the hero. And has Cap not stood for truth and justice all these years?[52]

This is especially evident in the Canadian and British nationalist superheroes, although tensions still emerge because of the genre's links to American hege-mony and the international interventions it justifies:

> *Captain Britain* writer Paul Cornell: "The trouble with Captain America is that he almost *is* the authority. He represents it to an extraordinary degree. [. . .] With Captain Britain, I think we're more comfortable with the idea of—well, it's a socialist thing—the authority feels elected by us. There's something [of] the bunker in Utah about the superhero myth. [. . .] I didn't think [having British superheroes work for the state] was too controversial, but it was controversial [. . .] because the readers of this are from way within the genre and they're used to the American version of "superhero versus authority."
>
> Me: They may have the British form of government in mind but they have an American form of superheroes.
>
> Paul Cornell: Absolutely.[53]

The complicity of nationalist superheroes (or lack thereof) with state author-ity is here shown to be complicated by the national contexts of representation, production, and consumption. The remainder of this chapter outlines the transnational diffusion of the nationalist superhero genre. These processes of transnationalism and localization are important, as they inform the analysis of subsequent chapters.

## Genre Diffusion

While the "American-ness" of the superhero genre is a central concern of the exceptionalist argument outlined previously, the origins of the superhero genre transcend national borders as does the appeal of superheroes. Canada even claims Superman as one of its own, based on Joe Shuster's Toronto birth[54]—but more significantly, Richard Reynolds sees the cultural antecedents of super-heroes as transnational: "Avenging 'Lone Wolf' heroes abounded in popular narrative of the 1930s and '40s on *both* sides of the Atlantic: from Doc Savage to Philip Marlowe, from Hannay in Hitchcock's *39 Steps* to the Green Hornet, from Rick Blaine in *Casablanca* to Captain Midnight of the radio serials."[55] Thus, any attempt to tie superheroes exclusively to the United States is thwarted, if not vanquished, by the historical evidence of transnational cultural flows both at the origins of the genre and now, with the superhero genre successful in many places around the world. Reader David Gordon-Macdonald wrote in to *Captain America* in 1982 and illustrates the transnational appeal of the nationalist superhero:

> It seems strange to me that I'm writing to the editors of *Captain America* as my premiere piece of feedback. I'm not even an American. In fact, I was not even born a Canadian, but emigrated from Britain. Despite these facts, Cap still speaks to me directly and not just because of incisive, moving scripts and expressive artwork. [. . .] The American dream is a human (and humane) dream which has been held as long as there has been freedom to aspire to. [. . .] The same dream is represented by Captain Britain—a man of peace and intellect who nevertheless fights to defend what he believes in from those who would destroy it. Alpha Flight represents Canada better than any one man could, as Canada is a mosaic, made up of many federated cultures. Such figures as Captain America, Captain Britain and Alpha Flight stand for the ideals of our Anglo-American culture.[56]

Therefore, what is interesting is how the *nationalist* superhero genre has been localized by creators and readers as it has shifted from its Jewish American roots in New York to new national contexts. This is intimately linked to the economics of comic book publishing, which make superhero publishing in both Canada and the United Kingdom risky propositions. Therefore complex interconnections exist between comics producers and consumers in all three countries. At some times Canadian nationalist superheroes have been published indigenously, and at other times they have been published by Marvel Comics, a New York–based publishing house. Similarly, the British nationalist superheroes studied in this book have been published by Marvel.[57] To add more complexity, these heroes have often been written and drawn by Canadian or British talent that has been hired by Marvel (such as the Canadian John Byrne or the Englishman Alan Moore). This makes the question of "authorship" an intriguing one, given the difficulty of teasing out the roles of publishers, writers, and artists in sculpting these nationalist narratives.[58] Instead of seeing this as a reason not to interrogate these issues or seeing these texts as a valid or invalid example of a singular, authentic, and autochthonous nationalism, however, I prefer to see the texts as enunciating a *particular* nationalism. Indeed, it is the details and peculiarity of production and reception that make this transnational process so fascinating.

## Canada

The economic relationship between the United States and Canada has long been asymmetrical. This extends into the realm of comic book publishing as well. In the late 1930s, when Superman and the other Golden Age heroes were first being produced, Canadians received their dose of action and excitement from the same place Americans did—New York publishers. American comic book producers had many ingrained advantages over any potential Canadian rivals—namely better market access and lower distribution costs. However, the entry of Canada into World War II changed the economic equation; the 1940 War Exchange Conservation Act restricted importation of nonessential goods so as to maintain Canadian stocks of American hard currency. In the sudden absence of the comics deluge from south of the border, four Canadian comics publishers emerged: Maple Leaf Publishing, Anglo-American, Hillborough Studios, and Bell Features.[59] Wartime rationing provided a brief respite from American domination, and a Canadian-based comic book industry effloresced. "While all four firms were to publish material in a wide variety of genres, they were also very much aware of the phenomenal success of the U.S. superheroes and of the need to provide Canadian fans with new superheroes."[60]

Early Canadian superheroes, such as Iron Man (from *Better Comics*, by Maple Leaf Publishing) and Freelance (from the appropriately named *Freelance Comics*, by Anglo-American) lacked a distinct Canadian identity.[61] However, the emergence of Nelvana of the Northern Lights in the August 1941 issue of *Triumph-Adventure Comics* marked the first Canadian nationalist superhero.[62] Created and written by Adrian Dingle, Nelvana was not a nationalist superhero via a connection in code name or costume, like the star-spangled Captain America, but rather through her unique relationship with Canadian landscape iconography. In fact, Dingle would later credit Franz Johnston of the Group of Seven[63] with the idea for Nelvana. "It seems that following a trip to the Arctic (probably in 1939), Johnston intrigued his friend Dingle with references to a powerful Inuit mythological figure—an old woman called Nelvana. Dingle thought that the Nelvana character had comic-book potential but decided that he would have to transform her, in keeping with the conventions of the superhero genre."[64] Dingle commodified and domesticated the aboriginal elements of the legend, turning Nelvana into a white Canadian heroine: "I changed her a bit. Did what I could with long hair and mini skirts. And tried to make her attractive[.] . . . Then we had to bring her up to date and put her into the war effort. And, of course, everything had to be very patriotic."[65] Dingle's vision of Nelvana was explicitly that of a nationalist superhero, appropriate to a country at war for the sake of its imperial connections and possibly its own survival. As John Bell argues:

> For over half a century before Nelvana's appearance, Canadian cartoonists had frequently personified Canada as a beautiful young woman named Canada or Miss Canada. [. . .] Nelvana, whom Dingle and Johnston identified as the daughter of Koliak, the King of the Northern Lights, clearly belonged in this same tradition. From the outset, it was obvious that Nelvana was intended to personify the North (she even drew her powers from the Northern Lights). [. . .] However, while Nelvana, the daughter of Koliak and a mortal woman, personified the North, she was very much a white goddess—not an Inuit. In choosing to portray Nelvana as white, Dingle was consciously casting her in the same mold as the many white queens and goddesses that had appeared in popular fiction since the publication of H. Rider Haggard's *She* (1886). Typically, these figures had names that ended with the letter "a," were beautiful and immortal, and ruled over "primitive" peoples (often lost races).[66]

Thus, the Canadian wartime Golden Age of comic book publishing could be seen as importing important genre elements but nevertheless hybridizing them with extant elements of Canadian identity to produce Canadian nationalist superheroes all their own.

After the war, when the U.S. comics market was shifting to romance, crime, and horror comics, the English-Canadian publishers shifted to reprinting this material for the Canadian audience. Even this, however, was not enough to save them when the ban on U.S. comic book imports was lifted in 1951.[67] The future of Canadian nationalist superheroes would not be found in mass market success, but rather in fan-oriented niche publishing. This niche publishing strategy, embraced decades before U.S. publishers would abandon their newsstand distribution, initially struggled to produce superhero comics: "One measure of the U.S. domination of the comics medium during the fifties and sixties is that when Canadian superheroes finally did return during the 1969–1974 period, the first characters were buffoons. It was as if Canadian comic book artists and writers recognized the absence of Canadian heroes, but could not quite— after a twenty-year diet of foreign comics—bring themselves to take such figures seriously."[68]

More long-lasting in significance was Richard Comely's creation in 1975 of Captain Canuck. Comely wanted to create a patriotic Canadian hero, and his is the most long-lived of all Canadian attempts to do so. Nevertheless, the publication history of Captain Canuck betrays the problems of Canadian comic book publishing in the post–World War II era. The first three issues were published in succession beginning in 1975, but then the character had to be revived in 1979 by a stable of artists working for CKR Publications. Fizzling out again in 1980, the hero had to wait until 1993 for another revival, this one only four issues published over four years. Finally, the most recent iteration of the hero is a limited series (originally three issues, but expanded to four) begun in 2004 and concluding in 2007.[69] Another limited series is, at the time of writing, stuck in publishing limbo. The economic constraints of comic book publishing in Canada take their toll on even Canada's mightiest hero.

It is perhaps indicative that the most commercially successful attempt at Canadian nationalist superheroes came from a U.S. publisher. *Alpha Flight*, from Marvel Comics, originated with Canadian writer/artist John Byrne and ran for 130 issues from 1983 to 1994. The original lineup of Alpha Flight can be understood as a Canadian nationalist super-team, as the heroes were consciously drawn from every region of Canada (notably the maple leaf–clad leader, Guardian, hailed from Ontario). Two revivals of the team have occurred but have been less successful. The first lasted for twenty issues in the late 1990s and the third for twelve issues in the early 2000s. The characters dated back to Byrne's early days within the comic book community, when he wanted to produce a whole array of Canadian superheroes: "Several members of what became Alpha Flight date back to my fan days. Guardian [the primary nationalist superhero of the team] is chief among them, being created when I was in my early 20s as the figurehead of a whole line of 'Canadian comics' I was hoping to produce."[70] After Byrne's departure from the series after issue #28, the series became notably less Canadian in its focus.[71] The relative commercial success of these (mostly) American-produced Canadian superheroes in comparison to the Canadian-made versions is indicative of the asymmetrical power relationships between the United States and Canada within the North American creative economy.

## United Kingdom

Unlike Canada, the United Kingdom has a long-standing tradition of comic book publishing. The United Kingdom had a thriving comics market outside the superhero genre, including long-running children's comics such as *The Dandy* and *The Beano*. The independence of the British comic book industry in comparison to the Canadian industry can be traced to differences in the scale of production and the greater costs of transportation from the United States. Nationalist (non-super) heroes were featured early and often, such as Biggles,[72] whose World War I and II adventures were eventually converted into comic book format, interestingly often by French artists. After World War II the British aerial tradition was expanded by Dan Dare, a futuristic space pilot who lived in the era of an ascendant United Kingdom, thus embodying the hopes of a Britain rising from austerity to experience newfound prosperity. Superheroes, however, were introduced to the United Kingdom via the local publication of reprinted *Captain Marvel* comics in 1953. The superhero genre quickly became accepted, and when the reprints stopped flowing, a local producer stepped in with the first British superhero, Marvelman. Marvelman was able to pick up where Captain Marvel left off and had a successful "indigenously produced" run of nine years.[73] Superheroes emerged as standard fare within the British style of anthology comics, such as *Valiant, Lion*, and *2000 AD*. The contrast between the proliferations of superheroes in the United Kingdom vis-à-vis their relative paucity in Canada is interesting. Canadian attempts at superhero publishing tend to be much more self-consciously nationalist; perhaps as a result of Canadian concern over being subsumed within American culture, the producers always seem to be contrasting the Canadian product with the American. As a consequence, virtually all Canadian-made superheroes can be categorized as nationalist superheroes while virtually all British-made superheroes are not.

While the thriving British comics industry was producing its own heroes, it was up to Marvel Comics to introduce the notion of nationalist superheroes such as those already found in the United States and Canada. In 1972 the Marvel UK imprint was created to sell reprints of U.S.-produced comics in the British market, a niche that had been unfilled for three years. These comics came in the form of British-style weekly anthologies, with titles such as *Spider-Man Comics Weekly* and *The Mighty World of Marvel*. These sold well, but British audiences cried out for local heroes, local villains, and local places in their weekly dose of superheroism. Marvel Comics turned to Chris Claremont to write a new United Kingdom–based comic book, relying on the fact that he had lived there as a young child to infuse the comics with Britishness. Turning to the nationalist superhero genre as a vehicle for penetrating the British market, Claremont created Captain Britain, lifting the military title and nationalist uniform from the model of Captain America but using the "flawed student with problems" model of narrative from Spider-Man. Beginning in 1976, Captain Britain occupied the first eight pages of his own self-titled comic book, yielding each week to more reprints from the United States. While there were some early problems with the American authorship of the comic (one embarrassing reference to a "soccer" match springs to mind), in general the character was embraced by comics readers, who seemed to view the American production of the comic as an egalitarian gesture, as evidenced by rapid calls (soon fulfilled) for a team-up between Captain America and Captain Britain.

Captain Britain's publication history, however, has been relatively shaky since then. The cancellation of *Captain Britain Weekly* in 1977 was followed up with a weekly story in the *Super Spider-Man and Captain Britain* anthology series and a brief run with Spider-Man in *Marvel Team-Up*. These stories were largely scripted by American talent. Following that, Captain Britain returned to his native land to be scripted by British talent for the first time, appearing within the regular *Black Knight* comic strip published in Marvel UK's *Hulk Comic*, and after that he had three other stints in U.K. comics, including another one self-titled, but monthly rather than weekly.[74] Since then, however, Captain Britain has been able to remain in print only as part of a superhero team, such as *Excalibur* (1988–1998), *New Excalibur* (2005–2008), or *Captain Britain and MI-13* (2008–2009). Although Captain Britain is now firmly part of the "mainstream" (i.e., United States–centered) Marvel Universe, he remains squarely in the second tier of heroes.

The other British nationalist superhero in the Marvel Universe was put retrospectively in World War II by comics writer Roy Thomas, who created a superhero team, the Invaders, from the Golden Age heroes Captain America, the Human Torch, and Namor the Sub-Mariner in 1976.[75] These heroes appeared in a superhero group called the All-Winners Squad during World War II with other heroes (themselves later resurrected by Thomas as the Liberty Legion). *The Invaders* was published from 1976–1979 and featured stories of the heroes based in the United Kingdom so that they could "invade" Nazi-occupied Europe. They were joined by British heroes Spitfire and, importantly for our purposes, Union Jack. Union Jack had no special powers but was a World War I "masked man" who fought against the Kaiser. After his death, other young men took up the mantle of Union Jack, and in the fictional Marvel Universe there has been a Union Jack defending Britain from Germans (and later, vampires) from World War I until the present. Union Jack has appeared in various comics since then but, like Captain Britain, always as part of a team, such as in *Knights of Pendragon* (1990–1993) and *New Invaders* (2004–2005). He has also starred in two self-titled limited series (1998–1999, 2006–2007).

The twentieth-century emergence of the nationalist superhero in the United States and its subsequent spread to the United Kingdom and Canada is indicative of the times; the prime modernity of the United States during its hegemony heightened the appeal of American cultural products in other parts of the world, however oddly these superheroes fit in with local forms of nationalism. The dependence of British and Canadian nationalist superhero comics on American capital and markets hints at the economic dimension of American hegemony in the twentieth century.

However, the spread of the nationalist superhero genre did not just illustrate American hegemony; it also incorporated realism (i.e., the quintessentially American paradigm of international relations) into the textual world of Marvel's superheroes. The realist paradigm asserts that the primary agents in global affairs are its states. These are formally equivalent and their relations are fundamentally anarchic; therefore, these relations are the natural result of differential distributions of power.[76] This naturalization of uneven power relations through theory is central to the justification of American hegemony.

In superhero terms, this meant that not only the United States, Canada, and the United Kingdom have nationalist superheroes, but virtually every other state has them as well. Therefore, we are introduced (often just in passing) to Shamrock (Ireland), the Scarlet Scarab (Egypt), Hauptmann Deutschland (Germany), Sabra (Israel), the Arabian Knight (Saudi Arabia), Red Guardian (Soviet Union and later Russia), and many others. While these superheroes never get their own comics in "our" world, their textual existence helps to reify the world as composed of formally equivalent units, each of whom is equipped with (su-per)power that can be used justifiably to advance its cause. This false equiva-lency elides the role of American power in producing its global hegemony.

Because this book addresses the nationalist superhero genre via analysis of its texts, it may seem to be reinforcing the realist paradigm: studying Captain America and his nationalist colleagues runs the risk of reproducing the state-centric assumptions of realism. After all, I am not studying Captain Casca-dia or Captain Euro.[77] Nevertheless, by paying rigorous attention to how the United States, Canada, and the United Kingdom are produced through popular culture, it becomes possible to break through the patterns of thought that state-centrism maintains and begin to imagine other geographies less exclusive and more just.

## Conclusions (and Beginnings)

As this chapter shows, the origins of the comic book industry in the United States during the Depression contributed to the superhero's unique relationship with power, morality, and authority. The crystallization of the generic conven-tions during a time when fascism had some appeal (before the war, anyway), as long as it was combined with democracy in some way, had long-term implica-tions for the superhero genre. Similarly, the crucible of World War II, which began in Europe even as superheroes were rolling off their freelance assembly lines in New York City, was key to the emergence of nationalist superheroes. It is difficult to imagine another subsequent era in which such a flamboyantly nationalistic hero like Captain America could emerge without irony.

Nevertheless, with the archetype of the nationalist superhero established during the war, it became possible for comic book producers (and readers), both within the United States and without, to continue to play with the subgenre un-til the present. As a language of politics and place, nationalist superheroes offer a metaphor for various political visions that seems hard to resist. In many ways, that is the story of this book.

Chapters 2 and 3 view the nationalist superhero through the lens of the body. The nationalist superhero subgenre invests the body of the hero as the embodiment of the nation, but that body cannot be universal—instead it is gen-dered and raced in particular ways. Chapters 2 and 3 consider how national-ist superhero narratives have negotiated questions of multiculturalism, sexual equality, and the nation-state. Chapters 4 and 5 introduce a concern with time, in particular the narration of nation over time. A perpetual concern with mak-ing the hero "current" can be seen to be in tension with the innate historicity of comic book continuity. Chapter 4 is concerned with origin stories and their relationship to the narration of nation, while Chapter 5 emphasizes how the nation-state is naturalized through the twin modalities of continuity and change.

Chapters 6 and 7 adopt more traditionally geopolitical concerns, emphasiz-ing the role of nationalist superhero narratives in locating the nation within particular spaces, both territorial and global. Chapter 6 considers how these comic books reify and naturalize the national territory, while Chapter 7 considers the narration of the nation-state within particular orders that invest particular states with geopolitical centrality. Chapters 8 and 9 conclude the book by breaking out of established continuity and considering alternatives. Chapter 8 looks to nationalist superhero narratives that use alternate timelines or new dimensions in order to consider counterfactual time-spaces. Chapter 9 breaks out of the canon considered in the previous chapters to address the deconstruction, critique, and parody of the nationalist superhero genre that has occurred within the industry, offering a brief tour of spaces of resistance to the genre's often stifling politics. The book concludes with a brief afterword that sums up this book's arguments. I hope that you enjoy reading the book as much as I enjoyed researching and writing it.

# Gendered Nation-state, Gendered Hero

aptain America's body was failing. The super-soldier serum that gave him his superpowers was breaking down after many decades of service. He had followed the supervillains Cobra and Mr. Hyde into the deserts of the American Southwest, but there his muscles gave out for the final time. He considered the impact of his muscular deterioration on his sense of self:

> What a complete and total waste I am. Anyone who ever admired or looked up to me is a fool. They backed the wrong man. They thought they were backing a guy who could win against anything life threw at him[.] ... [T]hey were wrong. I can't even win the fight for control over this useless body of mine![1]

Captain America's expression of self-loathing results from the centrality of his physical body to his identity as a hero of America. As fan Daniel Bigelow wrote regarding this story line:

> [Writer Mark] Gruenwald has pointed out a personality flaw in Cap that no one else has seen: his obsession with doing things himself and seeking physical solutions to his problems. This was not a problem when he could meet any threat with physical force. Now that he can't, he's on foreign ground.[2]

## Iconic Bodies

Of course, a solution was found to this particular medical dilemma, but the incident illustrates how the superheroic body is central to many analyses of superheroes; for instance, Scott Bukatman argues that "superhero comics embody social anxiety, especially regarding the adolescent body and its status within adult culture."[3] Bukatman's *embodied* relationship between the superhero and something beyond the realm of the text—for instance, the adolescent body or the body politic—hints that this iconic relationship can exceed simple metaphor. Extending Bukatman's argument, Marc Singer argues that super-hero continuity relies on metonymy rather than metaphor. Unlike metaphor, through which it is claimed two things are alike in some unidentified aspect, metonymy simply claims that "one term figuratively displaces another, closely related one."[4]

At the core of the nationalist superhero is the essential premise of the otherwise binary nation-state being identifiable in a single human body. This metonymic relationship poses many intriguing questions about nationalist superheroes, most obviously: why are they almost all male?[5] This chapter addresses this simple question from two perspectives: first by looking at the masculine superhero body in action, through which the state is produced as a "hard" masculine shell protecting the "soft" feminine nation. This material appreciation for the superheroic body is paired with a second perspective, that of the textual representations of domesticity and feminist values.

The remainder of this chapter begins with a review of the feminist literature on the intersection between the body, the nation, and the state. The empirical section that follows addresses the ways that gender is manifested within nationalist superhero texts, as well as occasional forays into readers' reactions as manifested in letters to the editor. Three themes are examined: masculinity and misogyny, hetero-heroism, and feminism.

## From Bodies Politic to Bodies on Parade

The nation has itself long been a profoundly gendered notion, with a particular relationship to the human body, often identified through the metaphor of the "body politic." Claire Rasmussen and Michael Brown have argued that this metaphor is not politically innocent.[6] The body politic works to take the complexity of a political formation, such as the nation-state, and reduce it to something of which we all have some experience—the human body. This metaphor long predates the superhero, but nationalist superheroes similarly take the modern, Western nation, with its complex histories, dynamics, and multiplicities, and reduce it to something familiar, tangible, and comprehensible. The body politic naturalizes ethical and political questions as health concerns, with the preservation of one's life legitimated under almost any circumstances. With this question of defense comes the gendering of the nation. For example, John Bell argues that early twentieth-century "Canadian cartoonists had frequently personified Canada as a beautiful young woman named Canada or Miss Canada. Often forced to spurn the advances of Uncle Sam (or Brother Jonathan), the demure Miss Canada was the Canadian equivalent of such established female cartoon symbols as Columbia (the U.S.) and Britannia (the U.K.)."[7] As this quotation indicates, nation-states often have both male and female personifications, each of which is used to reflect this notion of the state as something vigorously active and the nation as something to be protected (see Figure 2.1).[8]

Figure 2.1: "Trying Her Constancy, a Dangerous Flirtation," by Tom Merry, 1888. The gendering of national figures is important to the narration of international politics. (Courtesy of the National Library of Ireland. Used with permission.)

The anthropomorphic state has a long history, going back to the Greek city-states.

> Plato and Aristotle thought that, just like the body, the state should be protected from illness and injury. Just like the body, the state has a particular spatial constellation, consisting of different parts with different functions: a king, judges, soldiers, priests, etc. And just like the body, the state was to be governed by reason and care.[9]

Thomas Hobbes's later visualization of the state in *Leviathan* drew explicitly on this biologization:

> But as men, for the attaining of peace and conservation of themselves thereby, have made an artificial man, which we call a Commonwealth; so also have they made artificial chains, called civil laws, which they themselves, by mutual covenants, have fastened at one end to the lips of that man, or assembly, to whom they have given the sovereign power, and at the other to their own ears. These bonds, in their own nature but weak, may nevertheless be made to hold, by the danger, though not by the difficulty of breaking them.[10]

With this in mind, we might consider the nationalist superhero as one in a long line of embodiments of the nation-state, not the least of which is the sovereign himself (or herself). The word *state* itself comes from the Latin *stare*, "to stand." In medieval Europe, the sovereign's "standing" linked the bodily vitality and health of the king with his ability to maintain order; a strong king could enforce laws and ensure public welfare. This is carried forward in today's judiciaries, where if a court lacks "standing" it is not capable of adjudicating a case.[11]

Of course, there is a second, different genealogy to be traced for the embodiment of the nation. Elizabeth Gagen has argued that the body has two relationships to nationalism. The first is a performative, symbolic form in which human bodies "represent discourses according to the symbolic circulation of acts and practices"—Gagen sees connections here between Butler's performativity, Billig's banal nationalism, and Anderson's imagined communities.[12] Each relies on diffuse, everyday interactions to weave the personal and embodied with the national and abstract. In this context athletics becomes a site in which the gendered bodies of participants become a synecdoche of the nation—with men's athletics being a proxy for combat while women's athletics historically understood to be noncompetitive and focused on personal fitness, with its connotations of physical attractiveness and motherhood.

Gagen also articulates a materialist relation between the body and the nation, describing efforts at the turn of the twentieth century to provide physical education for boys and girls so that modern urban lifestyles would not undermine their vitality and undercut the national character. "When girls danced and boys sprinted, jumped and threw, in the eyes of reformers they were not representing abstract notions of gender and nation, they were actively habituating the ideals of those identities into their physical core."[13] Gagen argues that the parading of these youths during holidays was surely a symbolic performance of the nation via flags and uniforms, as per the first relationship, but also as per the second relationship was about harnessing these fleshy corporealities into a collective "we"—the future nation.

While the psychology behind such athletic practices has long ago been rejected, the notion within of the relationship between the body and the nation as more than symbolic—as metonymic—highlights the multiple ways that the gendered nationalist superhero relates to the gendered nation-state. The most obvious way is through the symbolic linkage—one look at the uniform of Captain America or Captain Canuck and it is clear that this person is linked to the nation-state.[14] However, Gagen's second relation between body and nation goes deeper than the surface inscriptions; it posits embodied equivalence. Captain America's sense of despair at his body's failure, with which this chapter began, is perhaps best understood in this sense.

## Gender and the National Security State

If gender is seen as central to many notions of nationalism, recent work in feminist international relations (IR) theory has emphasized the ways in which gender inflects both realist forms of international relations theory and cultures of national security.[15] As Simon Dalby argued almost two decades ago in referencing the feminist IR research of Cynthia Enloe:

> Women and children are scripted as the passive victims of international politics, requiring the masculine operation of diplomacy and military action to ensure their safety. National security is rendered as the masculine provision of safety for "womenandchildren." Apart from the possibilities of active female involvement in international politics being written out, also omitted is the obvious fact that it is usually from other males that the women, thus scripted, are being protected. Where women are given an active role it is only insofar as they are in positions of authority capable of being construed in terms of "honorary males."[16]

In this gendered reading of national security culture, it is the "soft," feminine nation that is to be protected by the "hard," masculine state. Among the implications of the troublesome term *nation-state*[17] is the heteronormative fusion of feminine and masculine functioning as the basis of modern conceptions of international relations.

Robert Jewett and John Shelton Lawrence's claims about the co-emergence of the western and superhero genres (see Chapter 1) here ground a feminist reading of both genres in parallel to the preceding critique of national security discourse.[18] Just as the cowboy served as a masculine source for (racialized) order on the western frontier, protecting a feminized "civilization" in regions beyond the reach of the state, superheroes serve as a masculine barrier between the vulnerable, feminized urban population and the chaotic savagery of criminals and supervillains. Cowboys, superheroes, and the national security state can each be imagined spatially as a hard body protecting the weak, feminized nation from external threats.[19]

While we can see the spatiality of the nation in the superheroic body, the dislocation of this body from within the national space is also important to appreciate. This distinction *from* the nation is key; just as cowboys must ride off into the sunset after defeating the "black hats," eschewing romance and domesticity, neither superheroes nor secret agents (the quintessential embodiment of the national security state in novels and movies) can ever fully participate in the domesticity they secure for others because they must always protect their secret identities, and this hampers the development of romantic and other attachments.[20] Their nomadism (whether literal or emotional) in each of these genres reproduces the very masculinity that causes it; suffering is a key part of the masculine heroic mythos and thus is a necessary component of narrations of both superheroes and national security.[21]

This reading of the superhero genre is not meant to be utterly totalizing; of course, many female superheroes fulfill the same discursive function as male superheroes, although often in slightly different ways. For instance, Mitra Emad, drawing on the work of Mona Domosh and Joni Seager in her analysis of *Wonder Woman*, argues that

> imagining nationhood as gendered often maps directly onto a doc-
> trine of separate spheres: feminine nationhood emerges as unchang-
> ing, natural, protective of children, a mother figure, while masculine
> nationhood emerges as political, volatile, official, and warlike. Wonder
> Woman [. . .] embodies historically specific mergings of these separate
> spheres. Whenever feminine nationhood threatens to become overly
> masculine, the images of Wonder Woman become increasingly sexual-
> ized and her body becomes subject to bondage.[22]

Nevertheless, Scott Bukatman is less sanguine about the confluence of female superheroes and the masculinist role they fulfill: "Overall the trend has been toward masculinized, even phallic, women—armed to the teeth and just one of the boys."[23] The connections to Dalby's earlier quotation about "honorary men" in national security culture are clear.

The dearth of nationalist superheroes who are women is chalked up by writer J. M. DeMatteis as simply part of the gendered patterns of production and consumption:

> I think it's simple: super hero comics began as a very boy-centric genre
> and that mentality has taken many, many years to begin to loosen its
> grip. It was entertainment for boys written and drawn by bigger boys,
> many of whom, in the early years, certainly, didn't have a clue how to
> write female characters.[24]

*Captain America* writer Steve Englehart argues instead that the gendering of narrative roles is central to understanding the lack of female nationalist super-heroes. "I think it's just what's ingrained in us, that men are strong and women aren't. [. . .] [T]here was Miss America, a Timely [Comics] counterpart to their Captain America. But basically, James Bond fulfills more archetypes than Modesty Blaise."[25] Of course, separating market "imperatives" and cultural constructions is a false dichotomy as they are both outcomes of everyday social processes through which gender is produced as a meaningful category. Regard-less, the general lack of nationalist superheroines was noted by readers of these comic books. In a 1977 letter to the editor, for example, B. Williams greeted the creation of the then-new Captain Britain with a call for more diversity: "Wom-en's Lib. I know it's almost a dirty word, but make a little girl's dream come true—give us a Welsh (why pretend? I'm a Taff through and through) female superhero! Please."[26] In the next section the three themes identified earlier are explored with the intention of drawing out the nuanced (and sometimes unnu-anced) interplay of gender and the nationalist superhero.

## Gender and the Nationalist Superhero

### Masculinity and Misogyny

The most obvious intersection between nationalist superheroes and gender comes in the repeated pattern of the superhero rescuing the woman in distress. This pattern is particularly strong in the wartime issues of *Captain America Comics,* in which an array of beautiful (and interchangeable) women feature in the adventures as women to be rescued by the hero and his sidekick, Bucky:

> **Captain America:** It's that same girl! She's in trouble!
> **Bucky:** Aw! Dames always are![27]

However, in *Captain America Comics* one woman became a recurring character, thus allowing for some character development and inversion of the usual gender roles. Betty Ross[28] was first an FBI agent; after the war she was a teacher with Steve Rogers (Captain America's alter ego) at the private Lee School; and finally she fought alongside Captain America as Golden Girl, his patriotic partner after young sidekick Bucky had been wounded. Betty Ross certainly fit the wartime stereotype of Rosie the Riveter, jumping in when her country needed her. While she often served the narrative by being in need of rescue, in dozens of stories she returns the favor by rescuing Captain America from certain doom, even if he remains the primary agent of salvation in their task.

By 1948 her relationship with Captain America had been transformed from the stereotypical Clark Kent–Superman–Lois Lane triangle to a more traditional romantic entanglement.[29] It is worth noting that during this time Golden Girl occasionally offered a different model of heroism, even if it was rooted in essentialized gender differences:

> **Betty Ross:** If we could only do something, Steve—to help! If instead of just jailing bandits and breaking up rackets, the team of Captain America and [Betty] Ross could only do something really constructive!
> **Captain America:** Constructive?
> **Betty Ross:** Well, maybe being your partner in crime-fighting is constructive! But so is helping young singers get their start in life! The way I look at it as a woman . . .[30]

There is, of course, a whole spectrum of ways that a nationalist superheroine could get by in such a masculinist field, and it is impossible here to document the characterization of every nationalist superheroine (even though there are relatively few). Instead I address two female embodiments of the nation-state who perform vastly different femininities: Miss America (classical femininity) and Sabra (honorary man).

Miss America was created in 1943 as a stand-alone wartime heroine, but after the war she was incorporated into the short-lived (and awkwardly named) superhero team known as the All-Winners Squad, which also included Captain America and other superstars from the Timely Comics stable. As mentioned in Chapter 1, in the 1970s writer Roy Thomas took Captain America from the All-Winners Squad and created *The Invaders*, a comic that allowed him to tell new stories from the Golden Age of comics in World War II. The Invaders were primarily shown fighting against the Axis overseas, and so Thomas created a domestic equivalent to the Invaders—the Liberty Legion was intended to remain at home and protect the home front.[31] Miss America and several other heroes who were left over from the original All-Winners Squad were incorporated into this new team. The parallels between Captain America and Miss America as nationalist superheroes were highlighted from the beginning, as were the gendered and heterosexualized roles each had to play:

> **Captain America**: Miss America? Now there's the kind of girl I ought to meet!
> **Namor (CA's teammate in the Invaders)**: You could hold hands while you sing the Star Spangled Banner.[32]

While Miss America is one of the most powerful of the Liberty Legion, with the ability to fly, as the only woman on the team she nevertheless also serves as the secretary at their meetings. While none of the Liberty Legionnaires received enough pages to flesh out their modern personalities, Miss America functioned as a point of romantic tension, especially in her relationship with the Whizzer (whom she eventually married). Her costume fit into the well-documented pattern from the 1940s of "part patriot, part pinup."[33] In many ways Miss America can be held as the icon of classically feminine nationalist superhero— subordinate to, and understandable in relation to, the men in her life.

Sabra, on the other hand, is an Israeli nationalist superhero who appears occasionally in various Marvel comics. Created much later than Miss America (1980), Sabra fights as an "honorary man" and has immense power at her fingertips. She is superstrong, very fast, and invulnerable to most physical attacks, including gunfire.[34] She also has special equipment that allows her to fly and fire blasts of energy from her hands. Her costume, while form-fitting (as most are, regardless of sex or gender), is not revealing by superhero standards.[35] She overtly works for the Israeli government, either with the Mossad or in a more freelance capacity.

Sabra appeared in this research via her appearance in the pages of *Union Jack*, in which she fought with Union Jack and another superhero called the Arabian Knight. Their dispute over gender roles served as a means of orientalizing the Arabian Knight[36] (in case his name alone did not accomplish the job) as well as positioning the heroes via "real-world" geopolitical identities:

> **Arabian Knight**: Perhaps you should embrace the sacred role of wife and mother, as God intends . . . [*Sabra attacks.*]
>
> **Sabra**: That "sacred role" was taken from me when Palestinians ambushed a bus full of Israeli schoolchildren. My son among them.[37]

Through this exchange a wide range of geopolitical scripting is accomplished, but central to the argument of this chapter is the way that Sabra simultaneously draws on popular conceptions of femininity (the emotional mother of a lost child) and escapes them, her lack of (living) children masculinizing her and "freeing" her from domesticity to fight alongside the men.[38]

If locating female nationalist superheroines on a gender spectrum is central to appreciating their sometimes awkward incorporation into the masculine spaces of nationalist superheroes, then considering the gendering of villains is somewhat easier. Almost always men, they are often marked as villains in part by their misogyny, which is externalized by the nationalist superhero (male or female) as an unacceptable behavior within the body politic. This takes many forms, most commonly the capturing of women as hostages (as described previously). However, a common theme has been the use of men's frustrated sexuality as a reason for their criminal activity.[39]

An example of this is the Jigsaw Man, a misogynist serial killer from *Knights of Pendragon*. He has left behind a trail of bodies, all successful women in their thirties. He is sought by Dai Thomas, detective of Scotland Yard and occasional nationalist superhero (as one of the Knights of Pendragon). Thomas correctly identifies the murderer via DNA evidence as Dolph, a former hit man who had been fired by his (successful, female, thirty-something) boss and is now homeless. Over the span of the story line Dolph slowly loses his mind, obsessing about ways to secure his male ego in the face of female threats. His attempts to do so, however, incessantly fail because the current object of his obsession is Kate McClellan, who is steadily gaining superpowers as the Pendragon force (the mystical essence of Britain that manifests, among other ways, as superpowers among select "knights"). He is repeatedly thrashed by the Knights and by Kate herself until he begins to manifest the powers associated with the Bane (the opposing force to that of the Pendragon). He is eventually killed by Union Jack.

Perhaps most significant as an expression of the role of misogyny in constituting villainous identities (and thus heroic identities as well) is the 1984 reworking of the Red Skull's origin. The Red Skull's origin has been retold in several ways over the last seven decades to establish new foundations for his role as Captain America's nemesis (see Chapter 5), but one of the most disturbing iterations in the narrative established a new relationship between the Red Skull's villainy and his sexuality. Johann Schmidt's mother had died giving birth to him. His father first tried to kill his infant son, but failing that (as a result of a doctor's intervention) he killed himself the next day. Many years later Schmidt escaped from his orphanage and took shelter from the harshness of reality in the shadows, which he said reminded him of the womb. Homeless and thirty years old, Schmidt attempted to rape a Jewish woman who had refused him, and in his rage he killed her, discovering pleasure in cruelty to others. Later, Hitler himself would see the rage simmering inside the bellboy at his hotel and would turn him into his most trusted lieutenant.

One does not have to have a degree in psychoanalysis to see how the Red Skull's previous origin narrative (which began with his being plucked from obscurity by Hitler in the hotel) has been inflected by misogyny and sexual frustration. Subsequent expressions of these elements in his personality included the Red Skull's request of his then criminal and sexual partner, the Viper, to put him on the Wheel of Sorrow and beat him so that he might become stronger. Similarly, when the Red Skull had a child of his own, a daughter, he almost threw her off a cliff because of his disdain for women. Her life is saved when a woman argues that any offspring of his is destined for greatness and offers to raise the girl herself.

Bondage is a relatively common theme when it comes to women in superhero narratives, given the scripting of women as objects to be rescued.[40] While most often the bondage is not overtly sexual, occasionally villains will obliquely refer to their sexual objectives for the women in their control, a point of contention for some readers' parents: "I am sure lines like 'You'll kiss back because I tell you to, witch' recited by panting, leering faces will help reinforce positive concepts of male-female relationships in my son's still muddled, evolving mind. Why not confuse and titillate all in one strike?"[41] In the 1970s this occasionally took on racial tones; for example, a 1974 story turned on the abduction of Leila, the sometime girlfriend of Captain America's partner, the Falcon. Visiting Lagos, Nigeria, the Harlem native Leila encounters Stoneface, an African American gang leader from Harlem who had fled to Africa after getting out of prison. When Leila's escorts are killed by Stoneface's goons, they lead her away, telling her to "keep [herself] warm for Stoneface tonight."[42] Such a relatively overt reference to rape was uncommon at this time and earlier and therefore seems to be related to the African context of the story. Rape as a narrative device has become more common over the last few decades as superhero comics have come to be written for a more adult audience.

In 1992, rape emerged as a fundamental element of the backstory of Diamondback, one of Captain America's girlfriends. Diamondback had been a criminal and member of the Serpent Society (a trade union for snake-themed villains) before meeting Captain America, who played an important role in her moral reform. Their relationship thus embodied patriarchal norms, with Diamondback always afraid of what Captain America would do if she ever reverted to her old ways; it also fed into an American narrative of redemption and second chances. In the narrative in question Diamondback is captured by Crossbones, a muscle-bound hit man and lieutenant of the Red Skull. She is imprisoned by him and then starved and tortured into revealing information about Captain America. It is revealed during this time that she and Crossbones know each other from their past; they had been teenagers in the same neighborhood, and Diamondback's brother had been in Crossbones's gang. During that time Crossbones had raped her, and that event sent her spiraling into her life as a criminal. The emotional complexities of their relationship are demonstrated when she has the opportunity to kill him but refrains; similarly, after he trains her to be tougher, she exhibits elements of Stockholm syndrome, both loving Crossbones and hating him for the things he has done to and for her. While clearly positioning the rape as a central event in Diamondback's downward spiral into criminality, the subsequent encounter with Crossbones introduces a disturbing element of "love through abuse." The power relationship that results is finally demonstrated when Diamondback tries to escape from the Red Skull's fortress, and responding to Crossbones's duplicitous offer of assistance, she is literally and metaphorically stabbed in the back.

While misogyny such as this is common (if usually more banal), it would be a mistake to see the readership as uniformly desiring and accepting such narratives. In particular, a 2006 narrative, also involving Crossbones, sparked a debate in the letters-to-the-editor pages that lasted for several months. In this narrative, Crossbones has rescued the Red Skull's daughter—Synthia Schmidt (a.k.a. Sin, mentioned in passing previously as an infant; she is now in her late teens)—from a SHIELD (a U.S. spy agency) "reeducation" facility. She had been brainwashed by the U.S. government into forgetting her past family connections, and Crossbones beats her mercilessly, wakes her up by dunking her head in water, and emotionally tortures her (he offers to free her if she will kill a captured night watchman and then kills him anyway when she refuses) in an attempt to have Sin abandon her newly learned pacifism. When Sin breaks through her SHIELD brainwashing, she climbs into Crossbones's bed and begins a romantic relationship. Like Diamondback before her, Sin responds to physical abuse by forming emotional attachments. This time, however, readers responded to the misogyny.

Rodney Boyce wrote to the creative team, arguing, "You spent twenty-two pages depicting a large man striking a defenseless woman repeatedly with a sexual undertone, and on the last page showing her enjoying it." He was joined by Daniel Braun, who claimed that the creative team "set out to entertain readers by showing them a woman being tortured, without trying to provide ANY sense of why this might be a bad thing." Ed Brubaker, the writer, replied, "I'm sorry if that subject matter was offensive to any of our readers, but it is hard to show evil people without them doing evil things."[43] Two months later the creative team confessed that they had been deluged with opinions on the matter, sparked by Boyce and Braun's letters. Five letters were published, four of which supported the creative team's rebuttal: that the images were meant to be repulsive, and seeing misogynistic violence does not produce misogyny. The remaining letter, by Pierre Comtois, criticized the editorial rebuttal as being "self-serving and facile. Creative freedom doesn't only give a person the right to do whatever he wants, it also gives him the choice *not* to do something."[44]

From the preceding discussion it is apparent that cultural understandings of masculinity as entailing the protection of women are central to an understanding of nationalist superheroes—even female ones; while this is true of the superhero genre in general, the metonymy of the nationalist superhero for the active, physical protection ostensibly provided by the state forecloses more active formulations of femininity. The nationalist superhero is predicated on the protection of female bodies, and conversely male villains are often marked out by their dysfunctional or misogynistic relationship with female bodies.

## Hetero-heroism

Hetero-heroism refers to the role of the nationalist superhero's body in representing the relationship between masculinities and heterosexual domesticity. Male superhero bodies, like the bodybuilding advertisements with which they shared the pages of comics in the later twentieth century, are meant to be gazed upon in awe, yet this requires that the female gaze be foregrounded so as to produce the superhero as a *heterosexual* object of desire. In this way, men's potential attraction could be safely bracketed.[45] For instance, consider this narration from a 1976 issue of *Captain America*: "The stranger [Captain America] comes forward in the dim light . . . he is like no man Carol has ever seen[.] . . . His garb is like none worn by any other man . . . he is like a fantasy which has finally come true."[46] The case of Captain America is a particularly interesting one with regard to his sexuality. Within the Marvel superhero continuity Captain America occupies the moral center of the universe; he is the character all others consider to be irreproachable. How, then, to deal with his romantic relationships?

In his early years Captain America eschews any romantic engagements, save an apparently chaste dating relationship with Betty Ross. Female hostages and villainesses alike fall for Captain America, but he avoids any entanglements (here distinguished from his relationship with Betty Ross by the need to negotiate a work/life balance) until his resurrection in the 1960s. Since then Captain America has had a series of (usually) long-lasting monogamous relationships, with SHIELD agent Sharon Carter, glass-blower and law student Bernie Rosenthal, the aforementioned Diamondback, lawyer Connie Ferrari, and commercial artist Rebecca Quan. His relationships are generally devoid of conflict except that caused by his career (more on this later) and thanks to the Comics Code, which was in effect for most of Captain America's post–World War II adventures, they are mostly sexless.[47] Given Captain America's iconic position as the moral center of the Marvel Universe, which itself stems from his role as the American nationalist superhero, his justification of this first documented dalliance is important as it establishes his (and therefore purportedly the nation's) moral boundaries:

> **Bernie Rosenthal:** And now it's my turn to impress you—with some
> gymnastics of my own! Mmmm. . . . Maybe we'd better head

> upstairs to the kitchen—'cause I'd hate to see you bounced out of
> the Avengers Mansion on an obscenity charge!
> **Captain America**: When two people love as deeply as we do—the word
> obscenity can never apply.[48]

A 2006 scene in which Captain America is in bed with Sharon Carter sparked two letters to the editor, each taking a different view on the issue. Dallan Baumgarten wrote, "After all that Cap has been through in the last 16 issues, he finally gets some action. [. . .] Steve needed that even more than you know," while Brian and Amy Cottrell argued, "Captain America is still supposed to be in the 1940s mindset. We don't think premarital sex would be the norm for Steve Rogers. He is a gentleman, one of the many traits that make him better than you and I." Writer Ed Brubaker, in turn, contested the nostalgia for a more moral era: "I'm pretty sure there were plenty of soldiers and civilians in the 40s who had premarital relationships. It's not exactly a twenty-first century phenomenon."[49] The shifting of Captain America's sexual morality was highlighted in 2003 when a villain known as the Interrogator attempted to corrupt Captain America to his own purposes by tricking the hero into sleeping with a beautiful woman and then highlighting the hero's moral relativity.

Captain America's modeling of heterosexual relationships is marked by his inability to fulfill his girlfriends' emotional needs because of his intense devotion to duty and the obviously never-ending requirements of his job. Nevertheless he often imagines the safe and secure domestic life that he provides for others, wishing that he could partake. These scenes usually include various aspects of the American Dream that Captain America claims to represent; for instance, a 2002 story line notably showed Captain America imagining a suburban house and a buxom bikini-clad woman. Captain America's American Dream seems to be a decidedly heteronormative one.

Captain Britain, by comparison, carries little of the burden of moral expectations. Unlike Captain America, he has always been envisaged as a flawed character rising to the challenge of his role as a nationalist superhero. His initial romantic relationship with Courtney Ross did not survive a turbulent period in the hero's publication history; costarring in other people's comic books, and therefore without enough pages to detail a romance, Courtney Ross disappeared and only reappeared as Captain Britain's lost love in the pages of *Excalibur* when he was already in his long-term relationship with the mutant Meggan. The relationship of Captain Britain and Meggan is intriguing both because it is exceptional in its duration and domesticity (the two were married in 1998 in *Excalibur #125* and remain so) and because of the reasons why the relationship has succeeded in a genre where such relationships are seemingly destined to fail.[50]

Meggan is a feminist's nightmare. Her superpower allows her to sense what people are feeling and expecting and then shape-shift to meet their needs. She was born to a superstitious Roma family who were anxious about her as a result of her birth near a British site associated with black magic. Meggan embodied their anxiety and fear as she unconsciously took the form of a demon. It was only when she gained a degree of self-understanding that she was able to take on a new, beautiful form that was perfect for attracting Captain Britain. Her mutant desire to please those around her (even by shape-shifting to be what they want to see) combined with a childlike naïveté (resulting from being hidden from view by her parents) to create a tabula rasa trophy wife, prone to walk around in lingerie and generally titillate a segment of the readership.

Readers were initially dismayed by Meggan's transformation into a traditional beauty, grounding their criticism in the larger representation of bodies within the superhero genre. T. M. Maple wrote:

> So now [Meggan] has an outer beauty to match that inner beauty. This seems to be standard for comics today, and indeed for all of popular literature: Beautiful people are good, and ugly people are bad. [. . .] How many ugly super-heroes or good looking super-villains (especially males) are there, for instance? [. . .] I only wish that if she had to change, her uniqueness had not been sacrificed for everyday beauty.[51]

It would be a mistake to think that Meggan appealed only to men's fantasies of a beautiful, childlike partner. One letter to the editor from Ian Watson in a 1992 issue of *Excalibur* illustrates the complex interrelationship of gender among readers and the gendering of the characters:

> Well, [my wife's] more mature than me. She doesn't need my boyish power-fantasies, so the rough, tough, killer characters do nothing for her. [. . . She] really enjoys the characters in Excalibur, especially Meggan's innocent delight at a world the rest of us take for granted.[52]

Meggan's innocence makes her appealing to both female and male readers but seemingly for different reasons.

If Meggan's fantasy-like, undemanding quality seems to have helped her dodge the curse of the nationalist superhero's unavailability for long-term relationships, it has not helped her enough. One fan, Jeff Kozzi, wrote in to request that the writers kill her off: "Coping with her sudden demise just may make Captain Britain interesting (i.e., maladjusted drunken blowhard) again."[53] The narrative imperative to have masculine nationalist superheroes who are not shackled to domestic life applies also to Captain Britain and Meggan; after marrying Meggan in the final issue of *Excalibur* in 1998, Captain Britain returned in the pages of *New Excalibur* and *Captain Britain and MI13* only after Meggan was revealed to have been dumped into the Underworld while guest-starring in another comic book. Therefore, Captain Britain is once again on his own throughout both of these comics' runs (they are reunited in the final issue of *Captain Britain and MI13*, by which time the writer knew the comic had been canceled).

The heteronormativity of the nationalist superhero is not limited to the male embodiments of the nation. The Canadian superheroes Nelvana of the Northern Lights and Snowbird in fact form a powerful narrative of heteronormative domestic life. Nelvana's father was Koliak the Mighty, an Arctic god who nevertheless saw the appeal of taking a human bride. For his "sins," Koliak was punished by the other gods such that he could never be seen by mortals again, except in the form of the aurora borealis. His daughter from this miscegenation is Nelvana, herself a demigod with elements of her father's powers. Despite her connections to the heavens, Nelvana too feels the pull of her human heritage, and she engages in a series of adventures with Corporal John Keene of the Royal Canadian Mounted Police. Here the gender roles are reversed, with Nelvana repeatedly saving Keene and at one point even fighting to save him from being married to the evil queen of the extradimensional world of Statica.

The inversion of the gender roles is refreshing, but the heteronormativity (even between gods and humans) returns decades later when Canadian writer John Byrne drew on the classic Nelvana comics to create Snowbird. According to the retelling of Snowbird's origin in *Alpha Flight #7*, a Canadian archaeologist named Richard Eaton uncovered a mysterious headband. When he put it on his head in the middle of the night, Eaton was visited by "Nelvanna" and "Hodiak,"[54] who asked for his "seed." Nelvanna then took the physical form of a transcendent beauty and consummated the new relationship with Eaton on the Canadian tundra. It fell to Michael Twoyoungmen, the First Nations member of Alpha Flight, to serve as midwife to this fusion of the Inuit gods and Anglo-Canadian settlers. He raised Snowbird as his daughter (Nelvanna having returned to the realm of the gods).

Cumulatively the saga of Nelvana and Snowbird embeds heteronormativity at the heart of the embodiment of Canada via the sexual union of Inuit gods and Anglo-Canadian settlers (with a First Nations shaman as a midwife, no less). Nelvana abandoned the heights of divinity to dwell among humans and eventually reproduce with them, facing possible punishment by the gods as Koliak/Hodiak had before her. The transitory nature of her domestic attachments is similar to that demonstrated in Captain America's inability to maintain romantic relationships and in Meggan's disappearance from the adventures of Captain Britain shortly after their marriage. Nationalist superheroes (and heroines) seem to be far better at enunciating heteronormative ideals than at actually achieving them.[55]

## Feminism

The final theme to be explored in this chapter's analysis of gender and nationalist superheroes is the manner in which the feminist movement is engaged. This section, rather than drawing on all three countries' heroes, focuses on Captain America, as his publication history enables the most in-depth analysis. *Captain*

*America* provides ample opportunity to reflect on the portrayal of the feminist movement in nationalist superhero comics as it is the only comic book studied here to be published continuously from 1964 onward.

Undoubtedly this record is dubious, although sometimes more well-intentioned than others. The introduction of SHIELD agent Sharon Carter in 1966 was connected to efforts to represent women as men's equals within superhero comics, but the masculinism of the genre made for some awkward moments, such as this 1971 exchange between Sharon Carter, Captain America, and SHIELD director (and grizzled World War II veteran) Nick Fury:

> **Sharon Carter:** I just know I've got bad vibes! There's something wrong!
> **Captain America:** You bet there's something wrong! The Falcon needs help—and he's gonna get it—this is no time to go feminine on me, honey! [. . .]
> **Nick Fury:** Sharon's head of our secret psyche squad.
> **Captain America:** What's that?
> **Nick Fury:** Ya can call it a hyped-up woman's intuition. Fer starters, she's got a PhD in metaphysical psychology.[56]

This ham-handed plot development, which both advanced women as heroic actors and also pigeon-holed them with stereotypical female characteristics, was quickly followed-up that same year with the creation within SHIELD of Femme Force One, an elite squad of all-female agents. It seems highly relevant that, shortly after their first appearance, Femme Force One disintegrates as Sharon Carter and another team member, the Contessa Valentina Allegra de la Fontaine, squabble over their romantic interest in Captain America.

Captain America's troubled negotiation of gender roles are emphatically on display during a long-running problem in his relationship with Sharon Carter stemming from the danger associated with their jobs. In 1969 Captain America sparks this argument by asking Sharon to resign from SHIELD because her job as a secret agent was too dangerous: "I'm serious Sharon! Every hour, every minute—I'm rubbing shoulders with death! I can't bear to think of you—facing the same dangers! And that's why—I want you to resign from SHIELD!"[57] She refuses, and several issues later readers hear Captain America's thoughts and see into his wounded male ego: "How can I marry a girl whose sense of duty equals my own? Who won't quit SHIELD as long as there's a need for her? And, what have I to offer her? Just the fading reputation of a battle-weary has-been!"[58]

Unable to get Sharon to resign voluntarily, Captain America goes to his old friend Nick Fury and gets him to reassign Sharon to safer duties. She greets this news with perplexing passivity ("If that's what you want, my dearest . . .") but Captain America then breaks up with Sharon anyway when he realizes that *his* job puts her in danger. Eventually they reconcile, and she resigns from SHIELD:

**Sharon Carter, to Nick Fury**: It's only that this crazy conflict between my love and my duty has got to end. I've hurt a lot of people by not taking this step before. [*Time passes.*]
**Captain America**: Little lady, I'm awfully proud of you!
**Sharon Carter**: Oh, Steve . . . you'll make me blush![59]

If this plot development and dialogue is not enough to make a feminist lose faith, subsequent events compound the state of affairs by turning the formerly heroic (if femininely so) Sharon Carter into the shrill girlfriend who wants Captain America to work less and spend more time at home, even considering leaving Captain America for romance with a conscientious objector to the Vietnam War. As one anonymous SHIELD pilot puts it, "Woman trouble! I bet he'd rather tangle with the Red Skull!"[60]

Feminine power is encoded as dangerous to the hero in many other ways during the serial narrative of *Captain America*, beyond being a threat to masculine freedom of action. For example, female villains often embody the notion of "feminine wiles" through their deployment of superpowers that allow them to control men's minds. This particular superpower appears astonishingly often, and the villains' names often reflect the male anxiety that this superpower symbolizes. For example, in a 1970 story titled "Suprema, the Deadliest of the Species!" the villain is taking over all the gambling and organized crime in the city by simply compelling men to do her bidding via "witchcraft." She is successful until she meets Captain America, who is immune to her powers as a result of his superior morality and discipline. The same powers are used on Captain America, and to the same effect, by Deadly Nightshade in 1975. In 1984 readers were introduced to the Sisters of Sin: Sister Dream, Sister Pleasure, Sister Agony, and Sister Death. Of these, it is Sister Pleasure who is capable of mesmerizing men ("When you die in Sister Pleasure's arms, your end is sheer ecstasy! My kiss . . . my touch . . . will melt you blissfully into oblivion!");[61] however, we never learn whether Captain America could resist Sister Pleasure because instead he falls victim to Sister Dream, whose victims see pleasant illusions—when he is caught, Captain America sees domestic bliss with his then girlfriend, Bernie Rosenthal (Figure 2.2). While Captain America can easily avoid sexual temptation, he falls victim to the (gendered, heteronormative) American Dream. In 1989 the Sisters of Sin return and we learn that their matriarch is in fact the aforementioned Suprema ("the Deadliest of the Species!"). The theme continues with Dansen Macabre, a nude woman who dances with ribbons that artfully cover her (again, we never learn whether Captain America is susceptible to her powers). A final example is 1990's Typhoid Mary, who complains that "this brazen Avenger [Captain America] resists my 'charms'!"[62] It appears that Captain America's iconic masculinity, with his emphasis on discipline, training, and personal responsibility, is seen as an antidote to feminine wiles. At a minimum it seems that representing him as under the spell of a woman is deemed unacceptable.

Figure 2.2: Captain America's dream of domestic life. (Copyright © 2012 Marvel Characters, Inc. Used with permission.)

The feminist movement became the focus of *Captain America* for the entire summer of 1991, this time explicitly as a villain. The story line for that summer began when Diamondback and some of her friends were kidnapped onto the SS *Superia*, a cruise liner full of superpowered women. Diamondback triggers a homing beacon that brings Captain America and his new ally Paladin (who seems to exist to make sexist comments the writer could not plausibly put in Captain America's voice) to the cruise liner. There they discover the women on board having a Power Pageant in which they compete via the demonstration of their superpowers. However, Captain America and Paladin are spotted and battle the fifty women in a fight scene laced with innuendo and sexism. The women can generally be sorted into two categories—beautiful women with sexy names and skintight outfits (the comic book standard) and large, masculine women with names like Battleaxe,[63] Knockout, or Titania. Overwhelmed, Paladin and Captain America are strip-searched[64] and then put into chemical baths that will, within forty-eight hours, turn them into women. Readers learn that the cruise ship is run by Superia, who tells the women on board that she is going to start a colony of women (imaginatively titled Femizonia) that will eventually take over North America, enslaving all men. Diamondback and her friends rescue Captain America and Paladin from their chemical emasculation, and subsequently Captain America overhears that Superia's plan is to chemically sterilize all the world's women outside Femizonia, thus turning the Femizonian women's reproductive capacity into a source of political hegemony. Superia's feminist motivations are not left to the readership's imagination, as illustrated by the following exchange with one of her female lieutenants:

> **Anaconda:** What's your big beef with men? Nobody invited you to the Senior Prom or somethin'?

> **Superia**: Men . . . are beasts, savages, brutes! They are far inferior to
> us and yet by force they've held sway over the civilization we share
> since ancient times! It is time for a change. It is time society recti-
> fied itself. It is time the world were ruled by those most fit to rule.[65]

Needless to say, the plot is foiled by the collaboration of Captain America with
the antiseparatist women on board (Diamondback and her friends).[66] However, the narrative all but names the feminist movement as a threat to America,
most graphically symbolized by the image of Captain America being chemically castrated (Figure 2.3). Of course, the inversion of domination advocated
by Superia is the antithesis of feminist thought, which advocates gender equality. Instead the narrative embraces conservative tropes of "man-haters" and the
subordination of men to argue for the status quo.

Superia returns in 1994, when readers are introduced to Cathy Webster, a
meek undergraduate. After volunteering for a psychology experiment to im-
prove her physical and mental capabilities, Cathy finds herself thrilling to her
new capabilities. However, Dr. Wentworth, the professor in charge of the project, is really Superia in disguise. Dr. Wentworth hires her to be the Free Spirit, a
symbol of women's equality, draped in red, white, and blue à la Captain America. She is unleashed on a toga party, where she confronts the men about their
sexism. Driven by subliminal antimen messages in her head, she beats the men
badly but leaves disgusted by her actions. Teaming up with Captain America,
the Free Spirit trains so that she can take revenge on Superia:

> I don't know who you are or what kind of twisted game you're play-
> ing, Wentworth! Why would someone with the genius to liberate my
> body want to subjugate my mind? Did you think I would be so grateful
> for my new physique that I would surrender my will to your anti-male
> agenda? Well, you have molded my body but my spirit remains free!
> You wanted me to be a champion of something, I will! But I'm the one
> who'll determine how I put my new body to use—I, the Free Spirit![67]

The Free Spirit thus offers a fusion of nationalist and feminist superhero (her
attire and rhetoric of freedom mark her as specifically American) that is genuinely feminist (and comfortably male-friendly) in comparison to Superia. Fans
mostly responded positively to the Free Spirit, with one reader even suggesting
her as an heir to the nationalist superhero himself should Captain America re-
tire. One fan felt differently: "Here are some reasons why I think that Free Spirit
is dumb: 1) Typical nerd-turned-super hero (can anyone say 'Peter Parker'?)
2) Feminist objectives."[68] Another seemed to miss the (feminist) point entirely:
"I really hope you will keep Free Spirit around. She is a real knockout and her
costume is perfect. I'll bet [Captain America's girlfriend] is going to be a little
jealous when she returns!"[69]

The feminist movement, as traced through these story lines from *Captain
America*, is generally seen as threatening to male ego, male freedom of action,

Figure 2.3: Captain America, held in a chemical bath that will turn him into a woman. This story turns on the fear of feminism castrating America. (Copyright © 2012 Marvel Characters, Inc. Used with permission.)

and ultimately the masculine nature of the state itself (via the literal castration of Captain America). Nevertheless, recognition of women's equality has been overtly on display in recent decades, even if fear of feminism as a project has been equally on display. The Free Spirit is an example of this, and in some ways Captain America's grudging acknowledgment of feminism can be seen as a sign of the progressive nature of feminism, as in this 2001 Captain America monologue:

If there were any female lawyers around in 1935 I never heard about them. Now, not only am I dating one—but two more sit on the bench of the Supreme Court. I've adapted to all the technological differences. [. . .] But it's the sociological changes that continue to amaze me most . . . that sometimes make me feel . . . old.[70]

Captain America's slow transition to acceptance of feminism was contrasted by one female reader with his ready acceptance of racial diversity and homosexuality: "Cap's not a sexist, any more than he's a racist, a homophobe, or any other kind of bigot. Since Cap's never had these thoughts before, please keep them out of his head now, especially if you want more female readers!"[71]

## Conclusions

This chapter began by highlighting the connections between the notion of the body politic and the body of the nationalist superhero. Captain America fan (and apparent student of Friedrich Ratzel)[72] James Fish made these connections explicit in a 1971 letter to the editor:

First off, America is an organism, and like any living organism possesses an identity [. . .] and holds a continual interaction with its environment. In an organism then, I venture to say that this interaction produces what we call thoughts, moods, emotions, and opinions, this is what I mean, applied to the America-organism, by the Spirit of America. Captain America is the symbol for this, and was intended to hold this place since his inception.[73]

Fish's biologization of America lacks gender (and race) until he arrives at its purported embodiment, Captain America. The chapter followed this thread to consider the masculinization of the state and consequent feminization of the nation, as understood in feminist IR theory. In this formulation, the state exists to protect the nation, and the active body of the nationalist superhero has come to personify one side of this dual gendering of the nation-state. Indeed, the masculine identities of heroes (even female ones) and the misogyny of villains (who threaten female bodies) have been amply substantiated in these comic books. Thus, the materialist understanding of the masculine body as in motion, flexing, and fighting to protect a more passive feminine body must be laid alongside the more representational coding of the body as belonging to the nation and either male or female.

However, the relationship of these heroes to heteronormative ideals of domesticity has been shown to be troubled, with romantic attachments a site through which the hero can be attacked. Further it can be argued that nationalist superheroes have moved beyond a simple reading as masculine defenders of feminine nations. Instead they simultaneously defend the feminine nation *and* defend the masculine state from femininity itself. Such a complex reading defies any simple categorizations of nationalist superheroes as feminist or antifeminist; the production of a feminine "other" as something to be held at arm's length (both in order to protect and to be protected from) must be viewed alongside (often ham-handed and reluctant) enunciations of gender equality. Rather, leaving that ambiguity intact, the focus of this book now shifts to another way in which the body of the nationalist superhero belies the complexity of the nation—through race and ethnicity.

# Embodying Multiculturalism

**Red Skull**: The America you knew is dead. The much heralded melting pot is little more than a lost ideal. Not unlike yourself. Think about it. You are white. Fit. I imagine if I were to pull off that face mask, your hair is blond. In every way, what Nietzsche described as "the Uberman." In every way, an Aryan. Join me. And fulfill your destiny.

**Captain America**: NEVER![1]

Chapter 2 shows the metonymic relationship between the nationalist superhero's body and the body politic to be problematic via its embodiment of the nation in a single sex (which can be sexed either male or female, but tends to be gendered as masculine regardless). However, as this chapter's opening quotation shows, similar problems are attributable to the racialized body of the nationalist superhero, with Captain America (in this case) trying to reject his association with whiteness in favor of a body politic lacking in racial attributes. However, whereas there are only two genders to be reconciled to the singular heroic body, the ethnic and racial complexity of any nation-state is far more complex.[2] Further, while there was little variation in the portrayal of gender in nationalist superhero comics published in and/or representing the United States, the United Kingdom, and Canada, the histories of colonialism and empire in each country (as well as their hegemonic narrations of those collective histories) ensure that race and ethnicity are treated quite differently in each case.

## Race in a Four-Color World

Whereas Chapter 2 explores the relationship of gender and nationalist superheroes, this chapter expands the field of analysis by tracing the various ways in which the nation's embodiment within a (racialized) corporeal form both contributes to the metonymic racialization of the nation-state but also provides narrative opportunities to negotiate and narrate the race/nation relationship.

## Raced Bodies within the Body Politic

Taking forward Elizabeth Gagen's notion of the corporeal nation (discussed in Chapter 2), Emily Grabham has noted that while scholars in whiteness studies often argue that "white" is understood as the nonethnic and the invisible, "it is more productive [. . .] to think about how whiteness is reiterated as an always visible corporeal norm."[3] It is with this in mind that the almost unanimous whiteness of the nationalist superheroes documented in this book must be considered. The nationalist superhero body is a spectacle; the use of costumes and masks only emphasizes that the body is a vision meant to be beheld (if not fully comprehended). Always highly visible but with their race generally deemed tacit and unworthy of attention, nationalist superhero bodies are constitutive of the larger (racialized) bodies politic with which they are aligned.

Drawing on the work of Sara Ahmed, Grabham argues that "whiteness is a habit, [. . .] an accumulation of 'gestures of "sinking" into' a space. When bodies do not 'sink into' spaces, they are perceived as out of place. Racialized bodies, in these terms, may 'sink in' or not, depending on the styles of embodiment that they repeat or do not repeat."[4] White bodies "sink in" to the body politic (at least in North American and European contexts), while racial and ethnic others are often exteriorized. As one explanation, the whiteness of nationalist superheroes can be traced to the production processes of comic books themselves:

> Comics are a medium that tends to use earth tones and shadows in the backgrounds in order to create atmosphere.
> Yes, there are times when the stories will call for the heroes to skulk in the shadows or blend into the crowds, but dramatic moments and fight scenes—of which there are many—work best when the heroes stand out.[5]

Artist Kyle Baker ran into this problem when trying to draw a black Captain America (more on this later): "If the person is dark-skinned, the only way to make him separate from the background is to make the background light. People are just not used to seeing this because there aren't very many Black people in comic books."[6] Literally then, white superheroes blend in via their visibility. Black superheroes do not "sink in" and instead seem out of place in a comics panel.

However, this technological/compositional approach only mirrors the larger cultural pattern rather than explains it. One reader complained to the creative staff of *Captain America* in 1974 about the yellow skin tone given to the Asian villain Yellow Claw. The editor's response indicates the difficulties of racial phenotype inherent to the medium, beginning with technological concerns that smoothly transition into cultural ones:

> The problem with coloring comics [. . .] is that the so-called "four-color" process we use allows only 32 possible color combinations—not nearly enough to make all the distinctions we'd like. We can get good approximations of Caucasian, Negroid, and American Indian flesh—but Oriental coloring is simply not available. [. . .] However, in the early days of comics (when there were only 16 colors by the way) the practice was to color Orientals solid yellow, and many people in the industry still automatically color that way [. . .] out of respect for convention. That's not a good reason, but it's the truth.[7]

As Steve Englehart notes, Native Americans have no such production-side issues, yet they too rarely appear as nationalist superheroes, unable to constitute national claims of their own. Instead, according to C. Richard King, "representations of Indians and Indianness in comic books have fostered the construction of identity, history, and community through the assertion of claims by Euro-Americans." This is accomplished by "mak[ing] claims about Native Americans: more natural, bellicose, spiritual, amodern, ahistorical, less than human, supplemental, inferior."[8] King has argued that the old stereotypical image of the Indian brave (popular especially in comics of the western genre) has been supplanted in recent years by the figure of the shaman (such as the aptly named Shaman, hero of *Alpha Flight*). This shift from the masculine (warrior) to the feminine (natural mystic) has been paralleled by the increasing deployment of female characters, "frequently noteworthy for their hypersexuality as well as their superpowers."[9] This confluence of race and gender in marginalizing nonwhite superheroes is not specific to Native American characters; indeed, in the following section our attention shifts from the constitutive role of bodies in relation to the nation to the discursive interplay of gender and race in delineating the nation.

## Gendered Races/Raced Nations

Writers of superhero comic books featuring African American heroes have often struggled with how to represent black masculinities. Jeffrey Brown has argued that

> the standard phallic version of the masculine idea is deeply grounded not just in misogynistic and homophobic ideology but also in thinly veiled racist terms. But not all Others have been constructed as equal by the dominant masculinist ideology. While the gay man, the Jewish man, the Asian man (and many other "Others") have been burdened by the projection of castrated softness, the black man has been subjected

to the burden of racial stereotypes that place him in the symbolic space of being *too* hard, *too* physical, *too* bodily.[10]

Anna Beatrice Scott argues along similar lines that creating a superpowered black man in a comic book is difficult because the black body has already been invested with supernatural qualities by a dominant, racist white culture. "The fearsome and overdetermined black body in a comic book is storyline, arc, setting, and character all rolled into one."[11] Whereas Adilifu Nama identifies Storm, who controls the weather and for a time led the X-Men, as "articulat[ing] a black womanist perspective,"[12] Scott is more skeptical, citing Storm as an example of the way in which black bodies are seen as *naturally* superpowered:

> Her body is drawn as a shapely soul-sister, not a rippling super[hero], bounding out of its skin with sheer possibility. When she begins to use her power [. . .] her body is not drawn straining under the force. It is natural for her frame. [. . .] Storm's lines in the panels in which she appears wrap her in the ordinariness of being a magical negress. She is so powerful that she need not force it since she is a force herself.[13]

Regardless of the possibility for racial progressivism in superhero comics, the key point here is that race and gender are intertwined.[14] Brown sees potential for black superheroes in the replacement of hypermasculinity with something more nuanced and "real"; similarly Nama tacks to the middle by applauding Black Panther's combination of supernatural Africana (femininity) with technological modernism (masculinity). Scott is more skeptical and still sees black bodies in superhero comics as overinvested with "naturalness" (which can be understood as clustering at either end of a gender spectrum, instead of tending toward the middle as advocated by Brown and Nama).

This gendering of racialized bodies, and the racing of gendered bodies, has important implications for discourses of the body politic. Metaphors of ethnic and racial purity within nations are by this point well documented, but it is worth reiterating that even "multicultural" societies remain tacitly raced, as the 2010 attempt by Arizona to racially profile Hispanic immigrants illustrates. Grabham argues that "the boundaries of the nation are [. . .] delineated *on and through* bodies," as these practices of exteriorizing racial otherness (literally, in the form of deportation) demonstrate.[15] However, it is through not only exteriorizing the racial other but also making visible the racial self that the nation becomes white. Nationalist superheroes are one such site on which national whiteness is enunciated and the body politic is cleansed of people of color.

The remainder of this chapter examines the relationship of nationalist superheroes to the racialized body politic. The chapter shows that nationalist superhero comics have been, and continue to be, embedded within racialized understandings of the nation-state, while nevertheless recognizing the increasing sensitivity brought to bear on the topic of race by creative staff and readers.

## Multiculturalism with a Racialized Nation

### Heroic Whiteness

It is by now not surprising that comic books created during World War II as a commercial venture, seeking to take advantage of nationalist sentiment, tend to express racist views.[16] Nevertheless, as the work of Caroline Bressey illustrates, it is not legitimate to say "that's just how it was."[17] Strong antiracist sentiment was expressed in opposition to the deployment of bigoted slurs in public, although public memory often neglects these events. The World War II tales of Captain America and Nelvana of the Northern Lights are awash in casual racism and orientalism; sometimes this was expressed as a belief in white supremacy, as in this quotation from *Nelvana of the Northern Lights*, in which a Canadian engineer is captured by the Japanese:

> **Japanese soldier**: Honorable Japs are here—for you! Up with hands!
> **"Spud" Jodwin**: OK chum! Even a white man can't argue with an armed battalion.[18]

The perception of World War II as a war between races was common, and this is reflected in *Captain America Comics*, where orientalist depictions of the Japanese dominated.[19] Both Captain America and his sidekick, Bucky, seem to view their enemies through the lens of race and ethnicity; their descriptions of the Japanese as "slant-eyed" and "yellow," of Malays as "monkeys," and of Arabs as preparing for holy war are clearly laced with orientalist imagery. It is unclear how much is intended as irony; naming a Japanese officer "General Sneeki" seems playful, while the following speech by Captain America to a crowd of Pacific Island "natives" seems less so: "And of course behind cold blooded murder, trickery, and deceit [. . .] [t]here is always the Jap!"[20]

Such racist language coming from the mouth of Captain America is virtually unfathomable to those who have read only the modern incarnation of the hero. A sign of the shift in attitudes among the writers and artists can be seen in a comparison of the portrayal of Japanese internment camps during World War II, and then thirty years later when the war was re-presented in the pages of *The Invaders*. The internment camps appear twice in the pages of *Captain America Comics* during World War II. In the first case, New York City is under attack by arsonists. These arsonists are exposed as opium addicts doing the bidding of Nogatomi, a Japanese specialist in chemical warfare who had escaped from an "American concentration camp."[21] Later, Captain America and Bucky uncover a plot by one hundred internment camp escapees to create a Japanese air base in Death Valley.[22] These story lines imply that the interned Japanese Americans were legitimate dangers to national security, if not individually then collectively.[23]

In 1978, however, the World War II internment camps were revisited in the pages of period-piece wartime comic *The Invaders*. When Toro, the teenaged

sidekick to the Human Torch, was badly injured in battle, he was rushed by
Bucky to California, where the famous Dr. Sabuki works. Arriving at Sabuki's
house, Bucky discovers that an opportunist has purchased Sabuki's house
cheaply because Sabuki has been interned. The man tells Bucky, "You could
tell he was a traitor just by lookin' at 'im! The only good Jap's a dead Jap—or
dontcha remember Pearl Harbor?"[24] Bucky heads to the internment camp to
get Sabuki, but when he arrives, Sabuki is not allowed to leave. Bucky battles
the guards, but they are interrupted by the arrival of Agent Axis, who kidnaps
Bucky, Dr. Sabuki, and Sabuki's daughter, Gwenny Lou. They are eventually rescued by the Invaders, Toro is healed, and Captain America berates the internment camp commander for his treatment of his charges. Thus, the narration of
the internment camps is reversed, from something commonsensical to Captain
America during World War II to something anathema to him. In a denouement,
the Japanese American teenager Gwenny Lou Sabuki and an African American
youngster named Davy Mitchell (who was also caught up in the action) gain
superpowers and team up with Bucky and Toro to form the Kid Commandoes;[25]
in this way the superhero history of World War II is revised to include the con-
tributions of ethnic minorities, in much the same way that Hollywood cinema
has been steadily reworking the cinematic history of key events in U.S. history.[26]
Both of these trends came together in the 2011 film *Captain America: The First
Avenger*, in which Captain America's World War II–era army unit was conspicu-
ously multicultural, even including a Japanese American soldier.

As indicated by the more ethnically conscious tales of *The Invaders* traced
previously, the early 1970s was a period in which mainstream American comic
book publishers turned away from the fantastic and tried to present their work
as being socially relevant. In *Captain America*, this occurred via the creation of
the first African American superhero in comics, the Falcon.[27] The Falcon served
to call into question the universalism of Captain America and his understanding of America. Introduced in 1969, the Falcon served as Captain America's
partner for 105 issues. Sam Wilson (the Falcon's alter ego) was a social worker
in Harlem, and as such his presence grounded Captain America's adventures
in the African American ghetto, in ways broadly progressive. These stories ostensibly decentered white narratives of America, setting the Falcon's loyalties
against those of his white allies. For instance, in one 1972 narrative, SHIELD
director Nick Fury invites the Falcon to join SHIELD, only to have him refuse:

> **The Falcon:** Fact is, my people need me a lot more than SHIELD or
> Cap! And I plan to see that they get at least one superhero to call
> their own—or my name isn't the Falcon!
> **Nick Fury:** Okay! Okay! You got yourself a point there—but I still wish
> you'd think about what I've told yuh! We're in a life-and-death
> struggle with Hydra—and if we lose it—your people are gonna suf-
> fer just as much as mine! I'm fightin' for the whole country—not
> just one group of citizens!

**The Falcon**: Maybe that's because you're white, Colonel—and don't understand how it feels to be on the other side of the color line![28]

Similarly, Captain America's whiteness positions him as the ethnic particular rather than the American universal. The Falcon and Captain America's relationship during this time is volatile and prone to miscommunication and legitimate grievance. Further, Captain America is identified by many Harlem residents as part of white power structures, with residents at various points referring to him as "nuthin' but a honkey in his long-johns" and "for us about as much as the Ku Klux Klan."[29]

Raising the problem of Captain America's white skin requires an act of racial recuperation, a suturing of the ethnic minority to the nationalist superhero. For African Americans this occurs primarily through the partnership itself, with the comic book even retitled *Captain America and the Falcon* for the duration. However, it also occurs through various exchanges in which the Falcon ostentatiously gives Captain America honorary ethnic status. For instance, in 1970 he tells Captain America, "Go in peace, my friend! Your skin may be a different color . . . but there's no man alive I'm prouder to call . . . brother!"[30]

A common story line for Captain America is of villains attempting to exploit racial divides in the United States to bring ruin to Captain America, the U.S. government, or the country as a whole. The first example of this appears in 1945, when German secret agents pose as injured veterans on hospital ships and, taking up positions in small towns all over America, stir up nativist sentiment and hatred for foreigners. They are stopped only because of the intervention of a blinded veteran (who cites the diversity of the U.S. Army as a reason for national inclusivity) and of Captain America: "Fellow Americans! This is our fanatical enemy! Dedicated to spreading hate! Pitting man against man! Race against race! And only thru [sic] united action by all freedom-loving people, will tyranny and oppression be utterly destroyed and mankind be rid of war and gain a lasting peace!"[31] This story established a model script, which would be repeated and elaborated on as the decades went by.

The first of many attempts by the villainous Red Skull to exploit American race relations occurred in 1971. The Red Skull crafted a disguise meant to appeal to the Falcon's Harlem neighbors; he became "The Man," dressed in a yellow jumpsuit with the image of a raised fist on his chest. As the leader of the People's Militia, he proceeded to work the African American residents of Harlem into a frenzy against white power structures, and a riot is avoided only because of the police force's "discipline" in the face of "emotional" provocation (see Figure 3.1). The Red Skull's plan crumbles when Captain America and the Falcon unmask the Red Skull and reveal his perfidy. By locating the source of emotion and danger in the Harlem ghetto, the self-professed liberal authors simultaneously express sympathy with the civil rights movement and position black power movements such as those led by Malcolm X as a threat to civil order (and American unity and strength).[32] Stories like this show that even if

Figure 3.1: The police force maintaining restraint in the face of Harlem's rioting African American population while Captain America and the Falcon attempt to preserve (racial) order. (Copyright © 2012 Marvel Characters, Inc. Used with permission.)

communism was rarely featured in Cold War tales of Captain America, the need for "containment" of domestic division and dissension was central to the Cold War geopolitical order (more on this in Chapter 7).

A similar plot was unveiled in 1979's "National Front" story line, this time led by the Red Skull's ally Dr. Faustus.[33] In 1996 the Red Skull attempted the ploy again, this time with his Nazi henchman Master Man undercover as the leader of the World Party, which promotes an anti-immigrant politics. While Captain America could defeat the Master Man, he could not stop the Red Skull from continuing to exploit American racism. Perhaps the most telling narration of American idealism and (fragile) multiculturalism can be found in a 2001 story line that has the Hatemonger (the life force of Hitler himself working for the Red Skull, literally fueled by the hate of those around him) instigating racial and anti-immigrant fury in Louisiana.

> **Captain America**: What's your game? A missile launch against Washington? Take out the governing structure so you can move in?
> **Red Skull**: Unnecessary. It's taken me a long time to realize it, but I have no reason to destroy America. Not when your pathetically diverse, patchwork country is capable of doing so—all by itself, from within. Your nation is a cauldron of hate waiting to erupt, a cesspool of violent thoughts looking for release. It's a fuse extending from one coast to the other, waiting for someone to ignite the flame. I shall be only too happy to do so.
> **Captain America**: Americans have moved beyond that, Skull. It can't be done.
> **Red Skull**: Watch me.[34]

The plan relies on the recently fanned hatred of the people in Louisiana to fuel a broadcast device that will spread the hatred from coast to coast. The Red Skull and Hatemonger capture Captain America and link him up to a machine that will amplify his hatred. However, there is no hatred to harness. Captain America frees himself and then lectures the Hatemonger's army of hateful people about being free from hate. Not knowing this, the Red Skull initiates the signal that links the Hatemonger with everyone on board; the Hatemonger disappears, dissolving in the lack of hate he found in the wake of Cap's lecture. The Red Skull is then quickly overcome and the plot foiled. These repeating scripts of American multiculturalism as fragile and in need of protection not only position American identity as virtuous and open-minded but also highlight the vigilance needed to police that identity.[35] Racial strife is instigated by America's enemies and is never a preexistent problem. This depoliticizing instinct is visible in Sharon Carter's comment about yet another impending riot: "It's unreal—that fellow countrymen could be so far apart! Simply because of the color of their skins! That's what it's really about—in spite of the other issues!"[36]

### Heroes of Color

Navigating the contradiction of the Falcon being both an African American man *and* superpowered was not a simple matter for the creative staff. Kobena Mercer argues that "shaped by [the history of slavery], black masculinity is a highly contradictory formation of identity, as it is a *subordinated* masculinity."[37] Avoiding this trap required careful narrative attention to the relationship between Captain America and the Falcon; for instance, the heroes are always described as equal partners despite Captain America's obvious seniority, and at times the Falcon strikes off on his own, quite successfully.

Still, the feminine/masculine binary embedded in the alter ego/superhero "secret identity" dualism takes on a special resonance for the Falcon because of his real-life job as a social worker. This job marks Sam Wilson (the Falcon's alter ego) as a passive, feminized individual within Harlem's racial and political polarization, as can be seen in this exchange at between Rafe, a neighborhood instigator, and Sam Wilson at a Black Revolution meeting:

> Rafe: What's he doin' here? Come to lay some welfare checks on us? Well, you can stuff 'em man—'cause we ain't buying that bit any-more!
> Sam Wilson: Just as reasonable as always, aren't you Rafe?
> Rafe: We been reasonable too long! You tell that to your pale-faced boss next time you're lickin' his boots![38]

Sam Wilson must exercise restraint in not revealing his identity as a "man of action," and so he is handcuffed to passivity in civilian life. This hampers his romantic relationship with Leila, who supports Black Power and comes by Sam's office to, in her words,

> see for myself what would make a big, strappin' brother like you waste all his talent in a place like this. Our people need heroes, man—not handouts[.] . . . I just came to tell you you're wastin' your time—we don't need no more social workers, we need fighters—to give our people pride.[39]

The emasculation and "whitewashing" of Sam Wilson takes its toll on his relationship with Captain America, who as the representative of an idealized color-blind America often struggles to see things from the Falcon's perspective.[40]

A more radical reworking of the white nationalist superhero archetype than anything attempted before was launched in 2003 with the limited series *Truth: Red, White, and Black*. The narrative of *Truth* follows several African American men who join the army when World War II begins but are quickly taken into the program to re-create the super-soldier serum that was used to turn puny Steve Rogers into Captain America (but was lost after a Nazi spy attacked the laboratory—more on this in Chapter 4). In a direct reference to the Tuskegee syphilis experiments,[41] three hundred African American soldiers are subjected to medical testing that kills most of them, leaving only the main protagonists, themselves distorted by overgrown muscles and mental deterioration. Only one, Isaiah Bradley, survives to get to the European theater of war, and once there he is sent on a suicide mission. Before leaving on the mission, he steals a Captain America uniform and therefore comes to embody a completely different kind of national narrative. "Where the original Captain America juxtaposed ethically pure Americans against a semi-demonic Nazi foe, *Truth* explicitly linked racial discourse in the U.S. and Germany."[42] The comic points to pre–World War II eugenics conferences, which were attended by representatives of the U.S., U.K., and German governments and sees in them the roots of the super-soldier serum that created Captain America. "Here the heroics of Captain America are shown to have their roots in a radical racist politics that paints the U.S. as more like and in league with the Nazis than different from and at war with them."[43] This point is made visually when Bradley breaks into a concentration camp on his suicide mission and is faced with a scene not unlike the one that made him.

*Truth* is a compelling counterpoint to the narratives of white nationalist superheroes and the struggles of heroes like the Falcon to fit in to those narratives. It is perhaps not surprising that *Truth* did not do well with longtime superhero comic book readers (although thanks to media coverage it sold well to non–comics readers).[44] It serves as a rejection of the universalizing narratives of national innocence, with the results etched onto the black-skinned bodies distorted by experiments. Grabham's previously quoted comment that "the boundaries of the nation are [. . .] delineated *on and through* bodies" here takes on an even more sinister meaning.[45]

In the United Kingdom, the narration of a multiracial society is far more recent than in the United States.[46] Thus, early debates over the embodiment of British nationalist superheroes were rooted more in questions of class and nationality (i.e., Englishness) than in race. However, the 2008–2009 publication of *Captain Britain and MI13* introduced Faiza Hussein, a British Muslim doctor. While tending to the wounded during a superpowered melee she falls victim to an alien blast, through which she gains the ability to heal people by taking their bodies apart and putting them back together again. She joins MI13, the British superhero team, using her abilities in battle to freeze enemies bodily; she refrains from hurting anyone as a result of both her Hippocratic oath and her religious sensibilities. The wizard Merlin persuades her to attempt to draw the sword Excalibur from a stone (as per Arthurian legend), and her nonviolent nature allows her to do so. When she and the MI13 hero Black Knight[47] go to her parents and show her father that Excalibur chose Faiza as its champion, Faiza's father couches this selection as proof of British multiculturalism: "Ahhh! I've never felt . . . I can feel it . . . it is of this nation . . . and thus . . . mine. Ours. Astonishing! I'm not a particularly religious man, [Black Knight], but I can feel it . . . this is . . . blessed. Faiza, do you know what this is? This is unconditional acceptance."[48] Eventually Faiza takes the name Excalibur as her superhero nom de plume and becomes romantically involved with the crusader hero Black Knight, embodying multiculturalism in a rather different way.

Faiza Hussein was the creation of writer Paul Cornell, who "wanted to write something genuinely multicultural without there being a big thing about it."[49] Unlike the Falcon, then, Faiza did not have to stand in for her entire ethnicity but still needed to be accurately portrayed as a member of the British Pakistani community. To that end, Cornell convened a panel of British Muslim women to serve as consultants. The effort paid off, even pointing him in new directions that he previously had not considered. For instance, he had previously thought that "getting Faiza into a romance would be a big thing, and I would save it until I had a bit of experience at this. But my Muslim ladies immediately said 'Oooooh! We like the look of the Black Knight; she ought to be with him!'"[50] Having a British Muslim become romantically involved with the descendant and embodiment of British Crusaders was obviously a daring move, but one that Cornell navigated successfully: "I haven't had a single letter of complaint from a Muslim. All I've had is positive stuff. Because, to be honest, any mistakes I've made in terms of head gear or language is nothing compared to seeing one of their own [wield Excalibur]." Excalibur is here conceived of as a metaphor for the idealized British color-blind society; Excalibur *chose* Faiza, seeing the essential goodness in her. Giving Faiza the archetypal symbol of British power and sovereignty inaugurates a different kind of nationalist superhero in which gender and race resonate in new ways; Faiza's perspective as an ethnic "other" and unwillingness to shed blood position her as an ideal representative of the multiethnic, multiracial Britain that Cornell is advocating. As Cornell explains, "[Excalibur] doesn't go to the big champion—Lancelot doesn't get the sword, it's the little guy because he deserves it."[51]

## Indigeneity

If the question of race in *Captain America* has often been asked with regard to African Americans (the lack of Hispanics within the comic book in comparison is stark), and if in regard to British nationalist superheroes the question has until recently rarely been asked at all, Canadian nationalist superhero comic books have struggled to narrate the relationship between the white nation (and its metonym, the nationalist superhero) and the indigenous "other."[52] *Captain America* has a similar problem, but this is a marginalized tension in comparison to its treatment of black-white relations.

North American nationalist superhero comic books first feature Native Americans and Canadians during World War II, with these indigenous North Americans scripted as points of vulnerability in the war effort because of their naïveté and, in some cases, racism against whites. Nelvana of the Northern Lights is kept busy in her role as protector of the Inuit, as the Japanese repeatedly attempt to persuade them to rise up against the white Canadian state, anonymously ruining the Inuit hunting grounds and then plying the people with food. Interestingly, the criticism of white Canada lodged by the Japanese mirrors postcolonial critique that would become popular much later, as in the following scene:

> Japanese officer: We realize that you have many problems—we are your friends, so we wish to warn you that when the white man builds roads through your country, you will be enslaved. We are distributing these "fire-sticks" [dynamite] and food to enable you to destroy the white man! Go! Spread news that your liberators have come.
> Narrator: To the simple Eskimo, the red disc symbol of the rising sun means one thing now—friendship! Did they not give him food and "blow-up" sticks to protect his family?[53]

Even if they are seen as a vulnerability in the war effort, the featuring of the indigenous "other" in nationalist superhero comics performed useful identity work. For instance, the use of the term *Kablunets* by the Inuit to describe "evil white men" (presumably the Germans) in Nelvana's tales is useful in establishing the paternal relationship between the Inuit and the Canadian state because it tacitly implies the category of "good white men," represented by people like Nelvana and Corporal Keene.

This paternal narration of the relationship between the white state (whether the United States or Canada) and the indigenous "other" is also produced by the stock character of the helpful native. For instance, in 1942 Captain America and Bucky are attacked by a secret society of Native Americans known as the Vultures, "bitter enemies of white men." While investigating, they encounter Little Moose, a man whom Captain America saved from gangsters when he visited New York City. Remembering this kindness, Little Moose points them in the right direction, and after Captain America reveals the leader of the Vultures to be Japanese, Little Moose's braves rally to Captain America's call for backup: "Foreign sneaks are pretending to be Indians . . . they are using the name of the first Americans to hide behind while they attack."[54] This particular enunciation of insider/outsider identities recuperates "good" Native Americans like Little Moose as within the nation while nevertheless marking their racial otherness ("Let's give their copper colored hides some exercise!" says the embodiment of the American Dream).

The "helpful native" appears in the 1975 opening sequence of *Captain Canuck*, in which the hero and his sidekick are in the Canadian Arctic, on their way to a government base when they are attacked by a polar bear.[55] They are saved by Utak, an Inuit man going in the same direction:

> Captain Canuck: I owe you much Utak. We have come to stop an enemy that have come to capture our land.
> Utak: I hear great noise from Alert Station. Utaks [*sic*] friends at station! We will make it a swift journey with my [dog] team! [*Takes the heroes to the base.*][56]

The narration of nation and territory found in this exchange folds indigenous difference into a friendly subservience in the face of external attack, as was the case with Little Moose and his braves thirty years earlier.

At the end of that decade, the creation of Alpha Flight augured a different take on the racialized nationalist superhero; instead of embodying the nation, each hero represented a province in a superheroic form of Canadian federalism. The team itself, in its plurality, embodied a multicultural Canada. This was an expansion of the attempt in *Captain Canuck* to acknowledge the Anglo-Quebecois divide via the addition of two sidekicks for Captain Canuck, known as Redcoat and Kébec (Figure 3.2). Whereas their difference (there was no hint of conflict) was subsumed under the federal paternalism of Captain

Figure 3.2: Embodying the Anglo-Quebecois divide in Canada: Redcoat and Kébec. (Courtesy of Richard Comely. Used with permission.)

Canuck himself, for Alpha Flight difference was constitutive of the national team. Included in this constitutive (and essentialized) difference was Shaman, the first aboriginal member of Alpha Flight. Shaman served both as a marker of aboriginal difference and as a symbol of the modernity brought to the First Nations by the Canadian state. In a flashback, Shaman is shown rejecting his grandfather's request to take up traditional medicine in favor of modern medicine. However, when his wife dies despite his best efforts to save her using modern science (on the same day his grandfather passed away), Shaman re-evaluates his stance and studies the magic of the Sarcee tribe. This magic is the source of his superpower, particularly a mystical medicine bag from which Shaman can draw magical objects to assist him in moments of danger. Shaman serves to incorporate the "natural" and thereby feminized First Nations into the Canadian state project through his willing participation in the Canadian nationalist super-team. This particular constellation of Canadianness was appreciated by Brandon T., of Calgary, who wrote in to say that "Your presentation of the Canadian hero is so much better than the normal stereotypical 'Renfrew, the Singing Mountie.' And I am equally impressed with your handling of the Native American cast in your book. You portray them as the proud, dignified people they are."[57]

It took until 2004's *Captain Canuck: Unholy War* for the postracial multiculturalism represented by *Captain Britain and MI13*'s Faiza Hussein to appear in Canada. Instead of Utak, the helpful native, this reboot of Captain Canuck incorporated Keith Smoke as the police partner of David Semple, the hero's alter ego (they are both Mounties, happily not singing ones). Smoke is significant not for any major actions within the story line; rather, he is significant because he is unmarked as aboriginal except by name and minor visual cues.

Perhaps most important, his job as a Mountie defies the conventions of Canadian national narrative: "The Anglo-Canadian, British, and American Mountie popular fictions of the late nineteenth and early twentieth centuries aided and abetted white empire/nation building, representing the Mountie as an idealized sign of a masculinized imperial order whose job was to expel Native peoples and 'foreign' villains."[58] Like a British Pakistani wielding Excalibur, an aboriginal Mountie turns national mythology inside out to create new narrations of multiculturalism.

The role of Native Americans in *Captain America* is relatively minor in comparison to its analogues north of the forty-ninth parallel. With the exception of the wartime concerns over Native American–Japanese collaboration, *Captain America* never really engaged with notions of indigeneity. This changed in 1984 with the introduction of Jesse Black Crow, who performed the same role as Alpha Flight's Shaman—essentializing and integrating the indigenous population. In the Black Crow narrative, Captain America finds himself hassled by a black crow, which the reader learns is really Jesse Black Crow. The reader learns via flashback that Black Crow had an accident on a construction site and now uses a wheelchair. However, he periodically transforms into the aforementioned black crow, remembering nothing of it until one day he has a vision of his people's history, which inspires him to action. Jesse Black Crow twice attacks Captain America in human form, appearing in the form of a powerful Indian warrior. The first time, he defeats Captain America and takes a lock of his hair. The second time he attacks, he leads with a lecture:

> When you die, Captain—the sins of your fathers die with you! The scales will have found balance—the restless spirits of my people will have found harmony once more! And in that harmony, the past and the present can merge . . . become transformed . . . and this land we love so can birth a future worthy of both our peoples! Such is the will of the Earth spirit! Such is our destiny![59]

In the subsequent battle Captain America is about to lose again when he willingly submits to his opponent. With that, Jesse Black Crow laughs, hugs him, and disappears, with the implication being that blood sacrifice (i.e., material reparations for past injustice) is unnecessary in the face of symbolic submission.

Readers seemed to appreciate this reconciliation, even as they worked to resubordinate Black Crow to Captain America. One wrote:

> The most interesting aspect of this story is that the Black Crow and Captain America are both symbols of America. Yet, the Black Crow represents an America unlike Cap's America. The Black Crow is the spirit of the old, pre-1500 America. [. . .] Also, the Black Crow said that Captain America represents the NEW America. This is a bit narrow-minded

on the Black Crow's part. [. . .] Despite the fact that he wears the colors of the new America, Cap wants to see ALL Americans achieve the fulfillment of the American dream, regardless of their ethnic origins.[60]

Even more to the point, one letter-writer argued, "It is good that the Black Crow explained his reasons for attacking Cap, but he should not talk too much. Silence is much better than words in some situations."[61]

Jesse Black Crow appears again later that year when Captain America has been poisoned and is dying. This story line rhetorically expands on the Native/white rapprochement offered in the earlier story line by having Jesse Black Crow receive a vision from the Earth Spirit that warns of Captain America's danger:

> You are the vessel for the power of the Indian nations! You are the protector of the dream! You are America as it was—and as it shall be! You are Black Crow! See now the vessel for the power of this modern age! He, too, is protector of the dream! He is America as-it-is—and as it shall be! He is Captain America! You are two in body—two in color—one in purpose! You are brothers—and your brother is dying![62]

In this passage the (white) ideal of the American Dream is grafted retrospectively onto Native American culture, and the purported continuities of Native and white political rule in North America are proffered, if tacit. Black Crow does as the Earth Spirit commands and tends to the dying Captain America with tribal medicine. While doing so, he incorporates his people into a liberal notion of citizenship even while conceding Captain America's right to embody the nation:

> You are the embodiment of America. The panorama of the country's history dwells within you. That is why you must not die. You must keep on fighting to make the American dream a reality[. . . .] Let me help you, my brother. Trust in me, your friends, in all Americans![63]

Just like the Falcon, Black Crow's deployment of the term *brother* links the ethnicities of America in a horizontal fellowship rather than a hierarchical set of power relations. In less than a year, the avenging spirit of the Native Americans had been converted into a mechanism for erasing ethnic difference.

## Conclusions

Chapters 2 and 3 highlight the various problems inherent in the idea of a single hero embodying an entire nation. The complex and specific interactions of race and gender in the United States, the United Kingdom, and Canada make for a wide array of narrative engagements on the topic of identity. Intriguingly, the comics illustrate how similar attempts to justify the white hero for a multicultural nation have gone through several stages in each country. The paternalism of the early heroes has steadily given way to more multicultural conceptions of the nation, represented by Faiza Hussein and Keith Smoke, but only after going through awkward intermediate stages, perhaps best understood through an examination of the Falcon.

Although this could be understood as a teleology of progress, it is important for critical scholars to remain focused on how "heroes of color" are used to recuperate racial others to national narratives in ways that are productive of geopolitical differences in legitimacy, modernity, and authority among and within states. For instance, it is well established that the United States, Canada, and the United Kingdom position themselves as beacons of human rights in the international realm and draw on this discourse for legitimacy. Therefore, the multicultural nation imagined via characters like Faiza Hussein, the Falcon, and Shaman is part of a discursive ensemble that produces geopolitical "power." Even so, these groundbreaking heroes, male and female, are embodied in feminine roles (e.g., doctor, social worker, medicine man) in contrast to the primary, white male heroes (who are often policemen, scientists, or other masculine figures). Therefore, the attempt to negotiate multiculturalism in this context has thus far reproduced some of the gendered/racialized understandings of the nation that the story lines were intended to overcome. Rather than accept this troubling "progress" as the outcome of a liberal "false choice" between ideals and reality, this analysis pushes further to bring to light how nation-states and their ideals are produced and made commonsensical. To this end, we now shift from a focus on superheroic bodies to national narratives.

# 4

## Origins

Brian Braddock: We fought together once, you know, [Captain America] and I. He had a presence that isn't easy to put into words. But whenever I hear the words "super hero," that have been used and overused until they seem to have no meaning anymore—I think of Captain America. And the American people loved him, Meggan, in a way I could never understand. It's not like I was revered when I was Captain Britain.

Meggan: Does that bother you, Brian?

Brian Braddock: Not really. Here and America are very different: two countries divided by a common language and all that. It's not in the British to love anyone that unconditionally.[1]

This chapter's opening quotation works both intratextually, as an explanation of the relative popularity of these two nationalist superheroes within their own countries, and extratextually, as a commentary on the struggle to transpose the American generic conventions of the nationalist superhero into new countries, each with unique national narratives already extant and with varying relationships to nationalism itself.

Connecting narratives of identity in the United States, Canada, and the United Kingdom with the specific origins of their nationalist superheroes has been uniquely challenging for creative staff. In the United States the relative publishing success of Captain America has meant that over time his origin narrative has had to be amended and embellished to keep up with more than seventy years of shifting national narratives. In Canada, contrary to the situation in the United States (and to a lesser extent Great Britain), the parlous economies of comic book publishing have led to frequent reworkings of superhero origin stories, which when commercially successful in engaging with Canadian nationalism have generally emphasized distinction from American superheroes, especially through the mark of Canadian "natural" heroism as well as good governance. Captain Britain, however, as the most-published British nationalist superhero, has suffered more than most from a perceived disconnect between his origin narrative and narratives of Britishness. Whereas Canadian nationalism has a long history of "othering" the United States, British nationalism has a more stigmatized place within British politics (as Captain Britain himself noted at the beginning of the chapter). In this chapter the importance of superhero origins in connecting to and shaping national narratives is explored via investigation of not only how nationalist superheroes in each country gain their powers and mission but also how those origin stories are modified over time to both resonate with readers' understandings of national identity and provide new narratives with which readers can associate themselves.

## Narrative Foundations of Identity

Homi Bhabha focused attention in the early 1990s on how nationhood is often narrated in ways that homogenize the national experience; in Bhabha's words, "the difference of space returns as the Sameness of time, turning Territory into Tradition, turning the People into One."[2] This is accomplished through the pedagogy of national discourse. In particular, Bhabha highlights the foundational narration of "out of many, one" as common to many narrations of nation (even serving as the national motto of the United States).[3] Indeed, within linear understandings of time, every story has to have a beginning, and that beginning is central to understanding all that follows.

   Of course, just as there is no single narration of nation, but instead a multitude coexisting, there is no single origin point for these narrations. As Edward Said argued, "To take account of this horizontal, secular space of the crowded spectacle of the modern nation [. . .] implies that no single explanation sending one back immediately to a single origin is adequate."[4] For instance, Thomas Schlereth has shown that the selection of origin stories in the United States was laden with sectarian and ethnic import. For nineteenth-century American Catholics, the celebration of Christopher Columbus's "discovery" of the Americas served as a foundational counternarrative to the landing of the Pilgrims in New England 128 years later, which had dominated national mythology. This historical outflanking of New England Protestantism's centrality to America was one-upped by the 1887 erection of a statue in Boston of (the Protestant convert) Leif Eriksson, who had purportedly landed in North America several centuries before Columbus. To overcome the (now) Canadian location of Eriksson's exploits, a faux-Scandinavian rune stone was planted on a Minnesota farm sometime during that same decade.[5] These various origin narratives were not purely about sectarian pride but were wrapped up in the increasing flows of immigrants from southern and eastern Europe during the latter half of the nineteenth century, which called into question the Anglo-Saxon domination of the country. Political power in the United States, then as now, was co-productive of historical narrative; in that struggle for which moment really mattered can be seen a struggle for which population groups and countries of origin really mattered.

The way in which national origins are negotiated is caught up in the circulation of media artifacts. For instance, Robert Burgoyne argues that Terrence Malick's film *The New World* (2005) "both challenges and reinforces the traditional story of the encounter [between Native Americans and English settlers at Jamestown], depicting it as both harrowing and full of utopian possibility, presenting the narrative as a tone poem of contrasting and dissonant parts."[6] The film uses traditional narratives of colonist and Native American harmony through its narration of the romance of John Smith and Pocahontas (each a stand-in for their societies, their coupling an origin story for the nation); it also decenters the colonists' experience by presenting Jamestown from the perspective of Pocahontas, making the colonists seem foreign and out of place. Unlike the aforementioned sectarian contest over which naval landing to prioritize, Malick manages to reimagine this origin moment as something else: the end of indigenous civilization as it existed before.

Nationalist superheroes clearly embody the nation in ways less subtle than John Smith and Pocahontas. A fundamental part of a superhero's narrative is the hero's origin, which "effectively locates them in the super-hero universe and defines who and where they are in relation to established characters, events, and plot lines. An important feature of origins is that they are drawn from a range of cultural resources, including science, but also magic, religion, myth, legend, folklore and so on."[7] Origin stories of superheroes are important because they frame the actions that follow; they provide not only a motivation for what is certainly an unusual vocation but also a context in which action occurs. A commonly cited example is Batman; Bruce Wayne decided to become Batman as a result of his parents' murder at the hands of Gotham City's criminals. His desire to strike fear into the hearts of the underworld led him to self-consciously adopt his dark and fearsome appearance and motivated his intense training and fitness regimen (he has no actual superpowers, beyond unlimited industrial wealth inherited from his parents). His nemesis, the Joker, can be seen as flowing from this origin story. Where the hero adopts a dark and nightmarish exterior, the villain adopts a comedic, light visage; where the hero seeks to impose order on the city, the villain embodies entropy and chaos. Everything flows from the origin story.

While usually not making historical claims about when or how the nation's overarching story began, nationalist superhero origin stories can make claims about what makes that nation distinct and that point of distinction forms a different kind of origin story. A parallel can be found in Frederick Jackson Turner's frontier thesis, itself a kind of origin story: the frontier is the site at which Europeans are transformed into Americans. The frontier thesis is not about a foundational point or a historical origin understood in the sense of linear time, but it describes a set of processes that transform people from a banal identity to one spectacular and valued, somewhat like a superhero origin story: "A character's origin can be thought of as defining the initial *moment of transformation*, when their status as 'super' is established, instituting a shift from the ordinary to the extra-ordinary."[8] It therefore becomes important to pay attention to not only how nationalist superheroes come to be so but also how that story is modified over time and how readers react to these modifications. This chapter engages in just this task, organizing the nationalist superheroes in question in accordance with the nation they are narrating.

## Genesis

### United States

A brief story found in *Captain America Comics #1* sets the stage: with Nazi spies attacking the U.S. defense industries in anticipation of eventual American intervention in the war, President Franklin D. Roosevelt comes up with a plan. Later, frail Steve Rogers, desperate for American intervention in the war but categorized 4F by the military and thus unable to serve, is offered the chance to take part in a top-secret army project. Given the top-secret super-soldier serum by Jewish émigré Dr. Reinstein (an obvious reference to Albert Einstein), Steve Rogers is transformed from a frail, sickly boy into the pinnacle of human athleticism. He is to be the first of an army of super-soldiers, but a Nazi agent among the spectators suddenly opens fire, killing Dr. Reinstein, the only person who knew the formula for the super-soldier serum. Steve Rogers is placed undercover as a private in the U.S. Army, where he is one day discovered by the camp mascot, Bucky Barnes, when changing into his uniform.[9]

This origin story, as initially told, is only eight pages long. Together he and Bucky defend the United States against "fifth columnists" and then, with the U.S. entry into war, start to fight overseas with U.S. troops (interspersed with domestic adventures). The defensive orientation of Captain America, and thus America itself, is narrated in this origin via his lack of superpowers (while an Olympic athlete in his strength, stamina, and quickness, Captain America has no more glamorous powers like Superman's flight or superstrength) and the fact that his primary accessory is a *shield*.[10] This section of the chapter focuses first on the retelling of this origin, with the slight modifications that were introduced over time. Then we move on to discuss the significant additions and elaborations made to the origin story over that time, and finally we focus on a particular story line that used Captain America's origin as a focal point for the interrogation of American morality.

The 1964 revival of the character in the pages of *Tales of Suspense* marks a break with the previous incarnation of the hero. The abandoning of wartime xenophobia and Cold War McCarthyism prompted the development of a more thoughtful, liberal Captain America. However, it was difficult to reconcile this new "man out of time" American ideal with his wartime origin story. Indeed,

Captain America's origin is retold twice in 1965 (one an original reenvisioning, the other a reprint of the 1940 original), and again in 1969, 1970, 1974, 1981, and 1985, and then only occasionally until the present. As comics writer Paul Cornell has argued, "[Writer] Stan [Lee] is desperate. [. . .] He keeps going back to the origin to try and tweak it slightly to find some way that this is going to work."[11] The flurry of retellings of Captain America's origin in his first decade of the current publishing era signify an attempt to come to find some narrative purchase on the character, and over time this was achieved by an array of slight modifications and larger elaborations on the initial origin story.

For instance, one small facet of the initial origin story that has been changed over time relates to the Nazi assassin who kills Dr. Reinstein. In the 1940 version, the newly turgid Steve Rogers attacks the spy after the murder, and in the melee Rogers punches the spy into some electrical equipment, which electrocutes him. However, in the first retelling from 1965 the assassin runs away while spouting the rhetoric of Nazi supremacy, only for him to be accidentally electrocuted by running into an "omniverter."[12] This detail would remain in place until a 2009 trip back to Captain America's origin moment when once again the assassin is thrown into the electrical equipment by Steve Rogers.[13] This small detail is important because it traces the willingness of (Captain) America to exert lethal force against enemies.

The role of Captain America's wartime sidekick Bucky over this period is also subject to incremental change. The 1964 reworking of Captain America's continuity established that a 1945 mission led to Bucky's seeming demise and to Captain America's immersion in the frigid North Atlantic. He was frozen in an iceberg for almost two decades, only to be discovered and defrosted by the superhero team he would later lead, the Avengers. Captain America's emotional life in the 1960s and 1970s is tied to mourning Bucky and blaming himself for the loss.[14] In the original stories from World War II, Bucky is an enthusiastic youngster who tags along with Captain America and joins in on the missions, spraying machine-gun fire and hurling insults and grenades at Nazis. Just as Captain America's violence in World War II had been sanitized (e.g., the electrocution of Reinstein's assassin), it would not do to have Captain America bringing a young adolescent into battle with him. But whereas Captain America was made more *idealistic*, Bucky had to be made more *realistic*. The original story had Bucky as the camp mascot, but by 1999 Bucky was understood to be an operator who worked the camp's black market. By 2004, the discovery of Captain America's identity by Bucky was tweaked such that it was followed by a meeting with a general, in which the army offered Bucky the chance to be a propaganda figure in opposition to the Hitler Youth by serving anonymously alongside Captain America. This authorization of Bucky's wartime exploits takes the onus off Captain America for leading Bucky into battle (he is even seen protesting to the general about child endangerment). Just a year later Bucky's role was elaborated yet again, only this time we learn that Bucky was a virtual killing machine, trained by the British Special Air Service (SAS) at age sixteen, forced on an unwilling Captain America by the U.S. Army to do the killing that Captain America, as a symbol of American virtue, simply could not be caught doing. The initial discovery of Captain America's secret identity is now revealed to be simply a cover story designed for media relations.[15] This change was contested by one reader, Jesse Ojeda, who was

> troubled about [. . .] how you'd have Captain America letting a 16 year-old kid do all the killing and maiming of people as he looked away. [. . .] It was certainly the great war and ugly things needed to be done, but you made Cap seem like a coward, knowing what Bucky is doing but looking the other way because of his ideals.[16]

Another key modification to Captain America's origin is the role of the Red Skull, who does not feature in the 1940 origin story (although *a* Red Skull does appear in the first issue).[17] By 1987 the military project that produced Captain America was being narrated as a response to the fearsome appearance of the Red Skull, as Captain America describes here: "The [Red] Skull became such a potent symbol for the cause of Nazism that some anonymous bigwig in the U.S. War Department came up with the idea of creating a counter-symbol to represent freedom and liberty[.] . . . I guess you could say that in a way Captain America owes his existence to the Red Skull." Collectively, these three changes to the origin story produce a Captain America who is less concerned with warfare than with American identity itself. By pushing Captain America out of the material world of World War II and into the symbolic world of American identity, and by seeing this as a response to foreign propaganda, Captain America was detached from his wartime role as super-soldier and instead renarrated as the embodiment of the American Dream, despite the narrative possibilities of deploying him to various geopolitical hotspots as a proxy Cold Warrior. Of course, policing American identity was just as much a part of the Cold War as military action against communists (a point well known by George Kennan and many others).[18]

This American identity should be understood as related to, but not identifiable with, the U.S. government. One significant elaboration on the origin story that has taken place over the last seventy years is the steady darkening of the U.S. government's role in the creation of Captain America. In the 1940 *Captain America Comics* origin, the government is an unambiguously positive source of scientific modernity. However, over the past seventy years the portrayal of the U.S. government has steadily soured. The first hint of this in relation to Captain America is Project: Tess, which was revealed in 1986 to be the opposite number of Project: Rebirth, the project that led to the creation of the super-soldier serum. Tess was a robot warrior created out of President Roosevelt's concern that the super-soldier serum would lead to a master race attempting to gain political power. The fascist overtones of the super-soldier serum are here positioned as of concern to the U.S. government.

However, the U.S. government's interest in fascism is an element of the origin narrative that emerges in part because of an unintentional change in the origin story when it was renarrated in 1965. Writer Stan Lee changed Prof. Reinstein's name to Dr. Abraham Erskine, thereby losing the overt connection to Albert Einstein (and Jewishness).[19] The loss of the Einstein connection enabled Erskine to be a more nefarious character, as seen in the miniseries *Truth: Red, White, and Black* (mentioned in Chapter 3). In this story we discover that the Germans, the British, and the Americans met before World War I to discuss "racial hygiene" policy. Hitler sent his top scientists to meet up with American eugenicists and share their revolutionary medical techniques—hence, Project: Super Soldier was born. Therefore, the U.S. government's attempts to create a super-soldier are complicated by connections to not only militarism but also eugenics.

The darkening of the U.S. government role in Captain America's creation sharpens the contrast with Captain America. This is accomplished not only by changing the emplotment of the U.S. government in the origin of Captain America but also by fleshing out the character of Steve Rogers (before being Captain America) in a way not attempted in 1940. A 1991 limited series titled *The Adventures of Captain America* filled in the backstory of his selection for the super-soldier serum. This story continued to flesh out the qualities of Steve Rogers that allowed him to become Captain America. He was in competition with a Harvard physicist, a Notre Dame fullback, and a racist. Rogers is by far the weakest, and he struggles in the physical testing yet never gives up; however, the physicist ends up being a hemophiliac and the fullback injures his knee in a fight with the racist. Given the two remaining, the military chose Steve Rogers despite his weakness:

> **Col. Fletcher:** What we have left is courage and calamity.
> **Prof. Reinstein:** Und you fear the possibilities regarding Mr. Hodge [the racist]?
> **Col. Fletcher:** The soldier in me says go for courage every time.[20]

This renarration of the origin story allows the character of Steve Rogers to be seen as central to his later success, taking away his reliance on the super-soldier serum for his distinctiveness. While President Roosevelt would be quoted as saying, "You became Captain America long before they pumped you full of any chemicals,"[21] Steve Rogers is not shown as a static character; rather, he is shown as a socially awkward, puny muralist for the Works Progress Administration slowly growing to be the icon of a nation.[22] Together, these modifications and elaborations on the origin narrative allow the character of Captain America to be productive of peacetime American identity in ways completely different than during World War II. Maintaining continuity, and yet keeping a superheroic origin relevant to storytelling, is not always easy, as a final example from *Captain America* demonstrates.

A 1990 story line titled "Streets of Poison" connected President Reagan's war on drugs with Captain America's origin in a manner uncomfortable for the star-spangled hero. Captain America finds Fabian, his mechanic, looking thinner, working long hours, and paranoid, having become hooked on "Ice" (seemingly a stand-in for crack cocaine). Taking the moral high ground, Captain America suspends Fabian from his job and gets him into rehab, but only after this exchange:

> **Captain America:** Besides the harm you're doing to yourself, there's another consideration. The Avengers are role models to the nation. We simply cannot tolerate unhealthy, illegal substance abuse to go on among us.
> **Fabian:** But, Cap . . . what about the super-soldier serum? Don't you owe your very powers . . . to a drug?
> **Captain America:** That's . . . uh, different.[23]

In one fell swoop Fabian has brought into focus a contradiction in the narratives of Captain America; in World War II Captain America symbolized American scientific modernity (combined judiciously with American courage), with the super-soldier serum both the marker of, and guarantee for, American geopolitical superiority. However, another American narrative often harnessed by Captain America is the virtue of hard work, which was effectively circumvented by the serum.

Deciding he needs to do something about the high rate of addiction in New York, Captain America traces a drug distribution network back to a booby-trapped stash house. When the bomb inside explodes, Captain America is exposed to Ice, which bonds to the super-soldier serum in his veins and causes him to start acting erratically (Figure 4.1). He is captured by his friends as he descends into hallucinations, and they give him a total blood transfusion that removes the Ice from his system, as well as the super-soldier serum.

Waking up, Captain America worries whether he can keep on being a superhero without the serum in his blood; he ventures out to prove himself, eventually battling the Red Skull's goon, Crossbones, and defeating him in a difficult battle. With renewed confidence, he returns to his base and refuses the offer of his blood returned, clean of Ice: "I found out something important tonight. I don't need the serum to be Captain America. Perhaps I once did, to give my non-athletic body what nature did not. But that was a long time ago. Now I am what I am with or without the drug in my veins. I don't need my old blood back. I don't want it either. [. . .] Hey, if I can't just say no, who can?"[24] As it turns out, however, Captain America's moral stand carries no cost, as he soon discovers that his body has been genetically modified by the super-soldier process and his cells now produce the serum on their own. He regains his prior strength and agility soon enough, newly confident that Captain America is the product of character and hard work, not steroids. This earned the disdain of reader

Figure 4.1: Captain America, addicted to Ice in a plotline that interrogated the ethics of the hero's origin. (Copyright © 2012 Marvel Characters, Inc. Used with permission.)

Ali Kokmen: "I smell a cop-out! Making the super-soldier serum a permanent fixture to Cap's physiology thoroughly undercuts any and all anti-drug sentiment in the 'Streets of Poison' tale."[25] Most fans, however, appreciated the story line, with Howard Kidd writing that the "portrayal of drugs [. . .] has virtually never been explored in this type of fiction through the hero's eyes" and with Kent Lowther arguing that the story line redeemed Captain America: "You did it—you explained that the Super-Soldier Serum/virus is not akin to steroids or the illegal recreational drugs. There is more to the Serum than physical enhancement and you have wonderfully explained that."[26] Of course, the story line did not actually do either of these things—but the character of Steve Rogers was seen as being more important to the emergence of Captain America than drugs. Nevertheless, Lowther's argument shows the anxiety that could be found in any equation of Captain America with drugs because of its implications for the war on drugs and the carceral state produced through that war.

## Canada

Because of their generally weak publishing history (with the exception of *Alpha Flight*), Canadian nationalist superheroes either never get the chance to have their origin stories elaborated in the extensive manner just described, or they are stopped and reimagined so many times that it is hard to find a coherent thread through the character's history. This is certainly the case with Captain Canuck, whose uneven publication history has led to his (re)introduction four times over the past thirty years. The initial run of *Captain Canuck* under creator Richard Comely in 1975 lasted three issues; issue #4 did not come out until 1979, as part of a relatively stable run of twelve issues that were produced by the larger stable of CKR Productions that year and the next. A four-issue run was sporadically produced by Richard Comely between 1993 and 1996, and then the character lay dormant until 2004, when the hero was resurrected by Riel and Drue Langlois in a four-issue series titled *Captain Canuck: Unholy War*. In these four series, there are three different Captain Canucks, each with his own origin.[27]

The first issue of *Captain Canuck* clearly owes a debt to the Captain America archetype of the nationalist superhero, although with some clear distinctions. The comic book is set nearly twenty years in the (then) future, during a period of Canadian global hegemony. This hegemony, however, differed from the American (nonfictional) hegemony with which it is obviously to be juxtaposed. The source of Canadian hegemony is not imperialism but rather high demand for Canadian natural resources: "The predictions of Canada becoming the most important country in the world became a reality in the 1980s. This posed new threats and problems for Canada's leaders and for the countries that depend upon Canada's supply of natural resources."[28] This sense of natural abundance carries over to the origin narrative of Captain Canuck. Unlike

Captain America's origins in the military-industrial complex, Captain Canuck initially has no superpowers at all and is "naturally" super. Creator Richard Comely said as much in his letters-to-the-editor column: "Captain Canuck's tremendous strength and endurance come from a good wholesome diet and lots of exercise. His alertness and determination come from having a strong, clean mind."[29] Letters written by readers regarding this origin confirmed the pleasure they took in this sense of Canadian-ness. John Deyarmond wrote that the origin of Captain Canuck "indicates a humaneness and profoundness that puts your comic in a class by itself. It is this, I believe, that makes it distinctively Canadian."[30] John Toews similarly argued, "I like the idea of a Canadian hero not using sorcery or something phoney [sic] like that."[31] This rejection of American origin narratives in favor of something more Canadian can be seen as a commentary on the American-ness of the superhero genre itself, with this notion of American-ness defined as excess and artificial grandiosity.

When *Captain Canuck* continued in 1979 after a publishing hiatus, the comic was retooled to be more profitable in a competitive North American marketplace. One of the changes made to the character was the revelation that, without his knowledge, Captain Canuck had been given his fighting capacity by an alien ray from space. This change in his origin story undercut many Canadian readers' identification with the narrative of Canadian identity that Captain Canuck embodied. Reader Jim Bell wrote in to complain: "As for Captain Canuck, I was sorry to see that his strength is not all 'good clean living,' as you stated in one of your earlier issues. To me, this makes him seem phony. It lowers him to the level of the American superheroes, and he becomes just another of the horrid mess of ridiculous characters with impossible powers."[32] Juxtaposing Bell's letter with Deyarmond and Toews's letters from five years earlier is instructive; what has been seemingly lost is a sense of Canadian naturalness in the face of an encroaching American baroque.

The relaunches of Captain Canuck in 1993 and 2004 each incorporated a new title character, purportedly inspired by the earlier *Captain Canuck*. Darren Oak and David Semple each come to the role in different ways. Darren Oak and his brother Nathan came from a wealthy Ontario family; Nathan plots to take over the country by inciting civil war between Anglophone and Francophone Canadians.[33] Darren realizes that he must take up the mantle of Captain Canuck after reading his deaf son's school report titled "My Country Canada," thus being moved to preserve the federal state from his brother's machinations (Figure 4.2). Darren Oak, as Captain Canuck, returns the character to his "natural," nonsuperpowered roots. David Semple similarly lacks superpowers, but also any fighting skill. The Langlois brothers effectively satirize American superheroes by trying to capture a sense of realism. David Semple needs no angst, no crisis, to become a superhero: "My parents *weren't* murdered in front of my very eyes . . . no one killed my partner. I'm *not* part of a top secret government project. So what makes a guy put on a costume and fight crime? What if a man became a superhero just because he knew he could?"[34] Pushing this realism

Figure 4.2: Darren Oak, moved by his son's school report about Canadian multicultural-ism to become Captain Canuck. (Courtesy of Richard Comely. Used with permission.)

further, writer Riel Langlois sought to defy the stereotype of the nationalist superhero through his narration of Captain Canuck as a poor combatant:

> In real life, a skilled martial artist can't really fight a whole bunch of guys simultaneously—they just overwhelm him. I think we all know that on either a conscious or subconscious level. That's why Jackie Chan movies work so well: Jackie Chan is always running away from large groups of people, and a lot of his stunts center on that. David Semple believes in the myth that one man can fight a gang, but *Unholy War* is about his gradual realization that he has to become more tactical.[35]

*Alpha Flight* similarly wrestles with the question of what it means to be a Canadian superhero in a genre dominated by Americans. The nationalist superhero on the team (although collectively Alpha Flight can also be understood as a nationalist superhero team—see Chapter 3) is Guardian.[36] Canadian artist John Byrne eventually invented the whole team but conceived Guardian first as a character to appear in *Captain America*, in a story where he went north to meet his opposite number in Canada. While the story was never published, the character was eventually used in a story in *The Uncanny X-Men* in which the Canadian government sends a superpowered agent to hunt down Wolverine, an X-Man who is the product of the Canadian iteration of the super-soldier project that created Captain America.[37] The rest of the team was invented to help Guardian battle the X-Men; when fan reaction sparked the idea of an *Alpha Flight* comic book, the characters were all blank slates to be filled in by Byrne. Guardian's 1983 fleshed-out origin centered on Jim "Mac" Hudson, an engineer for the Am-Can Petroleum Company. Hudson devised a powerful suit to explore for oil in Alberta and built it using Am-Can money. However, the CEO of Am-Can tells Hudson that the suit is to be turned over to the U.S. military to be used in the war in Vietnam because most of Am-Can's investors are American. Hudson refuses, stealing the suit and destroying the blueprints: "I designed this rig to expedite oil exploration—but if it could be used for offense, it could also be used for defense . . . Canada's."[38] He and his girlfriend (later wife), Heather, turn to the Canadian government, who agree to the (false) story that Hudson has been working for the Canadian government for the past six years, and therefore the suit is theirs. Hudson goes on to wear the suit as the superhero Guardian and to form Alpha Flight around him under the aegis of the Canadian government. Guardian's origin, and to a certain extent Alpha Flight's as well, has a narrative focus on the vulnerability of Canadian sovereignty to American capital, and on the beneficence of the Canadian government (versus the imperialism of the U.S. government). "Mac" Hudson would soon die and Heather would wear the Guardian suit; under her leadership Alpha Flight would become less an arm of the Canadian government and more a team of outlaws, like the Canadian X-Men. However, in Byrne's original formulation Guardian and his superhero team were explicitly part of the state apparatus.

Like Captain Canuck, Guardian and Alpha Flight emphasize the role of the state in protecting Canadian sovereignty, especially vis-à-vis the United States; central to this is the Cold War context of Canada as at times uncomfortably integrated with U.S. hemispheric security plans, including the emplacement of American nuclear missiles.

The origins of Nelvana of the Northern Lights date far earlier than those of Captain Canuck or Guardian and leave behind the scientific modernity embedded in the origins of Captain America and the other Canadian heroes (even Captain Canuck's much-loathed alien ray from space falls under the category of science fiction). As stated earlier, she is the daughter of the god Koliak, who mated with a human woman. The god/human liaison (or alternatively, rape) is a classic trope of myth and legend to explain the arrival of a hero, from Zeus and Danaë to the Christian God and Mary. The relationship of Nelvana to the nation is less obvious here than in the other heroes' origin stories. Nevertheless, her connection to the Canadian landscape (see Chapter 6) and her role as the protector of the Inuit (which parallels the paternalism of the Canadian state— see Chapter 3) identify her as an agent of Canada (later she makes it official by moving south and becoming an actual wartime agent of Canada). The mythical nature of her origin story itself makes claims about Canada, giving the Canadian state divine sanction (here Nelvana's whiteness is relevant as a cultural marker) and producing Canadian-ness as a transcendental identity. Unfortunately, Nelvana's publication record is too scant to allow for elaborations and amendments that would show how this origin narrative would advance. However, this kind of origin story, rooted in myth and magic, is more fully explored in the superheroes of the United Kingdom.

## United Kingdom

Debates over the (dis)enchantment of modernity have generally passed superheroes by, although Simon Locke has argued that "science, or its representation, is central to the constitution of the fantasy worlds ('universes') that superheroes inhabit."[39] Richard Reynolds highlights the juxtaposition of science and magic in superheroes' worlds; while the generic history of superheroes owes a great deal to the world of science fiction, Reynolds's labeling of superheroes as a "modern mythology" hints at the ineffable powers attributed to some of these characters.[40] Locke concludes that within superhero comics, "science is commonly treated as one means to attain an enchanted condition that brings contact with a transcendent cosmological order in which all ways of knowing and being are accorded their place."[41] While he is undoubtedly correct that science and magic are seen in superhero comics as two paths to the same enlightenment, for nationalist superheroes, it matters which path brings transcendence.[42] Indeed, as we have seen previously, the way in which a superhero's power is gained is a key part of the narration of national purpose and power.

Captain Britain's origins veer back and forth between science and magic during his over thirty-five-year career.[43] As with Captain Canuck (but to a lesser degree), this alternation between the twin poles of science and magic is partly attributable to the hero's checkered publication history. His marginality within the larger Marvel Universe meant that Captain Britain has always suffered from too much or too little character development. The first issue of *Captain Britain* introduces Brian Braddock, a Ph.D. student from Thames University working at the Darkmoor Research Centre. There he and his supervisor are working on a fusion reactor that will solve the world's energy problems when they are interrupted by the villainous Reaver, who wants to kidnap the scientists and make them work for him so that he can dominate global energy markets. Brian escapes on a motorcycle but crashes within a mystical circle of stones. Merlin and his daughter Roma appear within the circle, and Merlin offers Brian a choice—he must choose either the amulet of right or the sword of might.[44] Inexplicably, given that he is surrounded by the Reaver's men, he chooses the amulet and is immediately transformed into Captain Britain. Roma gives him his charge and situates him within a mythic Britishness:

> Rejoice, my son, for thou hast chosen the Amulet of Right over the Sword of Might! Therefore, let there be beauty and strength—power and compassion—honour and humility, mirth and reverence—within you[.] . . . Be one with thy brothers of the Round Table—with Arthur and Lancelot, Gawain and Galahad, with them all[.] . . . Be thou what they were—a hero! Strive forever to maintain the rule of right—of law and justice—against those who live and rule by might.[45]

This magical origin, however, was quickly contested by reader Keith Sparrow, who argued that "the obvious choice for a British superhero's origin was medieval backgrounds, but let's see something other than that, huh? Freak chemical explosions happen over here as well, y'know?"[46] At least with this reader, the lack of modernity implicit in Captain Britain's origin seemed to set the United Kingdom apart from the United States in a way that rendered the country static and museum-like, despite the prominence in the story of nuclear fusion and Braddock's scientific proficiency. This initial conflict over the meanings associated with Captain Britain would continue to the present.

After the initial run of *Captain Britain* petered out, Captain Britain returned in his own title in 1985.[47] Writer Alan Moore had taken over in the interim and had begun to trial the literary deconstruction he would perfect in the superhero genre over the next few years.[48] He began by highlighting the science/magic ambiguity of the hero's origin. In Captain Britain's words, "They made me choose. But there was no choice. They dipped me in magic and clothed me in science. They made me a hero."[49] Further, by taking the emphasis off Brian's choice (the amulet or the sword), his own moral claim to heroism is deemphasized. Moore's next move was to make Brian Braddock even more a victim of circumstance by introducing the idea that Brian is only half human; his father had been one of Merlin's chosen guard and had left the mystical realm of Otherworld to prepare the earth for Merlin's arrival. His powers are *now* derived from this alien heritage rather than solely from the amulet of right. Like Captain Canuck's earlier inclusion of alien origins, this met with some dubiousness from readers: "Not too sure about Brian Braddock and family being aliens," wrote Damian Spencer.[50] A further development was the addition of a new highly technological Captain Britain uniform, which was given to the hero by Merlin and amplified his alien powers. While Alan Moore's contribution to superhero comics is virtually unmatched, according to writer Paul Cornell the effects of Moore's work would wreak havoc on Captain Britain: "I felt that for the longest time he'd been disassembled. He was the first hero that got the big questions asked of him. 'What is this genre about?' [. . .] And it never stopped. He was never put back together again."[51]

Later, during Captain Britain's membership in Excalibur, other writers toyed further with the origin of his powers, trying to synchronize them with his role as Captain Britain. In 1986 Captain Britain is able use his powers without his uniform and he begins to think it was a placebo; in 1989 he loses his powers only to regain them when dumped in the Thames River—*now* his powers are rooted in Britain itself, and the uniform works as a battery to store the magic of the nation (which his powers use up). In 1991 this is updated: Captain Britain *now* gets his powers from the friction of various astral dimensions rubbing against one another; these dimensional interfaces are all over the planet but the unusual quantity and proximity of the fields in the British Isles account for the importance of place to his powers (more on this in Chapter 6). In this iteration the uniform works as not only a battery but also an antenna. Captain Britain has by now come a long way from his magical origins as a knight of the Round Table. In March 1994 Brian is reinvented as Britanic, a silent, stoic figure who knows the future; by February 1995, less than a year later, Brian stops being Britanic *or* Captain Britain and just starts inventing things in a lab as former Ph.D. student Brian Braddock: "As he [Brian Braddock] steps into the sky, his powers ignite—the powers of the Captain Britain he once was, a fusion of wild genes and old magic. But he had given the names and costumes and wars up. He was happy just to build things."[52] This whipsawing of the character's origins irritated many readers who attributed this to the comic's authorship, such as Tony Ingram of England, who complained vociferously about Captain Britain's shabby treatment and the erasure of his Britishness:

> It seems that since Excalibur became more a part of the X-Men's world, no one has really known what to do with Brian. First, he was dumped in limbo for months. Then, he was stripped of the Captain Britain name (which I personally found rather insulting—how would you like it if a British creative team got hold of Steve Rogers and gave him some

meaningless, generic name?). That was when I gave up on this title. [...]
Please, either put Captain Britain back where the action is and try to
flesh his character our a bit, or write him out so that at some time in
the future, a writer who cares about him can restore him to his former
glory.[53]

After losing and regaining his powers a few more times, Captain Britain returned to heroic form in *New Excalibur*, particularly in a story line in which he
(and the rest of the team) face off against Albion, a villain who chose the sword
of might rather than the amulet of right. This return to the *mythic* qualities of
Captain Britain's first origin simultaneously returns him to the role of iconic
nationalist superhero by emphasizing his morality rather than the technologies
of his power:

> **Captain Britain:** Just because our path was laid by Merlyn and Roma...
> doesn't mean we're committed to it. We have minds and souls of
> our own. We can forge our own destiny!
> **Albion:** Why should we follow your lead, Braddock? It's a harsh omni-
> verse. Could you follow mine, if it came to that? Here's a thought—
> perhaps the sword is needed more today than the amulet?
> **Captain Britain:** And perhaps the essence of true leadership ... is to
> learn from what's gone before ... in order to make a better future?[54]

This trend continued in *Captain Britain and MI13*, but with a twist. Writer Paul
Cornell decided to re-origin Captain Britain, clearing away the convoluted continuity of aliens, antennae, amulets, and astral dimensions. He did this by having Captain Britain die heroically while trying to save the Siege Perilous (site of
his original transformation and a center of magical energies in Great Britain)
from an alien missile strike. The voice of Merlin intones, "My champion, my
Captain. The young lion of London. You were always full of doubt. The doubt
appropriate to a hero of many worlds. But the time for doubt is done—and NOW
is the time of sacrifice."[55] This being the world of comic books, he is dead for
only two issues before Merlin smashes his staff in the geographical center of
Britain, causing all the flags of Britain to converge on the resurrected figure of
Captain Britain. With a new uniform and a new relationship to his powers (his
power surges and ebbs with his self-confidence), this new origin for Captain
Britain firmly ensconces him in the world of magic and wipes clean the convoluted prior narrative (Figure 4.3). Paul Cornell explains his reasoning: "It's
entirely fitting that he's tied in with Merlin and the matter of Britain. This is
the point of British heroism; the Arthur myth is so fundamental."[56]

From this it is clear that many writers have struggled to link Captain Britain's origin and powers to a coherent narrative of Britishness. In part this seems
to come from a disjuncture between notions of proper British identity and the
idea of a nationalist superhero. Interestingly, in a 1978 effort to expand Captain

Figure 4.3: Captain Britain's rebirth, in which flags from all over Great Britain converge on his location. (Copyright © 2012 Marvel Characters, Inc. Used with permission.)

Britain's readership, he moved to New York and lived with Spider-Man in the pages of *Marvel Team-Up*. Here, when Brian tells his (first) origin story to Peter Parker (Spider-Man's alter ego) some new dialogue is inserted, not found in the original text, in which Brian and Merlin argue over British nationalism:

> **Merlin:** As in days long past, the people of this land we cherish need a champion, a symbol—a paladin who will stand for the values and beliefs that transcend time. Be that champion, Brian Braddock.
>
> **Brian Braddock:** What are you talking about? I'm no hero. I'm a student, a . . . scholar. That's all I ever want to be. And besides, the people you want me to fight for, they—we—have outgrown the need for that sort of symbol.
>
> **Merlin:** Have you, sirrah? I'd think again lest thy hasty words condemn thee.[57]

The dialogue can be understood as an extratextual call by the publishers for British audiences to warm to the genre despite its roots in American notions of patriotism. This ambivalence about nationalism in 1978 was still a part of British culture that Captain Britain writers were trying to negotiate with readers in 2008. Paul Cornell explains:

> There was a telling point on the [Internet fan] message board—in a scene when a flag gets snatched out of the old folks' hands [to go resurrect Captain Britain], I thought that was a parade. And it was drawn as the Royal British Legion parade, World War II veterans who always carry Union Jacks. Who I thought would be, during the [alien] invasion, out in the streets being patriotic. I thought that would be a very positive group of people to have the flag snatched from. But on the message board someone assumed that because they had all those flags that they must be in a National Front parade, or the British National Party [an anti-immigrant party in British politics associated with racism]. And I thought yeah, this is what the flag has come to symbolize. We've had our flag stolen.[58]

Cornell's attempts to reground Captain Britain within a national narrative of British magic and heroism rather than American technological modernity is an attempt to claim a distinct and iconic space for Britishness within the Marvel Universe, but also within British society itself. Although well aware of the small readership *Captain Britain and MI13* had, he saw his writing as a way of taking back British nationalism from the far right of British politics. The subsequent cancellation of *Captain Britain and MI13* may indicate the lack of resonance between Cornell's vision and British sensibilities, or it may speak more to the long odds of survival for a British comic in a largely North American market.

## Conclusions

The importance of the origin narrative, to both Bhabha's theorization of nations and the superheroic avatars of these nations, cannot be understated. The process by which the ordinary is transformed into the extraordinary is not just a means to an end but must also serve as a legitimation for the exercise of superpower(s). In other words, the particulars of these story lines matter, and in the case of nationalist superheroes they must resonate with not only national narratives but also the economics of transnational comic book markets.

For Captain America, whose relative success in publishing has generated a long continuity, wartime origins associated with scientific modernity have required nearly continuous renegotiation. The outcome of these renegotiations is inseparable from the larger processes through which American identity itself is negotiated. For Captain Britain and Captain Canuck, whose publishing history is both spottier and more concerned with transnational processes of production and distribution, origin stories are subject to frequent revolution rather than revision. This is because these origin stories are required to feel authentic to British and Canadian readers and also to appeal to the larger American market, in which superhero comics are understood to live and die. Because Captain America serves as the archetype for the nationalist superhero, he serves as a magnetic pole that both attracts and repels these British and Canadian heroes; because he is their generic forebear, by definition they must adopt some of his conventions. However, they must be distinct in some way so as to legitimate the hero among domestic audiences. *Alpha Flight* and *Excalibur* also demonstrate this pattern, making initial claims to national distinctiveness but eventually falling into the orbit of the popular Marvel Comics *X-Men* titles (interestingly, both make it about sixty issues before turning solidly in this direction). *Nelvana of the Northern Lights* is something of an outlier and in any event did not last long enough for these changes to become apparent (if they were going to do so).

In Chapter 5, we examine how nationalist superhero narratives co-produced the nation as a continuous, stable identity while nevertheless adapting through constant change. Appreciating this narrative flexibility is key to understanding how Bhabha's idea of the pedagogy of national discourse works in practice.

# Narratives of Continuity and Change

Once there was a mighty empire, whose lands reached around the globe, and upon which the sun never set. Strong it was, and powerful, and never did it meet defeat at the hands of any other nation! Time passed, and—bit by bit—the empire was whittled away, until it was but a fraction of its former size. Today, the empire is all but gone, and some say that the glory and the grandeur of that mighty realm, that England, is gone forever. But the people of that fabled land live on . . . and they are still a good people, a people possessed of all the strength, might, and indomitable will which forged that empire of days gone by. And as long as that people endures . . . as long as a few of those valiant hearts and minds and souls persist—then shall the spirit of Union Jack live on![1]

This narrated exposition, concluding a two-issue story arc in which Captain America travels to England to team up with Union Jack against the Nazi vampire Baron Blood, illustrates how national narratives and superhero narratives intertwine. In particular, Union Jack is portrayed as the embodiment of a national spirit that is essential to British identity: a good people of strength, might, and will. However, even as the narrator asserts this timelessness, the decline of British geopolitical fortunes is also foregrounded. This chapter continues the thread of Chapter 4 by showing the paradoxical centrality of change in nationalist superhero narratives to the stabilization of that national identity over time.

## Negotiating Narratives

Chapter 4 documented the importance of the nationalist superhero's origins to the kind of national narrative that spooled out afterward, and further it illustrated the need for constant renegotiation of that origin in order for it to continue resonating with readers. This chapter continues that theme through the continuity that unfolds from the origin point. For superhero comic books, this narrative takes the form of a serial narrative, or one that unfolds in small doses over time.[2] National narratives can also be understood as serialized; instead of being experienced as a timeless essence, the nation is constituted through regular episodes that constitute a continually shifting story line in which certain fundamentals remain the same even as characters may grow, change, establish relationships, or disassociate from each other.[3] This serialized narration of the nation takes place in a variety of overlapping temporalities, materialities, and performances, such as the nightly news, weekly magazines, monthly comic books, quarterly economic forecasts, two-year Congresses and four-year presidencies (in the United States), and the uneven duration of parliaments and monarchical reigns (in countries such as Canada and the United Kingdom).[4] These episodes are socially constructed and rendered into texts or other media, such as documentary films and national history books. As Homi Bhabha argues, "The steady, onward clocking of calendrical time [. . .] gives the imagined world of the nation a sociological solidity; it links together diverse acts and actors on the national stage who are entirely unaware of each other, except as a function of this synchronicity of time."[5]

The temporality of nationalist superhero narratives has both a linear component and a cyclical one. In the first temporality, issues are released one after the other, marching forward through time; this is epitomized by the issue number, which locates each issue on a time line vis-à-vis other issues.[6] This temporality adds to superhero continuity, either telling new "presentist" stories or adding to and modifying old continuity. The second temporality is cyclical, in that characters are meant to be relatively consistent, and in the case of nationalist superheroes so are the national identities with which they are in dialogue. In both cases (superhero and nation) the essential characterization is heavily policed by fans. Therefore, the characters themselves seem to take on a reality off the page that must be taken into account when considering the authorship of these serial narratives. Consider the following comment by *Captain America* writer J. M. DeMatteis:

> Whenever you're writing a serialized character like Cap—one who was around decades before you took the assignment and will be around decades after you're gone—you have to work within certain limits. You can't just go in and tear down everything that's come before, you can't totally change the character and his reason for being. You can push the edges [of the character], certainly, but you have to do it carefully and with character-logic.[7]

Each story line must roughly end up where it began but not exactly so. This is true of national narratives as well; narratives that are relatively well developed and generally accepted are more subject to regular revision than rapid revolution. For instance, the shifting of British national narrative from one that is openly imperialist to one that (at least publicly) eschews empire is an ongoing process begun fifty years ago and still not complete today. Because the revisions are each relatively small and commonplace, produced through everyday conversations and interactions (in the preceding example of empire, often involving the subtle changes of pronoun such as from *our* to *their* in regard to former possessions), they can be difficult to witness. This has given the impression to scholars such as Samuel Huntington that macro-scaled social identities have a seemingly monolithic and implacable quality, but this is simply not true.[8] Superhero and national narratives each have both the linear and the cyclical, change and continuity. As Charles Tilly argues, "Identities are social arrangements reinforced by socially constructed and *continuously negotiated* stories."[9] *Captain America* writer Steve Englehart describes the way superhero narratives and national narratives evolve together in ways that are co-constitutive:

> I was very aware when doing Cap that I wanted to rehabilitate him as a character, and that meant facing up to his particular ambiance, which was Classic Americanism. It seemed to me that he stood for something—had to stand for something—because of who he was (if you accepted his origin story). I always "believed" in my characters as I did them, so I accepted his origin, and felt that he stood for the New Deal Americanism that's part of our history and was in existence when he had his origin—the idea that America stood for something great, that Americans could accomplish anything they set their mind to. The fact that I was writing him in an era (1972) when America was learning a whole new side of itself, when Americanism was in disrepute, just sharpened his focus, as far as I was concerned.[10]

Englehart's ability to tack between different narrations of America, from the gung-ho patriotic "classical" to a more reflexive, liberal "New Deal," illustrates not only the multiplicity of nationalist discourses but also the bounded nature of change within nationalist narratives. Englehart successfully boosted sales and made Captain America resonate with contemporary concerns, but he did so through incremental change over time.

The remainder of this chapter illustrates the ways in which nationalist superhero narratives remain stable over relatively long periods of time, yet paradoxically do so through the incorporation of subtle changes. Given the inconsistency of Canadian superhero publishing, I have excluded Canadian superheroes from this chapter. While British nationalist superheroes also have difficulty maintaining a market niche, they alternately enter and are withdrawn from participation in the relatively stable British portion of Marvel Comics continuity. Captain America obviously has the easiest time of it, having been continuously published since 1964, as well as periods of consistent publication in the 1940s and sporadic publication in the 1950s.

## Continuity and Change

### United Kingdom

If Captain Britain, as seen in Chapter 4, struggled to link his origins to a narrative of Britishness, Union Jack has had few such problems. In part this may be because Union Jack's origins are themselves less important than the hero's serial narrative; he is less an individual superhero than a British tradition (the repetition of practices through time). Union Jack debuted in *The Invaders*, itself a comic that dwelled in nostalgia and the passage of time. The first Union Jack was Lord Falsworth, and he is an old man at first introduction, telling of his adventures in World War I:

> I fear I had no such formidable superpowers as you [Invaders] possess, however; I was merely a special secret operative of His Majesty's government . . . making such use of my fists as I could . . . and a pistol and dagger, of course. My mission on such forays was to strike terror into Bosche [German soldiers'] hearts by appearing the very personification of the British flag and nation. I daresay it all proved quite effective.[11]

Union Jack is the retroactive placement of the World War II nationalist superhero archetype into the action of World War I, just as the Invaders was the retroactive placement of the superhero team (a 1960s innovation) into the action of World War II.[12] This extension of Union Jack back through time, with no definable origin (at no point does Lord Falsworth say why or how he came to be Union Jack beyond his relationship with the British government) is congruent with Bhabha's claim that "nations, like narrative, lose their origins in the myths of time and only fully realize their horizons in the mind's eye."[13] Like Falsworth's aristocratic title (another connection to British tradition and timelessness), the role of Union Jack is meant to be handed down. In a 1976 issue of *The Invaders*, Lord Falsworth is crippled after donning his costume to fight alongside the Invaders against his brother and longtime nemesis, Baron Blood. The role is taken up by his son, Brian, who joins the Invaders, and eventually is passed on to Joey Chapman, the best friend of Lord Falsworth's grandson, in a 1981 issue of *Captain America*.

In passing the role and costume of Union Jack from one man to the next, the masked hero is given an ageless quality, linked as he is to cyclical time (generations). An outsider would be unable to tell when one Union Jack ends and another begins. However, the identities of the men within the Union Jack costume illustrate the passage of linear, national time. Lord Falsworth is represented as a throwback patriot of the Edwardian era, temporally distant even within the anachronistic *Invaders* comic book. His son, Ken, is a man embedded in the times in which he lived; thrown out of the house by Lord Falsworth for supporting Chamberlain's late 1930s appeasement policy, he was brought to see Hitler's threat and fought with the German Resistance prior to becoming Union Jack. He is also an ardent defender of empire.

However, the return of Union Jack after *The Invaders* ceased publication marked a new era for the character and the national narrative when Joey Chapman took the role. Instead of being one of the aristocratic Falsworths, Union Jack has been a working-class hero ever since:

> Eight hours a day. Five days a week. Most people work for a living. In factories. Mills. Shipyards. Hard work. But there are a select few who, for generations, have labored in less taxing pursuits. They while away their leisurely days with sport and high tea and not much more. What distinguishes one group from the other is an accident of birth. A separation of social and economic class that's gradually becoming more trivial.[14]

Here, Union Jack's intratextual narration and embodiment of a shift in British social structure illustrates how national identities are reified through small narrative changes. This one had been suggested by Calum Fraser, a reader of *Captain Britain*, four years before the introduction of Joey Chapman as Union Jack:

> I hope that another British hero is added to Marvel's line-up soon. When you do this I hope you give the superhero a working-class background, in contrast to C.B.'s upper class roots, as I think the average reader, being mainly working-class, could identify better with him or her.[15]

On the one hand, the introduction of class is merely a practical way to distinguish between the two British nationalist superheroes; *Captain Britain and MI13* writer Paul Cornell described the problem of two British nationalist superheroes created roughly at the same time by American writers:

> The trouble is [Union Jack's] wearing Captain Britain's costume. [. . .] It's always been a big problem, because [Marvel has] two people trying to occupy the same niche. [. . .] To make Joey (or Joe—nobody in Britain is known as Joey). . . . To make Joe working class was a very good previous writer's solution to how to differentiate the two.[16]

On the other hand, it is also an attempt to tinker with the narrative of Union Jack to heighten the resonance with modern readers and raise a different set of political issues. In regard to resonance with modern readers, the shift seems to have been popular among readers. For example, Steven Chapman wrote in a letter to the editor to *Knights of Pendragon* that "Union Jack is an example of what Larkin called 'the Displaced Working Class Hero,' who was rampant amongst post-war British Fiction. It's nice to see how he interacts with his more middle-class team members; there could be some interesting tension there."[17]

Making Union Jack working class also put a different twist on the stories that could be told with him. The narrative of Union Jack continued to revolve around vampires, but rather than emphasize the Nazism of the original Baron Blood, a 1999 story line revolved around Baroness Blood (wife of the original) and her plot to merge her vampire lineage with the aristocratic Falsworth bloodline. Having a working-class Union Jack battle against patrician, hierarchical (British establishment) vampires is a great plot, if you are trying to narrate a different Britain than that of Captain Britain (who lived in Braddock Manor and inherited a position in London's Hellfire Club). Similarly, a 2007 story line involved a group of supervillains plotting a terrorist attack on London; having gotten wind of it, British intelligence refuses to warn the citizenry because it would alert the terrorists that they have been discovered. Union Jack agrees to this, but when he notices government officials and wealthy people leaving the city, he becomes furious and announces the situation on television, eventually confronting his intelligence contact, Gavin:

> Union Jack: You should've told them, Gavin. All of them. Not just the rich and powerful. I can understand evacuating Parliament. But every guest in that posh hotel was heading for high ground. It's happening all over the city. I won't stand by while aristocrats jump ship, leaving the rest of us to our fate.
> Gavin: Well, aren't WE the champion of the down-trodden![18]

The story line ends with Union Jack, sporting broken ribs and exhausted after a day of saving London from terrorist attacks, about to be killed by a robotic Dreadnought in Trafalgar Square. However, the Dreadnought is distracted by a crew of construction workers with a wrecking ball, giving Union Jack the opportunity to impale the robot on a flagpole (with an actual Union flag on the end). This synergy of nationalist superhero and working class is the latest episode in a narration of Britishness that has been ongoing for thirty-five years but accounts for almost a century of change in British identity.

As Chapter 4's discussion of Captain Britain's origin(s) illustrated, the association of Britishness with Arthurian myth, at least within the world of nationalist superhero comics, is significant. Whereas in Chapter 4 this reliance on mythology was seen as illustrative of Britain's narration as a magical nation in contrast to a North American scientific modernity, in this chapter the monolithic nature of this narration is unpicked by closer analysis of the Arthurian myth within the pages of *Captain Britain*, *Excalibur*, and *Knights of Pendragon*. The malleability and polyvalence of Arthurian myth allows a continuous Britishness (or alternately, a British continuity) dating from the sixth century to be asserted, yet also accommodates a wide variety of narratives.[19]

Arthurian legend exerts itself most obviously through the presence of Merlin as an actual character within narratives of *Captain Britain* and *Excalibur*. Merlin and his daughter Roma are central to the creation of Captain Britain, having set out the sword of might and the amulet of right after the fall of Camelot as a shibboleth, indicating the rise of a new knight who would choose life over death. Indeed, from the beginning Captain Britain is narrated by Roma as a knight of the round table: "Thy test is over, Brian Braddock. Thou hast proven thyself worthy. Thy destiny awaits thee . . . wilt thou pick up the gauntlet, young sir—and become the champion of good 'gainst the forces of evil? Or dost thou refuse such noble service?"[20] At two points subsequently, Merlin both resurrects Captain Britain from death and grants him new costume and powers (in 1979 and 2008). The revelation that Merlin is not a human wizard but rather a cosmic figure that operates on many worlds paradoxically does not locate Merlin within the frame of science fiction but instead produces him as a divine figure. This interpretation is bolstered by Merlin's rule over another dimension called Otherworld. Arthurian legend also bears concrete connection to these comics through the introduction of Excalibur (the sword, not the superhero team) to story lines at varying moments. As early as Captain Britain's second appearance, the narration of Arthurian myth had taken on a particular meaning: "Strive forever to maintain the rule of right—of law and justice—against those who live and rule by might."[21]

Using a superpowered individual like Captain Britain who is more or less untethered to democratic institutions as an example of the rule of law over the powerful is not an intuitive maneuver, but effectively connects Captain Britain to a classic narrative of Britishness (Arthur and the Round Table) that resonates with contemporary political thought. This interpretation of Arthurian myth is returned to, and twisted slightly, with the foundation of Excalibur (the superhero team, not the sword) in 1987. An ad hoc collection of superheroes, linked only through their relationships to the then-deceased mutant superhero team the X-Men, gather in London to battle supervillains and commiserate over the loss of their friends. The X-Men were led by Professor X, the leading proponent of peaceful mutant coexistence with humans; he has been considered by some to be the Martin Luther King, Jr., of the Marvel Universe, with the X-Men a stand-in for persecuted minorities from homosexuals to African Americans.[22] The foundational moment for the superhero team Excalibur draws on the Arthurian myth, but braids it with an X-Men-based message of tolerance and multiculturalism:

King Arthur had a dream, [like Professor X]. Of a world where might served right, instead of subjugating it. His knights of the round table were the agents of that dream . . . and his sword, Excalibur, the symbol of it. He died, the table was destroyed, his knights mostly slain—yet the dream survived. They became legend—and the sword, the means of keeping the legend alive and vital through the ages. The X-Men thought enough of Professor Xavier's dream to offer up their lives. Is it so much to ask that we fight to preserve it? The sword, Excalibur, represented hope. It was light in the darkness of fear and ignorance and hate.[23]

If this seems an inauspicious bit of intertextuality for the start of a British superhero team, it did in fact foreshadow the eventual conversion of Excalibur into a European branch of the X-Men (it could not even be called British, as most members came from the United States or continental Europe). This process was inextricably linked to the difficulty of integrating Captain Britain into the story lines, travails that were outlined Chapter 4.

When *New Excalibur* was launched in 2005, it was distinctly more British in terms of both team composition (although still sporting some Americans, of course) and Arthurian content. The formation of the team, engineered by British government agents, hinged on persuading Captain Britain to lead the group. When he finally acceded, it was with his original Arthurian mandate in mind: "Captain Britain, first and foremost, is champion of this realm. [. . .] Now, as before, Excalibur stands for an ideal—might in the service of right. Let's go do some good!"[24] Taking the Arthurian elements of the narrative seriously was a hallmark of this short-lived comic book, with one story line even involving time travel into the past so the team could forestall the "real" Camelot's premature collapse. This particular iteration of Arthurian legend, however, is found only in stories that include Captain Britain as a significant player.

In both volumes of *Knights of Pendragon*, Arthurian legend is taken in a completely different direction. More than in *Excalibur* or *New Excalibur*, *Knights of Pendragon* represents a more comprehensive attempt to create a British nationalist superhero team. This is done through the embedding of the entire team within Arthurian archetypes. The team consists of some characters known previously, such as Union Jack and policeman Dai Thomas, but mostly of characters created for the comic book. These characters begin to manifest powers associated with the Pendragon force, which, as the heroic (if awkwardly named) Peter Hunter explains,

is the power that invests certain individuals when it becomes necessary for them to take a stand for the common good. It makes champions of exceptional men . . . and women. And it's been doing that since the days of Arthur . . . or even earlier. It attunes the individual to the natural cycle, urges him or her to defend the essential fabric of all that is important . . . all that is "good" to use an inadequate word. And it teaches us to recognize the threatening foe in its true form. Each Pendragon carries with it the past incarnations of its champions.[25]

The *Knights of Pendragon* thus engages in a double move vis-à-vis Arthurian myth. First, it repositions Camelot not as a British origin myth but as the *effect*

Figure 5.1: Knights of Pendragon from all periods of history converging to battle the Bane. (Copyright © 2012 Marvel Characters, Inc. Used with permission.)

of something else constitutive of the British whole. Second, it contextualizes the conflict as environmental, and therefore, while framed by British myth, ultimately a matter of global contestation. This becomes apparent as an older Pendragon describes when he first encountered the Bane (the antithesis of the Pendragon force) during World War I:

> My foe was a youth in the tunic of the British Expeditionary Force, and so my true foe was not some warrior of a foreign power, but the dark side of humanity itself . . . the love of war, of winter, of destruction[.] . . . Then I knew the nature of the eternal war, and saw the awful truth of the conflicting parties so tritely labeled good and evil.[26]

While this could be seen as abstracting the conflict from the British context (and also deterritorializing the Arthur myth), at moments of crisis the Pendragon force draws on its reserves—long-dead knights from various epochs— and fields an army of British subjects from all of history (Figure 5.1).

The Pendragon force works on behalf of the Green Knight. The Green Knight is an integral part of Arthurian myth, drawn from the tale of Gawain and the Green Knight.[27] In *Knights of Pendragon*, the Green Knight resides in the Green Chapel, in the extradimensional land of Avalon. The original Green Knight myth involves an offer by the Green Knight to let any of King Arthur's knights chop off his head if he is allowed to do the same to the knight a year later. Gawain agrees, and having cut off the Green Knight's head, he is shocked

Figure 5.2: The Lady of the Lake, corrupted by the imbalance between modernity and the environment. (Copyright © 2012 Marvel Characters, Inc. Used with permission.)

to see the knight pick it back up and replace it. A year later, Gawain ventures off to meet his fate at the hands of the Green Knight, who pardons him after testing his courage and fidelity.[28] In *Knights of Pendragon* this is told as a bargain between humanity, in the form of Gawain, and nature, in the form of the Green Knight. Neither can take more than the other can give. In the world of *Knights of Pendragon*, humanity has not kept its end of the bargain; the Lady of the Lake has been transformed from the beautiful female form familiar to Arthurian enthusiasts into a rotting organic figure (Figure 5.2). As a consequence the Green Knight has been killing polluters and poachers. Dai Thomas becomes possessed by the essence of Sir Gawain and goes to offer himself as a blood sacrifice to reconsecrate the bargain. He does, only to be resurrected. Other Knights are inhabited by the Pendragon force, and like Dai Thomas/Gawain they are doubles of Arthurian archetypes: Guinevere, Lancelot, Perceval, and even Arthur himself. The Knights of Pendragon gather around the obligatory round table in order to battle the Bane, who serve the Red Lord. Thus, even by comic book standards *Knights of Pendragon* is Manichean in outlook, pitting good environmentalists against evil exploitation. This seemed to be appreciated by readers; Ellen Foley wrote a letter to the editor in appreciation:

I usually cringe at the idea of socio-political themes in comics. It is normally achieved in such a haphazard and band-wagoning way, but you have handled the predictable environmental issues in an innovative and exciting way and allowed Mother Nature to fight back with a vengeance.[29]

However, *Knights of Pendragon* offers a narrative that diverges from most superhero comics; drawing on both the Green Knight myth and environmental discourse, the resolution of the initial all-out brawl between Pendragon and Bane is not jeremiad and extirpation, but conversion and balancing. Adam Crown (Arthur) tosses Excalibur aside, and the leader of the Bane sees his essential goodness and casts the demonic Bane out of her body, eventually becoming a Pendragon herself. Her underlings similarly are freed of Bane influence, and the Red Lord is forced to withdraw from the field of battle. Adam Crown explains:

I remembered what the pitiful Lady of the Lake had told me . . . balance . . . equality . . . the Red Lord and the Green Knight must coexist, and could do so as long as man didn't outweigh the scales to either side . . . for too long, too much of mankind has been seduced by the easy riches of the Bane way. Steel couldn't save our race. Only a willingness by the masses to forego greed. [. . .] I let the [leader of the Bane] feel what drove my soul . . . she saw it. [. . .] The heart of me had made my sword redundant.[30]

Such a speech, in a mass-produced paper product[31] and in a genre that requires regular doses of cataclysmic violence, is perhaps hypocritical but definitely refreshing through its subversion of genre expectations.

In summary, British nationalist superheroes have a number of possible connections to essentialized British identity; two such sources of continuity are the idea of Union Jack as a tradition going back through time, like the aristocratic titles of the Falsworths, and Arthurian mythology. Even as there are multiple continuities of British identity with which to link, those discourses can themselves be altered to narrate multiple forms of idealized Britishness (e.g., Union Jack's various class positions) and various political engagements (e.g., *Captain Britain's* and *Excalibur's* social justice or *Knights of Pendragon's* environmental justice).

## United States

In the case of Captain America, the connection of the nationalist superhero to national continuity comes from his own origins in World War II, a war that occupies a privileged position in the narrative of American identity. Both a war that is seen as fundamentally moral (especially in contrast with later wars) and the war that thrust the United States into its role as a global hegemon, World War II has long served as a touchstone for Americans seeking to ground an identity of both power and innocence during periods in which American power has been tainted or delegitimated (such as the post-Vietnam era).[32]

This link between Captain America and "the greatest generation" is narrated over and over again within the comic (Figure 5.3). For instance, an entire issue from 2000 tells a story that begins with Captain America being collected by SHIELD agent Cameron Klein; instead of starting him on a mission, Klein takes Captain America home to see his grandfather. Klein the elder had been telling his great-grandchildren stories from World War II, in which Captain America and Bucky had saved his whole unit during the Battle of the Bulge. However, during the storytelling he had a heart attack and was taken to the hospital, and it is at this point that Captain America arrives. Klein has the opportunity to thank Captain America for saving his life then, as he has had a very full fifty-five years since then; he then passes on. This story line occupied the entire comic book, including the flashback to Klein's war experiences. Other connections between Captain America and World War II are narrated more briefly:

> **Soldier 1**: Right this way, sir. Uhm . . . Time for an autograph?"
> **Soldier 2**: Me, too! My grandfather says you saved his neck at Normandy!
> **Captain America**: Some other time, fellas. We're in a real rush.
> **Soldier 1**: S'okay. It's an honor just to get to see you in person. Not just because of what you did for my family—but because of what you represent to all of us.
> **Sharon Carter**: Do you ever get used to that adulation?
> **Captain America**: It's not that. It's the respect for the nation that just happens to come my way, Sharon.[33]

One reader from the military wrote in to thank the creative team for Captain America's contribution to militarized patriotism:

> The fact that an icon like Cap actually broke down and cried [at Arlington National Cemetery] was something fans needed to see. [. . .] I'm only a Lieutenant, and have never seen war (and never hope to). If I ever have to, I hope I can remember the ideals that Cap has laid down for nearly 60 years.[34]

Beyond his connection to World War II, Captain America's continued, embodied existence produces a tangible link to the past that marks him as a distinct kind of symbol to which the more recent or intermittently published nationalist superheroes can only aspire. This is true both within the narratives and among the readers. Within the narrative, Captain America's continuity is associated

Figure 5.3: Captain America demonstrating his special relationship with World War II veterans and positioning himself as a point of continuity with America's past. (Copyright © 2012 Marvel Characters, Inc. Used with permission.)

with American continuity: "Captain America is more than a man—you're the one constant the American people can hold on to—a living reminder of a time when we took pride in ourselves."[35] Rashid Roby wrote in with a similar expression of continuity, but one that connects the personal and the political:

Happy 4th of July to everyone at Marvel including Steve [Rogers], the symbol of America himself! Today, my grandpop turned seventy-four on America's birthday and he couldn't be happier! Back during the days of World War II, he served as a member of the Navy and although he's not like Cap, he's a hero to me. Even though my grandfather wasn't into comics that much, Captain America was one of his favorites. In a way, grandpa kinda inspired me to start collecting and becoming a fan of Captain America.[36]

If Captain America and his relationship with veterans provide a constant link to a seminal moment in the narrative of American morality and hege-mony, then so does his ongoing conflict with his wartime nemesis, the Red Skull. If Captain America can be understood as an attempt to shore up an un-stable American identity by mooring it to "the Good War," then the Red Skull does the same by occupying a more ambiguous pole: that which is eternally un-American.[37] For several generations of readers now, the Red Skull has em-bodied a shifting set of values that were intended to resonate with readers as everything America is *not*, thus providing the effect of a constant and stable American identity in contrast to the Red Skull.[38]

The Red Skull first appears during the wartime *Captain America Comics* as a Nazi saboteur and assassin, focusing his efforts on killing American military officers and stealing war plans, only to be foiled by Captain America at every turn.[39] For instance, in a 1944 issue of *All Winners Comics* the Red Skull takes over a resort in upstate New York and converts it into a concentration camp, only to be thwarted when Captain America and Bucky (fortuitously) arrive on vacation. As such, he serves as a stand-in for Nazism, which is itself narrated as everything un-American. The Red Skull reappears during the short-lived 1953 revival of Captain America. In this iteration (coincident with the Korean War), the Red Skull is no longer a Nazi but has joined the global communist crusade against capitalism: "Flash! Here's terrible news, folks! The worst crimi-nal mind of all has come back to plague humanity! This time he's joined our red enemies to fight against America! Yes . . . the Red Skull is back!"[40] This time his plots include kidnapping the UN secretary-general to blackmail the world body, stealing the blueprints for a new plane, and stealing America's war plans; a similar modus operandi, if a different motive, in comparison with his World War II incarnation.

The publishing revival of Captain America in 1964 was not immediately matched by a revival of the Red Skull. Instead, the Red Skull haunts the hero, found in "flashback" stories told by Captain America to his new friends, and then finally through the fulfillment of his twenty-year-old plot to resurrect the Third Reich using time-activated robots referred to as the Sleepers. The Sleep-ers emerge from underground to wreak havoc on West Germany, activated by Nazi sleeper agents who have been dormant in German society since the war. Together these human and robotic sleepers signal the return of Nazi threat to the world of Captain America, finally embodied in the Red Skull himself. The Red Skull finally returns as an active agent in 1966, explaining that he had been inadvertently put in suspended animation at the end of World War II by a po-tent combination of allied bombs and Nazi chemicals.

While the 1966 return of Nazism as a threat to the United States seems rather far-fetched, it makes narrative sense as a symbolic other for Americanism. During the 1960s (and later), counterpointing Captain America with communism or other "real world" threats to the United States would be unpalatable to vast swaths of the young, radical audience. Ian Jull wrote in to the editors to specifically request that Captain America not fight in Vietnam: "Formerly, if [Captain America] heard the word 'Communist' [he] would go into a patriotic flurry. But now, he is more compassionate, understanding, and open-minded."[41] However, Nazism had few overt supporters, then as now.[42] Indeed, the Red Skull, although still a Nazi (and marked as such by his swastika-laden jumpsuits), embodied a much more ambiguous form of anti-Americanism:

> Captain America: You were always a loser, Skull! Your own Third Reich was reduced to ashes by the very forces of freedom you so despised! And what of your beloved Fuehrer? He took the coward's way out while the Allied planes reduced his Fortress Europa to smoking rubble!
> Red Skull: No! No! Those are lies, do you hear? All lies! The war has never ended—and never been won! It was only the first battle that we lost! So long as evil lives—to muster the forces of bigotry, greed, and oppression—the fight goes on! So long as men take liberty for granted—so long as they laugh at brotherhood—sneer at honesty— and turn away from faith—so long will the forces of the Red Skull creep ever closer to the final victory![43]

Thus, in 1966 the Red Skull served as not only a particular character representing specific "un-American" values linked to the civil rights struggle (e.g., "bigotry, greed, and oppression") but also an avatar of the long-standing and never-ending nature of the battle to defend freedom against the many enemies of America. In this way, the Red Skull helped shore up a particular American identity that was useful in maintaining discipline on the home front of the Cold War, without having to engage with the messy politics of anticommunism and Vietnam.

If the continuity of both Captain America and the Red Skull from World War II to their modern incarnations embodies the narration of the American/ un-American binary and the need for eternal vigilance, then Captain America is meant to serve as a stable pivot around which the Red Skull can represent various iterations of "un-American" behavior. Indeed, freedom is a constant theme, with the Red Skull particularly obsessed during the 1960s with making Captain America his slave, either for his own personal pleasure or as a way of demoralizing the population of the United States. Melees between Captain America and the Red Skull always provide opportunities for the rhetorical framing of each character and their overarching conflict:

> **Red Skull**: Men were all born to be slaves! They're not worth your idiotic concern! Why should you care for them when they don't even care for each other? Look around you! The world is consumed by greed, crime, and bigotry.
>
> **Captain America**: Tyrants have always scorned their fellow humans! But still the race endures—while the despots fall! And those who would grind us underfoot—can never hope to keep us from reaching our eventual destiny![44]

Such a framing, of cynicism and selfishness versus freedom and progress, is typical of the Red Skull story lines of the 1960s. During this time the Red Skull's opposition to Captain America becomes more than ideological; it becomes personal: "Time and again, I had almost attained my eternal goal . . . the downfall of America . . . the crushing of liberty throughout the globe . . . only to have you snatch my victories from me!"[45] Plots are no longer about stealing American war secrets or the like, but instead about trying to drive Captain America insane or physically tormenting him.

This "Manchurian Candidate" theme continues in the 1970s, as plots to pervert Captain America's self-confidence and moral clarity by, for instance, tricking him into killing SHIELD director Nick Fury, putting Hitler's brain in Captain America's body, and revealing that his partner, the Falcon, was brainwashed by the Red Skull and planted as a double agent. The 1970s also see the Red Skull taking on a *Godfather*-like role to undermine America through a variety of criminal organizations that he bankrolls, exploiting American racial differences (see Chapter 3) and trying to undermine capitalism via massive counterfeiting and assassination of government regulators.

One such plot, from 1981, involved a film being made about the life of Captain America. The movie's filming is ruined by antagonists who claim to be nihilists but are really stooges of the Red Skull. The movie project is shelved, and word spreads that Captain America was "victimized" by the nihilists. Captain America discovers that the Red Skull is the studio head; he has pulled the movie from production and is now going to air a documentary about Captain America. He says:

> Yours is a nation of watchers, mein Kapitan—preyed upon by profit-seeking vultures! I knew that once news of your "victimization" broke, I could sell my "tribute" to the highest bidder! And the hundreds of millions that watched "Roots" and "Holocaust"—believing those verdammt lies about the Schwarzes and Juden—will again sit worshipping the great American God . . . television![46]

The film of the documentary has been chemically treated such that all who watch it will be compelled to riot.[47] Of course, Captain America defeats the Red Skull and burns the film so it can never be aired. This kind of story line, like those in which the Red Skull exploits American racial discord, allows the Red Skull to be used as a way of injecting a note of moral and political critique into *Captain America* in a way not seen before; in earlier story lines, what the Red Skull sees as weakness in America (multiculturalism, democracy) are exactly what Captain America sees as strengths. Here, Captain America does not defend America's emergent culture of couch potatoes and victimhood but instead must act to shore up this vulnerability in the nation he loves, with presumed moral implications for those reading.

Also, in 1981 the point is first raised that the project to create Captain America was begun in direct reaction to the Nazi creation of the Red Skull (as described in Chapter 4): General Phillips states, "The Skull has come to personify the evil of Nazism. We desperately need an agent who is his opposite . . . a man who will be a living symbol of life and liberty!"[48] While this retcon has the effect of shifting Captain America from being the prototype of an army of super-soldiers into the realm of symbolic politics (and thus orienting the character further toward peace than war), it also has the effect of sealing Captain America and the Red Skull into a constitutive binary. While still antagonistic, their relationship comes to be marked by respect. For example, in 1984 the Red Skull prevents another villain from killing Captain America because the villain had bested him through petty deceit.[49]

The Red Skull returns in 1988, his mind transferred into a cloned body of Captain America: "I am no longer an easily identifiable foreign agitator—I am now a disarmingly handsome American business man, turning the wondrous free enterprise system against itself!"[50] This brings Captain America and the Red Skull into narrative alignment as two sides of the same coin; no longer is the Red Skull a Nazi seeking the destruction of America but rather an extreme version of Reagan's America, an America that will eat itself:

> What a land of opportunity America is! How right I was to make my base here in the most influential, most affluent, most decadent country on earth! [. . .] I now embrace the American dream for what it is—the realization of one's personal ambitions by whatever means necessary! My American dream is no less than the denial of everyone else theirs! To achieve it, I will have to enslave every American citizen, and destroy America itself![51]

The Red Skull's reckless individualism is manifest through his involvement in organized crime, especially the illicit drug market, which he sees as yet one more technique to cause America to succumb to corruption and violent crime.

In 2005, the Red Skull is gunned down by a rival, corporate villain Aleksander Lukin; however, the Red Skull is able to transfer his mind once again, this time into the body of Lukin. The two rivals share the same body for some time and lead Kronas, a powerful transnational corporation. During this time they orchestrate a complex plot to plant their own presidential candidate in the

Oval Office and relocate the Red Skull's mind into Captain America's body (eventually failing in both). Still, the association of the Red Skull with corporate power only cements the transition begun in the late 1980s. Dovetailing with the 2008–2009 "credit crunch" and subsequent economic downturn, the Red Skull was scripted as being behind the then contemporary economic circumstances, as demonstrated in this fictional CNN anchor's coverage:

> Well, Tony, until there's some official explanation for Kronas's actions the past two days . . . all I can say is new CEO Morovin [the Red Skull] must hate the American people . . . while some of the homes being foreclosed on were part of the sub-prime lending scandal of earlier this year . . . most are simply homes of hardworking Americans who failed to read the fine print.[52]

The narration of contemporary corporate leaders as supervillains like the Red Skull rhetorically connects "real-world" fears of American economic collapse with the Red Skull's constant exploitation of American weaknesses, moral or political. As with the villain's earlier attempts to tear the fabric of America by exploitation of racial differences, drug addiction, or the passivity wrought by television culture, the Red Skull provides both a reminder that America will always need defending as well as a shifting sense of danger emanating from that which is narrated as un-American—fascism, racism, and greed. Nevertheless, the Red Skull also illustrates that some of these dangers are intrinsic to the United States itself. This puts the hero in a slightly different role; instead of needing the hero to protect us from villains, we need the hero to protect us from ourselves.

## Conclusions

This chapter has shown how narrative flexibility is key to making nationalist superhero narratives resonate with audiences over a long period of time, as a reading of Bhabha and Tilly would indicate. Shoring up national identities in uncertain times requires a sense of discursive stability even as the details of the narratives shift to maintain currency.

At the core of the narratives of Captain America is his relationship with the military and World War II. The lives of veterans stretched out from the time of the "Good War" and provided the temporal link to Captain America, the "man out of time." His relationships with veterans, couched in the military values of respect, camaraderie, and honor, reflect *cyclical* time and its sense of stability. Similarly, the maintenance of the Red Skull as a constant nemesis for Captain America provides a sense of eternal Manichean opposition to Americanism. The production of this constant oppositional force provides the illusion of a constant and eternal America, even as that oppositional force morphs into new, timely forms (that is, as it traces *linear* forms of time).

The constant negotiation between these two forms of time is also apparent in the British superheroes analyzed in this chapter. Union Jack embodied cyclical time, with the uniform being handed down from generation to generation. Nevertheless, the various Union Jacks collectively produced a narrative of change in British life, from the rural aristocracy and global empire to the politics and values of the working class. Similarly, the link to Arthurian legend stabilized the narratives of Captain Britain, even as that legend was reinterpreted in the various iterations of the hero. In each case the narrative strategy is to bolster the transhistorical nature of the hero, and the nation, by ironically appealing to its concreteness within specific time-spaces.

In Chapter 6 the argument shifts from the narration of nation, as an ethereal, rhetorical endeavor, to the way in which that nation is grounded in particular territories and spaces within the narratives and visual forms of nationalist superhero comics.[53] In doing so, my overall argument shifts from the terrain of the nation-state to the broader system of nation-states and how they territorialize the global.

# Grounding the Nation-state

This island [Great Britain] ain't been conquered in a thousand years.
What makes you chumps think . . . we're gonna let you ruin the streak?[1]

T his quotation (from Juggernaut, member of New Excalibur) provides a
taste of the emphasis given to territory and borders within the nationalist superhero subgenre. This emphasis has existed since the beginning of
the subgenre, given that the original purpose of Captain America was to catch
spies and saboteurs sent into the United States from Nazi Germany. However,
nationalist superheroes do more than defend their countries from attack. More
significantly, the subgenre reifies the connection of particular polities to specific territories through a variety of narrative and visual strategies. This chapter
analyzes these strategies, widening the methodological approach of previous
chapters to include the role of visual culture alongside narrative analysis. In
this way nationalist superheroes can be understood to contribute not only to
each country's territorialization but also to the broader international system of
nation-states that those territorializations comprise.

## Landscape, Territory, and the Nation-state

The rise of the modern nation-state to become the geopolitical default has been
the subject of extended historical analysis. Alexander Murphy, for example, has
traced the rise of the sovereign territorial ideal to west-central Europe, with this
ideal's slow eclipse of the decentered, overlapping medieval spatial order; fief-
doms, parishes, kingdoms, and bishoprics all contributed to a sense of spatial
fluidity and nonexclusivity.[2] This began to change with the rise of free cities
and their challenge to the feudal order; simultaneously absolutist rulers gained
the capacity to dominate their hinterlands, providing two models of spatial authority that had in common the exclusion of others' power within specific territories. By the signing of the Treaties of Westphalia, it had become increasingly

commonsensical that sovereigns should have absolute authority within their territory, at least in some matters. This view has been challenged many times over the intervening centuries, from the existence of extraterritorial empire to, more recently, Tony Blair's claim of a "responsibility to protect" human rights around the world that trumped notions of sovereignty.[3] This variability highlights the contingency of the sovereign territorial ideal and therefore demands attention to how this ideal is perpetuated in everyday life.

Arjun Appadurai's work on mediascapes offers some purchase on the role of visuality in the construction of national territories: "Media-scapes [. . .] tend to be image-centered, narrative-based accounts of strips of reality, and what they offer to those who experience and transform them is a series of elements [. . .] out of which scripts can be formed of imagined lives, their own as well as those of others living in other places."[4] While Appadurai may not have been imagining comic books when he wrote that, they certainly fit his description with their hybrid form of text/image, organized in sequence as a "series of elements." Appadurai is concerned with the role of mediascapes in deterritorializing and reterritorializing national spaces during our present period of advanced globalization. Recent work by Pauliina Raento and Stan Brunn has examined the role of postage stamps as a similar form of everyday text/image that connects the nation-state with particular territories, and of course this occurs in many other ways, both state sanctioned and not: national songs (e.g., "from sea to shining sea"), weather maps, and so on.[5] In that vein, I here argue that nationalist superheroes typically serve, perhaps unsurprisingly, as protectors of the notion of sovereignty and the preservation of territorial extent. This can take the form of either a (super)natural link between the hero and the national territory or the marking of the national territory as naturally united through some commonality.

The naturalizing of what are ultimately artificial boundaries has been the subject of recent work by Juliet Fall. She argues that "the idea of natural boundaries has created an inevitable link between a conception of the nation and its spatial inscription, doubly powerful for being rooted in the realms of both reason and feeling."[6] Indeed, the connection between borders and "coming home" has been *felt* by virtually everyone who has ventured through passport control in their hometown airport. More commonly experienced, however, are the everyday processes of boundary making described by Anssi Paasi:

> Boundaries penetrate the society in numerous practices and discourses through which the territory exists and achieves institutionalized meanings. Hence, it is political, economic, cultural, governmental and other practices, and the associated meanings, that make a territory and concomitantly territorialize everyday life. These elements become part of daily life through spatial socialization, the process by which people are socialized as members of territorial groups.[7]

Thus, it is the everyday experience of boundaries not-at-the-border that, for most people, situates them within national territories. This can occur through the consumption of nationalist superhero comics or other expressions of territoriality that connect identity to landscape.

*Landscape* refers to a visual tradition of apprehending nature that territorialized the nation via the production of "a visual totality with which people felt they could identify and to which they could feel entitled."[8] Linked developments in the artistic deployment of perspective and cartography were central to the development of national territories during the 1600s, especially in states such as Switzerland and the Netherlands that lacked a monarchical head of state as a unifying image. Landscape paintings typically locate the viewer as the (imagined) head of state, surveying her or his territory.

The existence of the state, viewable through its territory, relied on the efforts of Protestants in northern Europe to disenchant the national territory of its sacred association with saints and pilgrimage locations. This freed the land for reenchantment along nationalist lines, whether through the creation of monuments, the sacralization of battlefields, or the association of the nation with nature itself—seen in the modern creation of national parks, such as the Grand Canyon or Yosemite in the United States. Ken Olwig notes that the first American national monument was Virginia's Natural Bridge, which was personally purchased by Thomas Jefferson and donated to the newly founded state.

Without a monarch or any classical heritage, the United States took quickly to landscape art as a way of territorializing the state. Indeed, the associations of North America with nature (in contrast to a Europe marked by civilization) made it especially suitable for this form of territorialization. Several decades after Canadian independence, the development of the Group of Seven landscape painting school used these same romantic techniques to develop a Canadian territorial iconography. Not coincidentally, as mentioned earlier it was Canadian painter Franz Johnston of the Group of Seven who, upon returning from one of his trips to Canada's Arctic territories, told comics writer and artist Adrian Dingle about the mythological Inuit crone Nelvana.[9] The degrees of separation between romantic landscape painting and nationalist superheroes are just that few.

The remainder of this chapter focuses on how national borders and territory are discursively produced through the nationalist superhero genre. Juliet Fall argues that attention needs to be paid to processes of reification, naturalization, and fetishization:

> Reification, naturalization, and fetishization of boundaries happen simultaneously. [. . .] *Reification* involves taking objectification seriously in exploring how spatial objects are bounded and constructed, before being elevated to "real" things. [. . .] Exploring *naturalization* involves studying the very mechanisms that lead to equating nature and

politics. [. . .] Lastly, examining how these lines become quasi-sacred objects, venerated as true, means that *fetishization* should be examined, through understanding how borders, walls, technologies and other performances of power participate in making boundaries material, visible, and sacred.[10]

With this in mind, this chapter proceeds to a discussion of how borders, and the territories they delineate and suffuse, are reified, naturalized, and fetishized in the representations of nationalist superhero comic books. As indicated by the foregoing discussion of landscape art and mediascapes, attention is directed, in particular, to the visual elements of these borders and territories.

## Superheroes and Sovereignty

While the overtly nationalist focus of the superheroes analyzed here is by now amply evidenced, rarely are these superheroes called on to defend the international system of nation-states itself. However, just such an opportunity arose with the 1985 creation of a villain named Flag-Smasher.[11] Flag-Smasher grew up the son of a Swiss diplomat who was dedicated to peacemaking around the world; he followed his father around the world, learning languages and adopting a cosmopolitan identity. His father's death during an embassy riot, however, turned Flag-Smasher against pacifism, leading him to impose his antinationalist vision of a world united through force. Dressed in black and white, and with his belt buckle an image of a world without borders, Flag-Smasher visually contrasts with the colorful nationalism of Captain America.

Flag-Smasher first appears in an attack on the United Nations, in which he tears down the flags in front of the building: "The United Nations—feeble, pathetic farce! A misguided attempt to promote unity among peoples of the world! To think that good men with good intentions waste their time with such charades! If only I could open their eyes to the counterproductiveness of organizations like this!"[12] Flag-Smasher's antinationalism inspires his opposition to the United Nations, which is, after all, an international organization rather than a world government. Flag-Smasher's continued rampage[13] leads him into conflict with Captain America when he takes everyone hostage at a press conference being held by the hero. Using the assembled media, Flag-Smasher expresses his view that the very concept of nation-states is divisive and dangerous. Because Flag-Smasher is using classically villainous techniques, such as taking hostages and using force, he is clearly marked as beyond the pale and subject to Captain America's rough justice. Once Flag-Smasher is unconscious (and can no longer speak his views), a former hostage asks Captain America what he thinks about Flag-Smasher's views.

> **Former hostage:** What did you think of all the junk that creep was saying, Cap?

> **Captain America:** I believe my opponent was wrong. There is nothing harmful about having a sense of national identity or ethnic heritage. America is made up of a multitude of different ethnic groups, each of which has had its own part to contribute to American culture. Be proud of your heritage, but never let that pride make you forget that beneath it all, we are all human beings who have the same wants and needs and deserve the same respect and dignity. At least, that's how I see it.[14]

By shifting the frame of reference from the constitution of the global by the national to the constitution of the national by the ethnic, the nationalist hero situates the uncomfortable antinationalist rhetoric of Flag-Smasher within the comfortable discourse of multiculturalism (see Chapter 3). Readers took issue with the representation of cosmopolitanism in this story line; Paul Weissburg wrote in to argue, "It's ironic that Flag-Smasher's costume is black and white, since the whole issue of nationalism is presented in such black and white terms. [. . .] You didn't even try to give each side an equal chance." Roger Cadenhead similarly argued somewhat sympathetically, "Our invisible borderlines don't make us better or worse than others who share the same rock."[15]

Captain America and Flag-Smasher have several more encounters over the years, and each time Flag-Smasher becomes more embittered and ideological; he is always portrayed as a somewhat laughable figure of the far left. For example, while leading his terrorist outfit, ULTIMATUM (the Underground Liberated Totally Integrated Mobile Army to Unite Mankind), Flag-Smasher refuses to use weapons paid for by the Red Skull, as they are ideologically tainted. Captain America's ally, Battle Star, had this to say: "Let's see what his dossier says. Head of the terrorist group ULTIMATUM, that's trying to promote—ha!—world unity by attacking all governments! Sounds like a total nutcase, huh?"[16] Flag-Smasher is last seen (in the pages of *Captain America*, anyway) in 1999, serving as a thug for the CEO of Roxxon Oil. Flag-Smasher has suffered brain damage and is now controlled by the corporation through emotion-manipulating drugs. In the story he could have been replaced by any other goon, but his presence symbolically links the deterritorializing politics of the Cold War left with the equally deterritorializing politics of multinational corporations during the era of globalization. Each is portrayed as a threat to the territorial sovereignty of the United States through his opposition to Captain America.

The character of Flag-Smasher illustrates one way in which nationalist superheroes buttress the territoriality of the nation-state. However, in most examples this is not done through overt engagement with the nation-state, but rather through more subtle techniques.[17] The following discussion is structured according to Guntram Herb's notions of territorial differentiation and territorial bonding.[18] *Territorial differentiation* refers to the processes by which a bounded geographic entity is produced through the exclusion of other territories and the people associated with them. Territorial bonding, conversely, focuses analytical attention not at the borders but within localities and on the local processes that foster emotive connections between people and their territory.

## Territorial Differentiation

The cover art of *Captain America Comics* during World War II offers an interesting archive of visual culture through which to understand the changing wartime territorial imagination. The first two covers betray an anxiety over the national borders, with each image illustrating Captain America within Nazi military headquarters, discovering German plans for invasion of the United States—visually reproduced in the form of a map of the United States in the first cover and a globe in the second (with a Nazi flag helpfully planted within American territory). Given that this is before the U.S. entry into the war, and the interventionist stance of the creative team, this is perhaps not surprising.

However, with the U.S. entry into the war, the covers change to reflect the decoupling of territory from national borders; during the war the United States expanded its control (and in some cases, sovereignty) over territories well beyond its national borders. These active processes of territorial differentiation produced a rapidly changing set of territorialities manifesting through the cover art. This took the form of a visual style that relied less on cartography and more on traditions of landscape art. Like landscape art, key territories are featured within the scope of the viewers' gaze. These might be Pacific island beachheads (Figure 6.1), the Brenner Pass, the road to Berlin, or Berlin itself. However, unlike landscape art, the perspective is not that of the sovereign but of the enemy, German or Japanese, who is about to *lose* that territory. The geopolitical dynamism in each image is found in the body of Captain America (and to a lesser extent, Bucky), who leaps, strides, dives, or otherwise crosses the boundary from allied to enemy territory, which is usually occupied by soldiers visibly terrified by his incursion. The boundary between the two territories is represented by a no-man's-land between the two armies or occasionally by a body of water. This motif reaches its apogee with *Captain America Comics #13* (Figure 6.2), published shortly after Pearl Harbor, in which an enormous Captain America strides across the Pacific. Below naval battles rage and American armies mass for invasion, while above Captain America punches a subhuman Hideki Tōjō in the face. While it may seem paradoxical to locate the (presumed) American audience in the perspective of the enemy, it allows for the foregrounding of both Captain America and the landscape to be gained. As the war began to wind down in 1945, the covers became less territorially dynamic and returned to concerns over securing the mainland American territory from foreign sabotage, with the landscape helpfully labeled so viewers could comprehend the stakes. From the Boulder Dam Power Plant to the U.S. Air Force Gasoline Reserve to the vault in which atomic bomb prototypes are kept, each is saved from saboteurs in turn. The only "foreign" cover during this period is *Captain America Comics #47*, which features Captain America and Bucky attacking a V-5 rocket

Figure 6.1: The cover of *Captain America Comics*, issue 22. Note the arrangement of elements, with American troops crossing a no-man's-land toward the enemy (and the viewer). The hero, who also strides across the no-man's-land, is the most dynamic figure in the scene. (Copyright © 2012 Marvel Characters, Inc. Used with permission.)

Figure 6.2: The cover of *Captain America Comics*, issue 13. This cover expands the theme of Figure 6.1 to a continental scale. (Copyright © 2012 Marvel Characters, Inc. Used with permission.)

base. Even here, however, the threat to the territory of the United States is made explicit by the labeling of each rocket's destination (New York).

After the war, boundaries of control between states became static once again, and processes of territorial differentiation within nationalist superhero comics took narrative form. In particular, national borders were naturalized through their linkage with heroes' superpowers. For example, Alpha Flight member Snowbird, the daughter of Nelvana and therefore a demigoddess herself, has superpowers as a result of her divine ancestry (she is the granddaughter of Koliak, an Inuit god). Her powers are specifically linked to Canada; one of these is that she can take the form of any animal found in the Canadian Arctic. This means, hypothetically, that if she wanted to transform into an animal found only in, for instance, the Russian Arctic, her body would be unable to do so; this produces Canadian political boundaries as something natural that can be embodied. Taking this notion a step further, Snowbird's powers (as originally formulated by Canadian writer/artist John Byrne) recede when she leaves Canada, returning only when she crosses the politically and historically contingent forty-ninth parallel. The narrator describes this event: "She feels the radiant power of the north flow up to her, reach out to her like warm, enveloping arms, protecting her."[19] This magical link between the border and Snowbird's powers finds a parallel in her sense of responsibility: "The spell Shaman cast when he delivered a god-child bound me to the land—the Canadian land! My powers wane as I fly further from Canada! I cannot overtake the Hulk [whom she was chasing out of Canada]—and why should I? Let America deal with a monster of its own making! Alpha Flight's duty is to defend the Northland—is it not?"[20] Even if Alpha Flight did not always report directly to the Canadian state, the boundaries of that state are envisioned as a "power container," albeit not in the way that term is usually deployed.[21]

Within these comics, the reification of national borders does not take only the form of nationalist superheroes' jurisdictions, and the naturalization does not occur only through the limits of the heroes' powers. One 2009 story line from *Captain Britain and MI13* illustrates a different form of reification and naturalization, as Dracula prepares to launch an invasion of the United Kingdom from the moon. In a prologue, Dracula discusses his plans with the villainous Doctor Doom:

> **Dr. Doom**: Tell me, why do you want Britain?
> **Dracula**: It's the home of magic. The peasantry have a sensible knowledge of their past—an inclination to follow their betters. [. . .] Tell me, if I gain my new kingdom, will you then address me by my proper title?"
> **Dr. Doom**: Heh. Of course. You'll be a proper ruler then. I'll call you the little prince!
> **Dracula**: I am a prince only for my people. The vampire diaspora who will finally have a homeland.[22]

The embedding of Dracula's plan within a geopolitical imagination of diaspora, recognition, and sovereignty reifies states as a form of political organization desirable even for the undead as a way of securing their rights. Dracula's
anxiety for recognition, both of his own authority and of the nation he leads,
inspires him to declare war on the United Kingdom in hopes of generating a
governmental response (a performative act that would constitute the vampire
diaspora as a legitimate political actor).[23] The key to preventing the invasion is
the skull of Quincy Harker,[24] which is imbued with magic. While it is in the
United Kingdom, any vampire who wants to enter the country has to be individually invited (this is a scaled-up parallel to the legend that vampires must
be invited into the home). Dracula mistakenly believes that he has destroyed
the skull, when in fact it still exists. When Dracula's space armada arrives in
British airspace, his vampire hordes burst into flame (Figure 6.3).[25] Once again
national borders have been produced as something magically real, not the contingent product of human practices but rather a (super)natural feature of reality; the horizontality of Snowbird's limits, combined with the vertical ceiling
through which vampires cannot enter, form a territorial box within which the
nation-state is understood to exist.

Of course, territorial differentiation does not occur only as a function of
explicit bordering practices. The association of contrasting values with different places enables differentiation based on a sociocultural border that relates
to the political border but may not be congruent with it. Such contrasts are
common within nationalist superhero comics, not only because of the common
occurrence of the nationalist hero traveling to other countries, but also because
the visual form of a comic book allows for juxtaposition of images in ways that
produce territorial differentiation. One such example comes from a 2002 story
line in *Captain America* that drew on the real-world events of the September 11,
2001, attacks.[26] These attacks coincided with the relaunch of *Captain America*,
and so the original story line was quickly replaced with a new story line that
attempted to resonate with emergent geopolitical affects and narratives. The
first (right-hand) page of the comic assumes the perspective of a 9/11 hijacker,
with his hand holding a box-cutter in the aisle of a commercial jet, confused
and scared passengers in the middle distance. The narrator of the story intones: "It doesn't matter where you thought you were going today. You're part
of the bomb now."[27] The reader turns the page, revealing a two-page spread of
bearded men in robes, with assault rifles at hand. The narrator continues: "And
somewhere in the world—a handful of men with famished eyes sit around a
radio—or a telephone. Waiting. Twenty minutes—four thousand murders
later—They praise God for the blood which stains their hands."[28]

In this brief sequence, territorial differentiation takes place not only
through the narration of a series of binaries (innocent versus guilty, peaceful
versus violent, here versus there, us versus them) but also through the physical
act of turning the page, which is an integral part of the (literally) unfolding process through which the relevant geopolitical identities are produced. Without

Figure 6.3: Dracula's vampires bursting into flames as they enter British airspace, thus naturalizing the idea of territory as volume. (Copyright © 2012 Marvel Characters, Inc. Used with permission.)

mentioning Afghanistan, the Middle East, or any of the other places that would become so associated with the United States–led "war on terror," America is differentiated from its unnamed antithesis. This requires no specific focus on political borders but harnesses the discourse of American exceptionalism to imagine the United States as a peaceful place, protected by oceans from the corrupting influences of overseas conflicts.[29] Captain America, picking through the rubble of the World Trade Center, vocalizes his horror at the puncturing of this territorial bubble: "Oh, God—How could this happen *here*?"[30] Again, the visual form of comics emerges as important to the production of difference. The conclusion of a conversation between Captain America and another would-be rescuer is drawn from the perspective of a corpse they have found in the rubble, placing the reader in the scene as a victim of terrorism (Figure 6.4). The reader, wherever he or she might actually be, is placed within the space of "us," an innocent victim of "them."

### Territorial Bonding

If the lack of narrative specificity regarding the identities of the 9/11 attackers within the pages of *Captain America* produces a territorial differentiation that is abstract rather than absolute, then the subsequent narrative (in which Captain America battles terrorists led by a man named al-Tariq) linked clear social and cultural identities to those territories. However, it did so primarily through the deployment of mythic American landscapes that produce a geography, and affect, of vulnerability.

Territorial bonding in this story line is produced through the evocation of symbolic landscapes that connect with the notion of "American heartland." The terrorist al-Tariq chooses as his target the unlikely town of Centerville,[31] whose very name evokes the notion of "Middle America." The town is seated in an unidentified location away from the coasts and is apparently almost entirely populated by white people (only one African American is seen in the six-issue story line). The establishing frame for the events in Centerville does a lot of the work in linking the town to the heartland mythology (Figure 6.5). The image reveals a main street, with one-story commercial properties lining it; beyond this on either side are low, tree-lined residential streets in a grid pattern. A barn is visible in the distance. This depiction of a small town is unique in superhero comic books, which usually unfold in dense urban areas; therefore, the selection of this location for a terrorist attack seems like a deliberate attempt to harness the mythology of the American heartland and produce a visceral, emotional response to the attackers.[32]

Of course, the largest feature in the establishing frame is a product of the perspective; viewing Centerville from the top of the church steeple makes the Christian cross loom over the whole town, marking it as not only American heartland but Christian as well. This hybrid American/Christian identity is heightened by the lack of cars and people on the streets; they are all in the

Figure 6.4: The reader is offered the perspective of a World Trade Center victim in the 9/11 attacks. (Copyright © 2012 Marvel Characters, Inc. Used with permission.)

Figure 6.5: Centerville, the bucolic, Christian heartland of America. (Copyright © 2012 Marvel Characters, Inc. Used with permission.)

church because it is Easter Sunday. The sign outside the church says, "EASTER SERVICE: ALL ARE WELCOME," narrating the place as open and welcoming; this point is reiterated by the pastor's speech just before the attack by al-Tariq: "It's good to see so many visitors here this morning. Neighbors—you know we're always glad to see you. Strangers—we hope you'll give us a chance to know you better, after the service."[33] Just as these words have been uttered, al-Tariq and his men burst through a stained-glass window and take everyone prisoner in the church, holding them in their pews by deploying land mines with a web of trip wires across the hostages.

While Islam is never mentioned, al-Tariq's name and the jihadist language used by his men (one refers to a woman as a "whore with a painted mouth") establish a clear sense of distinction vis-à-vis the rustic, Christian Centerville. The emotive potential of the local to attach people to national territories, as in this comic book story line, indicates that analysis does not have to focus on the border in order to see the production of national territories. Territorial bonding can be seen working at multiple scales simultaneously.

At the regional scale, it is possible to discern the territory of the Canadian North as playing a particular role in processes of territorial bonding within Canadian comics.[34] On the one hand, the Canadian North serves as an internal Orient that bolsters a southern Canadian identity that is discursively produced as both more cosmopolitan than that of the Canadian Arctic periphery, but also produced as superior to that of the United States because of its association with that same Arctic periphery.[35] The colonial relationship between the Canadian South and the indigenous North is perhaps best found in the pages of *Nelvana of the Northern Lights*. The production of a white, patriotic Canadian heroine out of the northern Inuit legend illustrates the way Canadian national identity relies on the mythic power of the Arctic: "From the outset, it was obvious that Nelvana was intended to personify the North (she even drew her powers from the Northern Lights). This identification would be further underscored in issue #20 of *Triumph*, in which Nelvana goes south to civilization (Nortonville, Ontario) and adopts a new identity: Alana North, secret agent."[36]

Nelvana's link with the mysticism of the Canadian North is a pattern repeated throughout the past seventy years of Canadian nationalist superheroes. The Canadian Arctic is repeatedly portrayed as a space of fantasy that provides both danger and adventure to heroes. In one story, Koliak sends Nelvana to the timeless world of Glacia, which can be accessed only through a crevasse at the North Pole. Glacia, as its name implies, is a world that has been frozen for five million years and whose people do not recognize the passage of this vast amount of time. Instead, they hibernate simultaneously and wake together, experiencing each ice age as a group nap. Nelvana's body heat sparks the renewal of the frozen Glacia, and she is quickly caught up in palace intrigue as well as pitched battles against human-mammoth hybrids, yeti, and dragons. These fantastic adventures mark a strong contrast with her more mundane battles against the Japanese when she is above ground. Later, when a representative of the transdimensional Ether World wishes to lodge a complaint against the earth's production of radio signals, which torment his people, he does not go to Ottawa or Toronto to threaten war but instead appears in Corporal Keene's Royal Canadian Mounted Police (RCMP) outpost in the Arctic. Within the spatial grammar of Canadian regions, the appearance of the Etherian on Parliament Hill would be incomprehensible.

These themes continued in John Byrne's *Alpha Flight* through the character of Nelvana's daughter, Snowbird. Her personal mission is to battle the (fictional) evil pantheon of Inuit mythology, which include Tanaraq (a Sasquatch-like creature), Tundra (a monster who can reshape the land itself), and Kolomaq (the "living embodiment of winter"). Alpha Flight follows Nelvana's precedent by chasing these beasts through a hole in the ground in the far North, referred to by the Inuit as "the eye of the world." Through the incorporation of the Canadian Arctic into these narratives, in which southern superheroes (recall that even Nelvana is recuperated as a southern, white Canadian) contain dangers emerging from the fantasy world of the northern reaches, Canada itself is produced as an identity both superior to, and yet reliant on, the power of its Arctic territory. This paradoxical relation between Canada and its internal Orient is even evoked by an excerpt of a poem by Robert Service ("The Spell of the Yukon") printed on the first page of *Alpha Flight #14*:

> ... there's the land, have you seen it?
> It's the cussedest land that I know.
> From the big, dizzy mountains to the deep, deathlike valleys below.
> Some say God was tired when He made it, some say it's a fine land to
>    shun.
> Maybe. But there's some as would trade it for no land on earth,
> And I'm one.[37]

Together, these narratives illustrate the importance of particular regions to territorial bonding and highlight the fact that actually living in that region is not necessary for emotive connections to exist. In this case the iconic nature of the Arctic within the Canadian imagination is likely enhanced by the *lack* of personal experience most readers have of the region, which allows it to be narrated as a space of fantasy.

As noted in Chapter 4, the United Kingdom has often been narrated in the Marvel universe as a space of magic. *Captain Britain and MI13* author Paul Cornell has argued that Captain Britain's origin myth did not necessarily have to be Arthurian, "but from that body of magical origin myths, and in that Marvel way. Marvel has a way of getting rid of everything over-thought and tasteful, and too precious, and ripping the myth down to what it is originally."[38] The linkage of Captain Britain's origin to Merlin and Arthurian legend was a popular distinction from American superheroes but brought into play a particular territorial imagination, as represented in this letter from reader Peter Martin to the creative team: "The mystical touch to his origin was a brainwave, because, living in the North-East [of England], I am aware of the magical properties of this area."[39] The locus of magic within tales of Captain Britain is usually symbolized by a circle of stones, such as the one Brian Braddock crashes into when he receives his identity as Captain Britain.

These stone circles link to both the ancient history of the British Isles and the intimate connections between power and place, sorcery and site. Consider the initial exchange between Brian Braddock, Merlin, and his daughter Roma (initially identified as the "Lady of the Northern Skies"), especially the links between the magical figures, nature, and the stone circle:

Roma: I who am the beauty of the green earth and the white moon
amongst the stars and the mystery of the waters, and the desire of
the heart of man, I call unto thy soul to arise and come unto me . . .
for I am the soul of nature who giveth life to the universe; from me
all things proceed . . . and unto me all things must return. Welcome
to the Siege Perilous, Brian Braddock—welcome home.

Brian Braddock: Wha—? That voice—a woman's, but who?

Merlin: Be silent mortal, thou hast not been given leave to speak. Thou
art in a most ancient circle of power—and thou art here to be judged
on peril of thy immortal soul![40]

Stone circles feature in several other magically themed story lines. For instance,
Excalibur faces off against the villainous Demon Druid, who creates his own
circle of power at King Arthur's Seat in Edinburgh by magically transforming tourists into stone pillars. Seeking yet more power, Demon Druid starts to
create a new circle of power by replacing the cooling towers of Darkmoor Nuclear Research Facility (where Brian Braddock worked before becoming Captain Britain) with a complex formation of energy. Captain Britain expresses his
concern by identifying this location as central within an enchanted geography,
arguing that Demon Druid has created "a nuclear facsimile of Stonehenge over
one of the most significant focal points of arcane energies in the entire world!"[41]

This enchanted British geography, as described earlier in regards to the
changing origins of Captain Britain's powers, is more than just "magic" in the
traditional sense. These "focal points of arcane energies" are interdimensional
portals that are all over earth but exist in unusual quantity within Great Britain, causing their energy fields to overlap and synergize in ways not found
elsewhere. The relationship between these interdimensional portals and the
emergence of ancient monumental geographies is narrated through reference
to an enchanted premodernity that is incomprehensible to today's observers:

Captain Britain: I just never felt comfortable with all this olde worlde
magic hokum.

Captain UK: Arcane science, old knowledge . . . ancient man understood the multiverse and his place in it. They could sense the energy
matrix and mapped it with ley lines . . . marking each interface with
monoliths—stone circles—

Captain Britain: And towers . . .[42]

Captain Britain's final aside here hints at another form of magic monumen-
talism that is featured within this enchanted geography. In a 1986 story, Captain Britain buys a lighthouse as a new home for Meggan and himself, and this
eventually becomes the home for Excalibur. In 1990 it is revealed that the lighthouse itself sits on an interdimensional nexus, which enables many stories in

which Excalibur flits through various parallel dimensions, such as the afore-mentioned Otherworld (the realm of Merlin).

The 2008 launch of *Captain Britain and MI13* saw the magical landscapes of Britain take center stage as an alien invasion force heads to the Siege Perilous, where Captain Britain gained his powers.

> **John, MI13 agent:** Your new model extremist [alien], they're polite with it—but they're all about the wanting. They want summat we've got.
> **Pete Wisdom, MI13 leader:** What Britain has more of than anyone else—magic! They invade Avalon, they take the magic!
> **PM Gordon Brown:** All right. Not just us then. We have a responsibility to the world.[43]

Otherworld (Merlin's home) and Avalon (the realm of the Green Knight, from *Knights of Pendragon*) are described here less as other dimensions and more as something intrinsic to Britishness itself: "Avalon is the collective British unconscious. The soul of the nation. It's part of Otherworld, the access point to every other universe."[44] Nevertheless, this Britishness is instrumentalized by the aliens as a source of power ("Magic is just another force to be contained, controlled—put to the use of our God"),[45] and so they close the entrances to Avalon with military strikes and invade through the one remaining portal. The aliens kill the Lady of the Lake and the Green Knight, who were both disenchanted by the presence of alien technology and unable to fight back. The aliens smelt the amulet of right (from which Captain Britain was originally made), the sword of might, and the Holy Grail into a magical fetish with which the aliens hope to conquer the rest of the world. Eventually, however, the new magical artifact is broken by Captain Britain, freeing the magical creatures of Avalon, including the demon Satannish, to fight the alien invasion force and repel them, saving both the United Kingdom and Avalon at the cost of making the United Kingdom even more a place of folk creatures and quirky occultism.

The overall effect of these narratives is to produce the territory of the United Kingdom as (super)naturally magical and unique. Through this association, the inability of Captain Britain to maintain his powers for very long after leaving the country (at least without his uniform to serve as a battery), much like Snowbird of Alpha Flight, helps to reify and naturalize the national territory. Similarly, the territorial connection of sites in the United Kingdom to Avalon and Otherworld establishes Great Britain as the local and peculiar, discursively linked to the idiosyncrasies of magic versus the universal pretensions of science. The alien invasion force repeatedly frames magic as a tool meant to be used for grander purposes than those available within the circumscribed territory of Britain:

> Why did magic choose to be kept here? With such a small people? You venerate the small. You look no further than your shores. You make

epics of domestic trivia. You mourn your empire. You whine and complain. You do nothing.[46]

Applied science in the cause of our destiny will always triumph over this local, unorganized force you call—magic.[47]

This narration of the United Kingdom as the local and peculiar in opposition to the (unnamed) universal speaks to the role of magic in producing territorial bonding and a sense of British difference in a globalizing world. The alien invasion force's plans to "globalize" British magic was obviously a threat to the world's sovereigns, but more existentially it was a threat to take what makes Britain unique and disperse it across the globe.

A different version of territorial bonding can be understood as less rooted in the territory itself than in ritualized movement through it. This is the case with regard to *Captain America*, especially during the mid-1970s and the late 1980s. During both of these periods Steve Rogers gives up the role of Captain America and faces an existential crisis. In 1974 Captain America had traced connections of the right-wing Committee to Regain America's Principles (CRAP) to a shadowy organization known as the Secret Empire. Following the trail further (like his contemporaries Woodward and Bernstein), Captain America discovers that the Number One of the Secret Empire is, in fact, the president of the United States (while not seen, it is strongly implied that this is Nixon). Captain America was shaken to his core that corruption could reach so highly in the White House, as the story's narrator grandiloquently reported:

A man can change in a flicker of time. This man trusted the country of his birth ... he saw its flaws ... but trusted in its basic framework ... its stated goals ... its long-term virtue. Trusted. This man now is crushed inside, like millions of other Americans, each in his own way, he has seen his trust mocked! And this man is Captain America![48]

With these events, Steve Rogers retired, but after a few issues he returns as a new hero, appropriately named Nomad, the man without a country. This new hero, with his titular focus on mobility, is short-lived (lasting four issues), but in those issues he travels from one coast to the other and back, enunciating a different relationship between the hero and the polity. This relationship was the subject of great debate among those who wrote in. Reader W. James Grayson wrote in to sympathize with the hero:

Hate, wars, and government corruption had destroyed Steve Rogers's faith in America (as it has also done to us), the same America he fought for; the same America he symbolized because of faith in her. I don't really blame Steve for "resigning his office." Just think: everything he fought for blown away like smoke.[49]

Equally, fans applauded Steve Rogers's return to the role of Captain America, the story line having provided the catharsis through which readers could purge the national narrative of the taint of Watergate. Reader Bob Rodi wrote in:

> Let's face it, we all do love America, even though we realize she's not perfect. There is no Utopia anywhere. It is a reality to be faced. We are all like Steve Rogers, in a way . . . disillusionment and frustration make us divorce ourselves from America, but after weighing the alternatives, they just don't stack up. Using Captain America, a SYMBOL of our country, to illustrate this common feeling is masterful. [. . .] The concept has gone full circle. Captain America is not outdated. Captain America is rather indestructible . . . and I like that, a lot.[50]

This theme of mobility would be pushed further in the late 1980s, when Captain America is called before a high-level secret committee known as the Commission. They remind Captain America that he promised to follow the orders of the president in an official capacity until relieved of duty, and that the uniform and shield are the property of the U.S. government. They argue that to fulfill his agreement he must now take orders from them, but after taking a day to consider their offer, he resigns.

This time, Steve Rogers more completely adopts the idea of nomadism, even if he does not adopt the name again. He strikes out across the country in a van, growing a beard, and visiting his girlfriend in Wisconsin, and eventually he dons a uniform reminiscent of his old one (but in black) and decides to serve his country under the placeless name "the Captain." With some of his heroic friends in the van, the Captain heads off on a road trip, fighting the Serpent Society in Las Vegas, stopping a woman named Famine in the American Midwest, and then going back to Los Angeles to stop a supervillain breakout from a special prison. Finally, they head back to Washington, D.C., to foil an attempt to poison the capital's water supply. Eventually the Commission realizes that Steve Rogers is irreplaceable, and they ask him to come back to the job, with no strings attached.

While these story lines highlight the ritualistic tracing of the national territory that Steve Rogers engages in during periods of personal crisis, they are far from the only times that he leaves New York (his usual base of operations). In 1970 Captain America was struggling to adapt to being a man out of time, so he bought a motorcycle and headed out of town: "Any place is okay with me—long as I stop being a symbol, and come alive once more!" His itinerary reflects a far from random array of "real world" destinations: he attends a hippie rock concert, visits a liberal arts college, and ends up in San Francisco, all locations associated with comics readership in 1970.[51]

In 1985 Captain America receives a massive check from the U.S. government for back pay linked to his employment by the U.S. government since World War II. He uses the money to establish a national hotline through which citizens can call him and report troubles all over the country. He explicitly couches this as an attempt to remain in touch with the American people:

> Since first donning this star-spangled uniform more years ago than I care to remember, I have considered myself to be America's foremost champion and defender. And what is America? It is a land, a government, and a people. And while I cherish the land and think our form of government is one of the best ones yet devised, it is you, the people that I care most about. For without you this land is no different from any on earth, and this government cannot exist.[52]

The hotline eventually is converted into a computer network that serves the same function; in both forms, however, the hotline served the narrative function of getting Captain America out of New York and into regions of the country not often portrayed in mainstream superhero comics.

These examples illustrate the way in which touring America emerged as a narrative ritual through which Steve Rogers renewed his relationship with the United States when his relationship to the government, or his place within the polity, is troubled. This indicates a different narrative strategy for territorial bonding than that indicated in the comics of either British or Canadian nationalist superheroes. These tended to emphasize the land itself, or particular regions, as productive of national distinction. For Captain America, it is the process of moving through the landscape and getting in touch with the nation's people that is regenerative.

## Conclusions

Guntram Herb's framework of territorial differentiation and territorial bonding explicitly points to popular media as legitimators of state territorial projects:

> Mass education is crucial for the construction of national identity, but state-sponsored indoctrination with values that are divorced from existing popular ideas will be ineffective. Only conceptions of national identity to which the public is already attuned can be successfully inculcated through mass education and the media.[53]

Nevertheless, the state territory appears to be insinuated even in media that are absent active state intervention, perhaps because of the role of the state in the production of geographical knowledge.[54]

In this chapter, the role of both narrative and visual cultures in producing territorial imaginations has been explored via analysis of nationalist superhero comics. In this context, it is sometimes difficult to isolate one from the other; consider, for example, how quickly the image in Figure 6.6 switches from

Figure 6.6: Captain America couching the external Axis threat as jeopardizing the American land-scape. (Copyright © 2012 Marvel Characters, Inc. Used with permission.)

territorial bonding to differentiation. In this scene it is important to consider the interplay between bodies and the cartographies they emerge from and/or transgress. Clearly the "peaceful and beautiful" United States is drawn as distinct from its Axis enemies, and protected from them to some extent, by the surrounding oceans. The oceans however are no match for the transgressive, dynamic potential of the embodied Germany and embodied Japan, each threatening to stride across the oceans much as Captain America does in his wartime covers. The territorialization of the nation is not limited, then, to the cartographic but spills out into the corporeality of the hero and his rivals. Juliet Fall might argue that this conflation of body politic and "natural" boundaries, as well as the others illuminated in this chapter (such as the Canada-centric power of Snowbird or the vampire-incinerating borders of Britain), perform geopolitical work just "as mountains or rivers are presented as [. . .] uncontroversial and opportune political boundaries because of their intrinsic biophysical material-ity."[55] Having established how nationalist superhero comics produce particular state territories, we now turn to a consideration of how those territories are stitched to one another through narrative in ways that produce global geopolitical orders.

# 7

## Geopolitical Orders

Japanese reporter: And so you gambled on your instincts . . . and won.
Captain America: No gamble. The hostages were dead regardless. Only
   by forcing Akutagawa's hand could I even hope to seize control.
Japanese reporter: And Captain America in control is our only hope.
   We give you thanks.[1]

T his postcrisis exchange between the quintessentially American superhero
     and the Japanese media takes on a slightly different meaning than when
     Captain America is routinely feted by domestic news media. While some
may find the reliance of the United States on an unelected patriotic vigilante
named Captain America to maintain public order vaguely discomfiting, the
reliance by Japan on Captain America for the same thing raises many different
questions. As Neil Smith puts it:

> Put geographically, there is a trenchant contradiction between on the
> one hand the global promise of a certain kind of Americanism, to which
> people around the world can readily relate and invest in—the promise,
> and for no small few, the reality of a comfortable life—and on the other
> hand the exclusionary, elite and nationalist self-interest espoused as an
> integral part of this Americanism.[2]

Whereas previous chapters have primarily taken an inward-looking approach
to nationalism, focusing on intrastate narratives of national character, gender,
race, and territory, this chapter turns to the narration of the interstate realm.
Many of the intrastate narratives already described have explicitly relied on external others, such as the narration of America as a nation devoted to freedom
via its opposition to Nazi Germany, but this chapter shifts the emphasis firmly
onto the geopolitical aspects of nationalist superheroes, showing how these
stories discursively produce specific geopolitical worlds in which the United
States, the United Kingdom, and Canada are all ensconced in particular roles.

In doing so, I largely (but not completely) disregard the geopolitics of World War II, as the Nazis and, to a lesser extent, the Japanese have already featured heavily in the intrastate narratives and there is risk in repeating what is relatively self-evident.

Instead, I offer a contrast between the geopolitical narratives of Canada and the United Kingdom, which often rely on fantasy or science fiction to undergird claims of geopolitical relevance, with the geopolitics of Captain America, who has espoused a liberal internationalist geopolitical stance since the hero's return in 1964 (a period in which America's own superpower status has been relatively unquestioned). This contrast illustrates the complexity of nationalist narratives, which often bolster claims of national greatness but equally can work to hide power relations that might call national innocence into question.

## Superpowers or Just "Great Powers"?

The term *geopolitical order* has in the past referred to diagrammatic attempts to represent the distribution of power among various states.[3] However, such understandings of geopolitical orders tend to accentuate stability and structure, rather than the discourses and performances that give the *effect* of stability and structure. Just as preceding chapters have shown how national identity is not a taken-for-granted "thing," but rather something produced (among other avenues) through narrative, artistry, and consumption, this chapter calls into question how what is seemingly *obvious* (such as a geopolitical order) is made so.

Geopolitical orders often serve as (de)legitimators of various forms of political action. The Concert of Europe privileged consensus among an array of European Great Powers, where the term *Great Power* itself served as an exclusionary rhetoric distinguishing those whose opinions mattered from those who did not. Later formulations such as *balance of power* highlighted the aim of maintaining the status quo by paradoxically stigmatizing static alliances in favor of diplomatic fluidity. The bipolarity of the Cold War shaped global conflict along ideological lines, thereby bypassing tensions between global economic haves and have-nots. Recent debates over whether the world is unipolar, multipolar, or nonpolar are framed around power and domination rather than the alternatives to such an order.[4] All of these concepts privilege the state over other geopolitical actors.

In all of this it is apparent that geopolitical orders are themselves stories that we variously tell or to which we listen. These stories produce the world in which we live, attaching values to some places and ignoring others. Beyond the naming and valuing of places, these geopolitical orders also validate particular modes of engagement, whether state-to-state trade, military alliances, or nonrecognition of sovereignty. In short, they narrate people and places all over the world as having varying degrees of actorness; geopolitics is no longer about divining the structure that animates statecraft but instead becomes about emplacing and emplotting these actors.[5]

Considering geopolitical orders from such a perspective has become relatively commonplace; nevertheless, tracing such discourses into the world of fantasy and science fiction remains relatively uncommon. Klaus Dodds's work on James Bond films highlights how the fantastic can play a role in the production of geopolitical orders.[6] As he notes, the character of James Bond asserts the continued prominence of the United Kingdom on the world stage; while Felix Leiter and the Americans provide the money and the brawn, it is British intelligence that saves the day by uncovering transnational criminal plots. Bond embodies the notion that Britain remains equal partners with the United States in a special relationship, with his travels tracing the outlines of British Empire, formal and informal, in the tropics. Bond's (and Britain's) cosmopolitan mobility through these regions, with neither local accompaniment nor local sanction, annihilates the sovereignty of the (mostly) postcolonial states in which Bond operates. All together James Bond films portray a particular geopolitical order, in which shadowy criminal networks establish nodes in (scenic, adventurous) locations that Bond and his allies must find and root out. The example of Dodds's work on James Bond illustrates how particular narrations of Britishness rely on contrasts with a putative American identity on one side (e.g., Bond's style and sophistication) and contrasts with those presented as lacking in significant actorness on the other (e.g., postcolonial states or even other western European states).

This example illustrates how national identity and geopolitical order are co-constitutive, with performances of nationalism often requiring the narration of a particular geopolitical order that reflects the desired role for the nation-state. Such assertions need not be limited to boosterism, however. For instance, recent work on the spate of movies about the September 11, 2001, attacks on the United States show how the narration of national righteousness can occur through the *minimization* of a nation-state's role in the geopolitical order.[7] In the case of nationalism emerging from the September 11 attacks, this righteousness had as a prerequisite the assumption of national innocence, which was narrated, in part, through media such as film. The setup of a movie about the September 11 attacks isolates the events from a longer narrative that could be told of American intervention in Middle Eastern politics. Thus, there are no set formulas for the relationship between national identity and geopolitical order within a narrative.

## Finding a Place in the World

### Canada

The geopolitical order enunciated by Canadian nationalist superhero comics is in many ways more fragmented than that offered by the British and American heroes because of the diversity of publishers and variety of approaches over time and among authors. Nevertheless, there are some commonalities. These narratives construct Canada as a state caught up with the United States in various global struggles but fearful of being hugged too close. This anxiety is narrated through the assertion of Canadian sovereignty and technological superiority in the face of threats.

Even in World War II, Nelvana leads the charge against ambiguous bomber pilots from the North. Identified only as Kablunets (the purportedly Inuit phrase for "evil white men" used in *Nelvana of the Northern Lights*), with a lightning bolt logo on their planes, and led by an "air marshal" who speaks with what appears to be a French accent, the enemy is left ambiguous to the reader. They are stopped by the Royal Canadian Air Force (RCAF) after Nelvana tips them off; when the bombers get disoriented by the Northern Lights, the RCAF counterattacks in fighters made of plastic that are immune to the effects of the aurora borealis ("no-metal plastex 'dragonflies'").[8] This technological advantage leads to massive superiority and the defeat of the ambiguous enemy. This narrative of fantastic Canadian modernity continues in *Captain Canuck*, which opens with a statement of Canadian geopolitical supremacy: "The predictions of Canada becoming the most important country in the world became a reality in the 1980s. This posed new threats and problems for Canada's leaders and for the countries that depend upon Canada's supply of natural resources."[9] This proud statement of Canadian importance resonated strongly with the comic's readers, such as Damon Hartlin:

> A remark heard a few years ago was to the effect that it was too bad Canada didn't have big league baseball or its own comics. Well now we've got both and our neighbors from the south had just better watch out! Here's to success in making Canuck 100% Canadian—ads and all.[10]

The displacement of the United States as the global hegemon was not just a feature of the narrative but of the production process itself; the creation of Canadian superheroes was itself seen by readers as a statement of independence from the United States.

The arrival of *Alpha Flight*, published by the American company Marvel Comics, marked the end of fantasy regarding Canadian geopolitical hegemony over the United States, not only because *Alpha Flight* was to be read by both Canadians and Americans (and therefore had to be palatable to both) but also because the comic had to fit into Marvel's established America-centric continuity. Therefore, the international system found in *Alpha Flight* resembles that found in the realist paradigm of international relations, in which states are formally equal and free to exercise power to their own advantage (described in Chapter 1). This relative diminishment of Canada produced an artificial parallelism between the two countries. The United States had superheroes; so did Canada. The United States had Captain America; Canada had Guardian (the leader of Alpha Flight). Nevertheless, a sense of distinctiveness was fostered on the Canadian side. For instance, Guardian was originally named Vindicator, a term that was unpopular among both the creators and the readers. The act of changing the hero's name became itself an act of national narration:

> **Shaman:** You wear the flag of Canada as your costume. Wear also the spirit. You are our own Captain America, James. You represent the nation, and while you may feel you have much to vindicate, Canada does not.
>
> **Vindicator:** You're suggesting my name should be more in keeping with our image? Like . . . Guardian?[11]

This narration of national innocence sparked a reaction from at least one reader, Joshua Latten: "Shaman states in issue #2 that Canada has nothing to vindicate. Surely Shaman knows of the Beothuk tribe of Newfoundland, kinsmen to [Shaman's] Sarcee, who were wiped out in the 19th century? How about the white wolf; the black dog; the Ontario cougar; the Canadian lynx; the bobcat; the wolverine; bears; the harp seal? How about the timber wolf and the Arctic fox? The great auk? Whales? Moose? Canada's got nothing to vindicate? In the words of [Excalibur member] Kitty Pryde, 'Give me a break!!!'"[12] Still, the notion that Canada would have a different kind of nationalist superhero team was something the creators kept. The pacifism of Guardian's name and the anxiety over the dominance of the United States come together in Guardian's initial goals for Alpha Flight: "If I'm lucky I won't be fighting anybody. We've been putting together our little band of heroes more out of national pride than for any practical reason. Canada's just not the kind of country that breeds world-conquering types."[13]

This narration of Canadian diffidence was punctured when the original Guardian was killed on a mission in New York City. Although he would later be replaced in the role of Guardian by his wife, Heather, some readers, like Cory Caponero of Calgary, viewed this event through the lens of American cultural hegemony:

> I'm so mad right now I could burn an American flag, because you Americans think it's fun to spit on and desecrate our national symbol, the Canadian flag. First, when you made Guardian, I felt proud that Canada had its own "Captain America." The other characters didn't matter much—they were lucky to be with him. You people think that just because your country is older than ours it's better. Let me tell you, we know more about being proud of our national heritage than you do of yours. There are a few things that we know how to do better than you. We never slaughtered the Indians, or treated them and the blacks like they were cattle. I don't know if you guys keep in touch with what's going on up here, but our government is going to help the Indians develop their own self-ruling government. Let me see you guys do that (ha! ha!). There are a few people up here besides me who are upset that

you have killed off Guardian. I'm speaking for them. I hope you will see the error of your ways.[14]

The response from the editor emphasized writer John Byrne's Canadian nationality as a way of illustrating Canadian authorship of the comic, but clearly the American-ness of the comic's production was influencing the way in which *Alpha Flight* was viewed.

As mentioned earlier, Canadian technological superiority was one form of Canadian boosterism in tales of *Nelvana of the Northern Lights* and in *Captain Canuck*. This, too, was moderated to equality with the United States in *Alpha Flight*. Of course, the technologies available on either side of the border are fantastical by any measure (consider the powerful, yet still skintight Guardian outfit itself). The scientific prowess was seemingly doled out in equal parts on either side of the border, constructing yet more parallelisms. Whereas the United States had Bruce Banner and the Incredible Hulk,[15] Canada had Dr. Walter Langkowski, who replicated Banner's experiments and ended up as the heroic Sasquatch. A point of contrast with American scientific expertise emerges from the relationship between the Canadian state and the development of these technologies. Langkowski performed his experiments with government funding at a government facility in the Arctic. Similarly, the Canadian government funded the creation of the team, and Alpha Flight emerges as part of the Canadian military-industrial complex—for instance, in *Alpha Flight #26* when the team is used to test high-tech Canadian robot warriors. This extraordinary technology is developed "twenty miles south and west of Fort Albany, Ontario, [at] a vast, undeveloped area you will not find on any map. It is the ultra top-secret Albany River proving grounds, where most of Canada's secret military weaponry is tested."[16]

As noted in Chapter 6, the border between Canada and the United States looms large in *Alpha Flight*, and while the team's connection to the Canadian government would wax and wane, the team's affirmation of the southern border's fixity remained: "Yes, we recognize you—American-made mutant hunters who've plagued the X-Men over the years! But this is Canada . . . Alpha Flight's jurisdiction!"[17] Canadian readers, such as H. David Olivier of Toronto, urged the creative team to, among other things, take the defense of Canada more seriously: "Alpha Flight, as a team, is being funded by the Federal Government, purportedly to keep the borders of the nation secure against foreign superbeings' intervention, and to protect the populace from internal menace. If that is the case, then why is their base located off the coast of British Columbia, several thousand kilometers away from the main industrial/population belt, the Quebec City/Windsor corridor, and further still from both the Arctic and Atlantic coastlines?"[18] In short, while various individual story lines narrated the Canadian enemy as being from many different parts of the world, more energy is invested in managing the geopolitics of North America than any other region.

## United Kingdom

While integration with the Marvel Universe moderated Canadian geopolitical ambition, the British nationalist superheroes analyzed here have always existed in the Marvel Universe and yet this has rarely limited the scope of British geopolitical ambition within the comics. This is perhaps the result of the larger British market, which has been catered to more distinctly by Marvel executives. The creation of Captain Britain was the first attempt to create new content for Marvel UK, an imprint previously solely dedicated to reprinting Marvel comics in the United Kingdom.[19] Canada never received such a privileged treatment. As a consequence, Captain Britain's adventures were initially targeted primarily at British audiences; therefore, the worldview was fundamentally British (or at least an American company's idea of what it meant to be British). Rather than make the United Kingdom a periphery of the superhero world, the intention was to establish a privileged role for the country within the overall superhero-based geopolitical order.

The British Empire looms large in these attempts to give the United Kingdom a privileged role, either through the portrayal of its continued presence or through simulacra that reproduce British imperialism. Some early stories are predicated on the continued relevance of the empire, such as a 1976 story line that saw Captain Britain battling against Dr. Synne. The nefarious Dr. Synne saw domination of the British Empire as a jumping-off point for global hegemony: "Your dismal departure will usher in my master plan—to dominate first the entire empire—and finally the whole world!"[20] In these early stories, Britain is visible as a military power with the ability to intervene in postcolonial states. A 1977 story line centers on the villainous Manipulator, the former ruler of the African state of Umbazi, who is portrayed as a cruel tyrant: "He's ten minutes late! Were I still a power in Africa, I'd have his head on a pole for this insolence!"[21] The Manipulator uses a mystic gem to hypnotize Queen Elizabeth II at her Silver Jubilee and compel her to send the Royal Navy to conquer Umbazi and set the Manipulator back on the throne. Africa features repeatedly in Captain Britain's postcolonial adventures, such as in a 1985 story line in which Captain Britain heads to another invented African country, Mbangawi, to search for his kidnapped brother, Jamie. The emperor of Mbangawi is Joshua N'Dingi, also known as Dr. Crocodile, who was educated in England before ascending the throne. Captain Britain smashes into Dr. Crocodile's compound only to be gassed into submission; while under the spell of the gas, he has visions of the life of luxury he and Jamie have been living, which is based on the immiseration of others (images of white women sold into Arab slavery while black women are killed, murder, and starvation). However, Captain Britain denies he has done any of those things—and indeed he is absolved by Dr. Crocodile. However, he realizes that Jamie has indeed done those things, and so he leaves him to face Mbangawi justice. One reader enjoyed this twist:

At first it looked like Doctor Crocodile was going to be one of those Idi Amin type African despots. A valid sort of villain to be sure, but sometimes a bit over used and rather too smugly presented. But turnabout is fair play, and you certainly pulled a nice switch here.[22]

This story does highlight the continuing exploitation of informal imperialism but does so within a frame of British-administered justice; Captain Britain invaded the emperor's compound to take his brother home but was persuaded to leave him. He retains both his moral worth (by abandoning his brother to face justice) and his capacity and willingness to take action against postcolonial states should he deem them to be unjust.

A 1992 story line has Brian Braddock return to Africa, this time representing the family business—Braddock Enterprises. He is there taking part in a waste management project, which would see the world sending toxic waste to the state of Wakanda for high-tech neutralization. However, Wakanda is riven by political debate that is framed as modernization (via projects such as this) versus traditionalism. A former scientist with the name Icon (because of his face, which is a traditional wooden mask) attacks the meeting, holding everyone hostage: "I am the living embodiment of the Wakandan people as they should be! Pure. Primal. Prepared to wrest our country from the grip of the twentieth century world."[23] Unable to reveal himself as Captain Britain, Brian wears a loincloth and swings from the trees into battle with Icon, first calling himself Jungle Man and then later Captain Wakanda. He even speaks like Tarzan while rescuing the hostages, uttering nonsense like "Jungle Man no interest in political infrastructure."[24] In total the story line manages to both satirize the "white jungle lord" genre of pulp fiction and still unironically place in the role of antimodern villain all those opposed to Wakanda becoming the global destination for toxic waste processing.[25]

Thus, the role of empire and imperial relationships remain substantial in representations of Britishness within these comic books even after it was no longer deemed appropriate for heroes to fight for their state's advantage. It is difficult to point to the exact moment when this tipping point was reached, but two juxtaposed story lines illustrate the shift. A 1977–1978 story line in the World War II retrospective *The Invaders* featured the superhero team battling against both the Nazi army and the Scarlet Scarab, the superpowered defender of Egypt. Major Rawlings explains the situation to the Invaders upon their arrival:

To bring you up to date: Egypt has been formally independent since the end of the last war . . . but Britain has maintained a military presence there. At present, there are within Egypt two political factions—both of which wish their nation to achieve total independence by the end of this war. One group wishes to help us, while the other favors a German victory . . . in the mistaken impression that the Nazis will set them free![26]

The Invaders' first meeting with the Scarlet Scarab calls into question the geo-political legitimacy of their presence:

> Human Torch: All right, mister—give us the story—before we show you it takes much more than a gaudy costume to make a super-villain!
> Scarlet Scarab: Villain!? It is you who are the villains in this piece, Invaders! And you are aptly named, for you are invaders—the latest of a long line of conquerors of Egypt, all of whom are dead—as you soon shall be![27]

The story line concludes with a schism among the Invaders, with the English heroes (Union Jack and Spitfire) willing to battle the Scarlet Scarab to maintain control over Egypt and with Captain America content with Egyptian neutrality in the war. However, the schism was repeated in letters to the editor. Al Schroeder, an American, wrote in with the following:

> And it was a nice touch making the Scarlet Scarab a patriotic Egyptian, neutral toward both sides of World War Two, and despising the English for occupying his land. [. . .] One suggestion as a future foe for the Invaders: a super-"hero" called the Imperialist, who would act to put down any possible rebellions within the British Empire—in India, the Middle East, and Africa. A super-patriotic Britisher, who believes every word of Kipling, including the "white man's burden." It might be interesting to see Spitfire's and Union Jack's reaction to him, as they gradually begin to see the injustice of his ways.[28]

This intervention led to an arch reply by British subject H. S. Williams, who was overtly critical of American Cold War hegemony, both in the "real world" and within *The Invaders*:

> Particularly fascinating was a letter by a Mr. Al Schroeder III of Nashville. With reference to his novel idea of a superhero called "The Imperialist," I feel it would only be fair to include a new American hero to provide the same function for the Americans of the team as "The Imperialist" would for the British. [. . .] He could join the team later, and might I suggest the name "Big Brother," or rather "Biggest Brother," for him in the hope this would conjure concepts related to America for the reader: biggest weaponry, political pull, etc.[29]

This overt support for the British Empire (albeit in a retrospective comic book, perhaps deployed as a mechanism for showing how times have changed since World War II) can be contrasted with a 1993 *Excalibur* story line, in which a British intelligence agent, Peter Orpington-Smythe, creates an army of creatures with which to undertake a coup against the government. His motivations are basely geopolitical:

> I am a patriot, Captain. I make no apology. Perhaps you are not old enough to remember when Britain was an empire. Canada, India, Africa, Australia. All colonies of our proud democracy. But our glorious dream was corrupted by insidious forces intent on our destruction. They have reduced us to a historical curiosity. An insignificant island off the coast of Europe.[30]

This geopolitical order is rejected by Orpington-Smythe, who seeks to render Britain great again. However, he is undone by Captain Britain, who rejects the geopolitical logic of empire: "I was given my name and costume along with my powers. I'm not a patriot. I don't care about countries or governments. I care about people . . . justice . . . right and wrong—and you are wrong! Very wrong!"[31] While ostensibly the first story line associates British heroes with support for empire, it does so in retrospect, narrating the British rejection of imperialism in the (then) present. The second story line rather straightforwardly produces imperialism as deviant and associated with antidemocratic outcomes, both at home and overseas.

Of course, the British Empire is not the only way to signal the geopolitical centrality of the United Kingdom, whether that empire is actively invoked or simply evoked as an absent presence. Perhaps the most compelling way in which an Anglo-centric geopolitical order was narrated was through the architecture of the Omniverse. As outlined in previous chapters, Captain Britain gained his powers (for a period anyway) from the friction between various dimensions, which rubbed against each other to a heightened degree in the United Kingdom. This was true in the United Kingdom of every dimension, as the lighthouse owned by Captain Britain served as a central pivot point for all the dimensions. Merlin had set up this cosmic energy-production system to power not just Captain Britain, but the Captain Britains of every dimension, who served as his agents. Thus, Captain Britain is part of the Captain Britain Corps, which is composed of various agents who all chose the amulet of right over the sword of might when confronted by Merlin's choice; each Captain, however, reflects the historically contingent circumstances of that dimension (see Figure 7.1). Captain Britain's closest friend in the Corps, Captain UK (as the name implies, her world is not radically different than his), explains:

**Captain Britain**: I've never wanted any part of this constitutional clap-trap.
**Captain UK**: That's the problem, Brian. You are a member of the Corps. You have responsibilities, both as a guardian of the dimensional interface—the gateway between realities—and as a champion of the highest values of your earth's morality code.

Figure 7.1: The Captain Britain Corps as protector of both the interdimensional interface and local morality in every dimension. (Copyright © 2012 Marvel Characters, Inc. Used with permission.)

> **Captain Britain:** What is this morality code?
>
> **Captain UK:** Each reality has an accepted standard of morality . . . for instance, on Enforcer Capone's world, murder is legal . . . while in Sister Gaia's reality, plucking a flower is an act of gross brutality.[32]

Thus, the Captain Britain Corps not only serves as the linchpin of cosmic order through its defense of the interdimensional portals but also provides a strong, but geographically relative, force for morality and justice. Surely there is no more central role to play in geopolitics than for the United Kingdom to be the defenders of both the universal (or omniversal?) *and* the particular (each earth's morality).[33] I might add that Roma declares Captain Britain to be the strongest of the Captain Britain Corps and her champion, thus elevating *our* United Kingdom over that of all other dimensions.

Through both the construction and development of the Captain Britain Corps, as well as through earlier invocations of British imperialism, British nationalist superheroes narrate the power and relevance of the United Kingdom to the geopolitical order. Both Canadian and British formulations have been shown to rely on a sense of grandiosity and fantastic visions of technology and magic to situate them at the center of geopolitics. The next section demonstrates a contrasting strategy that has been relatively consistent for decades of *Captain America*.

## United States

Generally speaking, the geopolitical order expressed in *Captain America* is one in which the United States enacts a liberal internationalist hegemony. The world is envisioned as a realist one of sovereign and equal states, but the United States has a special role to play, purportedly as a result of its morality, objectivity, and power. Steve Rogers best encapsulates this geopolitical order, and its connection to violence, when he considers enlisting in the army before World War II:

I've always loathed the idea of war . . . of violence of any kind . . . and yet—! What if there are forces in the world—evil forces—that can't be stopped by any other means? Those newsreels . . . the Germans have gone mad . . . the Japanese have committed themselves to world conquest! And as much as I despise the whole militarist mentality—as vile as I find the notion of organized slaughter—dammit, there's no other way! Someone's got to put a halt to the lunacy that's gripped this planet—again! As one of the sane people—I'm obligated, like it or not![34]

This self-perception of being a reluctant public actor is manifest in republican notions of the citizen-legislator and also in American narrations of geopolitical intervention. As Neil Smith writes:

[The founding documents of the United States] mobilized the "natural rights of man," loudly proclaimed as universal, into the particularity of an Americanism which placed itself not simply as geographical but global historical alternative to inherited forms of social oppression, exploitation, and inequality. America was the future.[35]

This belief in the United States as not only a circumscribed geopolitical entity but also a beacon for the rest of the world is evident from the earliest wartime adventures of Captain America:

**South Asian man:** I have been to state school . . . I have read of you and your deeds! America is the hope of the world! Go free, brave Sahib, and crush the evil Fakir who sells us to the little brown devils [Japanese]!

**Captain America:** You bet I will! Get up on your feet! In America we kneel to no man![36]

This framing of American power as cultural and normative, drawing together a global constituency that (Captain) America leads against the minority of forces opposed to freedom, tends to ignore the political-economic advantages that produce such leadership. In other words, Captain America is imagined to exist in a world where American force is used only in self-defense or to protect public order (consider again the symbolism of his shield). This is manifested through two main narrative strategies. First, the United States is represented as a popular hegemon whose policies produce a safer world. Second, Captain America's relationship to violence and war is shown as complicated, despite his wartime origins. Generally though, since 1964 Captain America seeks peaceful resolution of conflict, resorting to violence only when necessary.

Captain America is often narrated as an ambassador of American values that wins over foreign observers. For instance, in 1970 King Hassab of Irabia toured the United States. Already captivated by what he saw ("I find America

a most fascinating land!"), when Captain America intervened to save his life
he was even more impressed: "Never have I seen such valor! If such as he truly
symbolizes America—"[37] Captain America's (and by implication, America's)
willingness to fight for others' freedom serves as a marker of difference through
which geopolitical legitimacy is earned. The universalism of this charge is
sometimes tacit, sometimes not.[38] Occasionally it borders on the ludicrous—as
in this 1942 exchange between Satan and Captain America:

> **Satan:** You have won, mortal! But I shall come again when the time is
> ripe, when there is no longer a Captain America to champion the
> good! I will come, if need be, again and again!
> **Captain America:** There will always be an American to fight for man-
> kind against the forces of evil![39]

In these and many situations like them, the American Dream is understood to
stretch far beyond the boundaries of the United States.

The narration of anti-imperialism explicitly requires the disavowal of
force, most especially when American authority around the world is understood to rest on a willingness to fight for what is right. Thus, precisely when
the United States is criticized as being imperialist, *Captain America* skews in
the other direction. For instance, during the war in Vietnam Captain America
traveled to the theater of war exactly twice. In 1965 he went to Vietnam, not to
fight the Vietcong, but to rescue a captured American helicopter pilot who was
lucky enough to be the brother of a soldier who had previously saved Captain
America's life. In 1970 he goes back, this time searching for Dr. Hoskins, a doctor who had tended to the wounded on both sides. Captain America suspects
both Vietnams of kidnapping Dr. Hoskins so as to scuttle peace talks. In both
cases, Captain America is not intervening in order to create American military
success, as he did in World War II, but instead is intervening for purposes of
peace and humanitarianism. There were, of course, good market reasons during the late 1960s and early 1970s for Marvel Comics to avoid implicating Captain America in the anticommunism and military interventionism that then
dominated American foreign policy; hence, the anachronistic concern over the
Red Skull and Nazis in the United States.

It would be easy to see this creative decision as the result of pure economic
interest on the part of the publishers; nevertheless, a counterexample indicates
that creative staff worked to sculpt a pacific United States through their deployment of the Captain America character. The 2003 invasion of Iraq stirred
up accusations of American imperialism but did so in a climate of patriotism
in which military adventurism was much more popular among comics readers than during Vietnam. A 2009 story line showed Captain America as go-
between again, arriving in Iraq shortly after the 2003 invasion.[40] While he
limits his military actions to saving the lives of American soldiers under attack,
most of the comic's events in Iraq revolve around Captain America's efforts to

Figure 7.2: Captain America drinking tea with an Iraqi mullah in an effort to resolve conflicts peacefully. (Copyright © 2012 Marvel Characters, Inc. Used with permission.)

show the U.S. Army how to end the insurgency peacefully—by visiting local mullahs and drinking tea with them (Figure 7.2). Together, the examples of Vietnam and Iraq indicate that the creative staff of *Captain America* is unwilling to use the hero as a proxy for wars that bear the whiff of imperialism.

Of course, for a superhero (and for a superhero story), violence is a regular part of life. As reader Steven Bennett noted, "Captain America seems incapable of surviving without a war. There has never been a peacetime Captain America. That's significant."[41] Captain America's efforts to resolve conflict without resorting to violence must fail most of the time, so that the spectacle of his fighting skills can be laid before readers. This was relatively easy during World War II, before the invention of the Comics Code and when violence against Germans and Japanese was licensed by the war.[42] Indeed, Captain America had no qualms during the war when he variously punched the criminal Killer Kole off a rooftop, pulled the pin on a grenade attached to a Nazi's belt, or machine-gunned a platoon of Japanese soldiers ("I hate to do this Bucky, but war is war!").[43] Perhaps most stunning is a 1944 story line titled "Tojo's Terror Masters," in which Captain America and Bucky pile dynamite in a Japanese tunnel connecting Japan to the United States under the Pacific. The explosion collapses the tunnel, killing one million Japanese soldiers. This is not a superhero whose hands are clean of blood.

With the resurrection of the character in 1964, the super-soldier was rewritten as "the American Dream," and Captain America became discursively linked to the liberal internationalist imperium.[44] The contrast of the hero's new take on war, in comparison to his World War II adventures, was appreciated by readers, especially Nils Osmar:

> I was worried about what Captain America's journey to Vietnam would bring, but you've restored my faith. For once, a Marvel hero fought overseas without political discrimination—without subjecting the

reader to propaganda—and it means a new dawn for Marvel. "Captured
. . . in Vietnam!" [the 1970 story described earlier] showed the war for
what it is—a fanatic, senseless struggle between two sides not clearly
discernable from each other. A cry is going up—not just in America,
but everywhere—for an end to war. The war hawk, the decorated hero
of the battlefield, is a fading remnant of yesterday. Captain America has
finally made the journey into the present, and—fighting only for peace
and the sacred right to live—he is welcome here.[45]

Of course, rejecting war is not the same thing as rejecting violence, as Captain America himself makes clear in 1971: "Mankind is sick of war! Nothing is
worth fighting for—except freedom and justice!"[46] This is a tension within the
characterization of the hero that is further examined during Steve Englehart's
run on *Captain America* as writer.

The introduction of pacifist Dave Cox critiqued the relationship between
Captain America's violence and the U.S. war in Vietnam in a way that the readership found acceptable. As Englehart himself describes, "I had a conscientious
objector as a character for a while, and he and Cap treated each other with
understanding and respect, and nobody said anything about it."[47] Cox was a
former prisoner of war who lost his arm in Vietnam and later became a conscientious objector.[48] Cox's principled objection to the war in Vietnam causes
Captain America to consider his position on the war, which he had so scru-
pulously avoided: "I can't stop thinking about that boy, Dave Cox—to be so
young and to have lived through what he has[.] . . . I was created to put an end to
things like that—to keep Americans safe from aggressors—but what can I do if
America herself—"[49] When the villainous Serpent Squad attacks while Captain
America is visiting Cox's house, Cox refuses to fight back:

> I told you before, Miss Carter: I refuse to participate in violence! I swore
> to myself and my God, who said "thou shalt not kill!" and "do unto oth-
> ers as you would have them do unto you!" Men talk of "using a gun to
> keep peace," of "fighting the war to end all wars"! Don't you see that it
> doesn't work—that violence only breeds violence![50]

Cox proves his courage by allowing himself to be tortured rather than give up
the location of Captain America and the Falcon; this affirms his masculinity to
Captain America's friend Peggy Carter:

> **Peggy:** I can't understand why a man like him [i.e., a pacifist] didn't
>     break!
> **Captain America:** Because he is a man like he is, Peg. He has his way,
>     and I have mine—but Dave Cox is no coward! He was willing to die
>     in order to protect us—without violating his beliefs! His beliefs . . .
>     aren't the ones I was taught—but I guess things do change with time.

However, the tension between Captain America's methods and those of Dave Cox continued to fester such that by 1975, Sharon Carter was tired of the hero's inability to make space in his life for her amid his adventuring. As mentioned in Chapter 2, the different form of masculinity that Dave Cox represents proves attractive to her, and their abortive relationship falters only because he leaves her, afraid of complicating her life further.

The character of Dave Cox proved intriguing to writer J. M. DeMatteis, who returned to the character in 1984 when Captain America visits Cox, to discuss their mutual past with Sharon Carter (then thought dead). This gives them the opportunity to respectfully rehash their differences:

> **Dave Cox:** Weird how fate threw us together, wasn't it? Dave Cox, Viet Nam vet and born-again pacifist—and Captain America, the greatest soldier who ever lived.
> **Captain America:** We're not that different Dave. I think we're both motivated by the same hopes . . . the same ideals.[51]

However, their meditations are interrupted as Cox is swept up in a plot by the villainous Mother Superior and Baron Zemo, who plot to break him of his idealism to prove the underlying evil of all mankind, thereby demoralizing Captain America—Cox is brainwashed and turned into a murderous zombie dubbed "the Slayer." However, he breaks through his brainwashing through sheer force of will, just as Captain America has so many times in the past. The two American heroes, pacifist and super-soldier, are each shown to be strong in their idealism and self-control. Cox's reclamation of his actions, instead of undermining Captain America, causes Baron Zemo to question his own views.

DeMatteis's resurrection of Dave Cox was part of an overarching narrative arc in which he wanted to have Captain America adopt Cox's philosophy:

> By the end of my run I was ready to turn Captain America on his head with a story line in which he renounced violence and set out on a new path. But that change came after a long build-up—there were (at least) a year's worth of stories pointing us in that direction. And, of course, in the end, the "Cap as pacifist" story was shot down by the Powers That Be.[52]

This reaction by the editorial staff is perhaps unsurprising, but it shows the fragmented nature of authorship in the mainstream comics industry. As noted in Chapter 1, the superhero genre is dependent on spectacular conflict, and *Captain America* was embedded within a discourse of righteous violence that has ties to domestic vigilantism and liberal interventionism abroad. Captain America's aversion to violence reached its apogee in 1986 when he shot an ULTIMATUM terrorist who was at that moment in the process of shooting hostages. Within the story line, this causes a media sensation (apparently these reporters do not remember his World War II adventures), and Switzerland (where the event took place) asks the United States to extradite Captain America to face trial. Captain America takes to the news media and explains:

> I believe killing is morally wrong, and that my actions should not be condoned or sanctioned by anyone. I am willing to go to Switzerland and stand trial for what I did if the Swiss authorities so desire. [. . .] What I ask of you is that you understand that I do not take lightly what I did, nor do I advocate murder as the solution to any problem. I also ask that you forgive me for letting you down.[53]

The controversy over this killing in the letters-to-the-editor column showed both a diversity of views on Captain America's sense of guilt ("How dumb can you get? He kills his enemy and *regrets* it!") and readers who attempted to reconcile his present aversion to guns with his wartime past ("He and the Invaders couldn't have gone that far behind German lines just using their fists!"). The editor's reply stretched continuity beyond belief:

> [Captain America and the Invaders] were never actively engaged in combat with the Axis *militia*, but concentrated their efforts against Nazi super-agents and their leaders. All this is to say that Captain America never sought to kill anyone on the battlefield. It probably happened that soldiers who shot at Cap were hit by their own bullets, but that's not the same as Cap shooting someone. We can't deny that Cap was at the center of a lot of bloodshed during the Big One, but he himself never intentionally shed another man's blood. The ULTIMATUM incident [. . .] was the first time Cap *intentionally* took someone's life.[54]

In the subsequent decades, Captain America is narrated as a character around whom others kill so that he does not. As already mentioned, Captain America's World War II partner Bucky was reinvented as an assassin who did the dirty work that Captain America could not be seen to do. Similarly, in a flashback readers are given insight into the early relationship between Captain America and Sharon Carter. Sharon, an agent of SHIELD, is meant to give Captain America an execution order signed by the president; instead she keeps it to herself, planning to kill the double agent herself:

> For as long as anyone can remember, you've been a perfect soldier . . . but never an assassin. You don't kill—not in cold blood. When I saw that you were being asked to choose between duty and conscience . . . I decided to spare you the burden. I'm a soldier, too . . . Steve. There are times I have to kill. I'm not proud of it . . . but my job gets dirty.

> Sometimes, the only way I can keep going . . . is to know that there's still
> one man who can always do the job clean.[55]

The schism between the violence Captain America can commit and the violence other agents of the United States are required to do to maintain the
geopolitical status quo steadily widens over the character's history, in what is
perhaps a tacit acknowledgment of the violence, or the threat of violence, at the
heart of American hegemony.[56]

Captain America has always been more circumspect about operating overseas than at home, especially during the Vietnam era and shortly thereafter.
This concern for sovereignty manifests in 1977 when Captain America is mistakenly kidnapped to a Central American country where the dictator rules
harshly: "Whoever runs that banana jail seems to get his kicks out of kicking
the inmates! This man they call 'the Swine' must be typical of the kind of bully
that flourishes in these two-bit dictatorships. But this is not my country and
not my place to fight for causes I know nothing about."[57] This discretion was
appreciated by at least one reader, Larry Lisowski: "On page 10, Cap thinks that
this foreign country's problems are out of his jurisdiction. At last, Cap is doing
some thinking along with his hitting."[58] Even here though, Captain America
does ultimately get involved (after freeing prisoners of the Swine) and argues
that the authoritarianism of the government is preventing development: "You'll
never bring new business to this area with that attitude!"[59]

A similar concern for, and then negation of, sovereignty can be seen in
a complex story line from 1986, in which a hero named Nighthawk traveled
from the earth of another dimension to see Captain America and his superhero
friends. Nighthawk needs help freeing his country from a group of superheroes
who rebuilt their country as a utopia—Nighthawk had fled because he opposed
the amount of social control that involved. Interestingly, Captain America
frames the request through the language of sovereignty:

> It's a difficult call. We're being asked to go to a foreign world and help a
> rebel change its form of government. This strikes me as wrong. We do
> not, after all, go around our own world and alter governments whose
> policies we disagree with . . . nor do we make it a practice to get involved
> in the politics of other worlds in *this* dimension. I must conclude that we
> don't have the right to go to another dimension and change its form of
> government . . . even though we all oppose the concept of dictatorships![60]

Later, however, Captain America changes his mind, deciding that he cannot leave
a tyranny unopposed—he agrees to help Nighthawk, but Nighthawk lets him off
the moral hook by getting help from others in his own dimension. In this case, as
in the last, intervention in others' affairs is seen as a reluctant, last step in the face
of oppression, yet one that is made relatively often: "Clandestine operations in
foreign nations aren't normally my style. But this is a unique situation."[61]

## Conclusions

The disavowal of generalized imperial interventionism, rapidly followed by the invocation of necessity and immediate exigencies, is emblematic of the liberal idealism that Captain America has embodied since the early 1960s ("the American Dream"). As Neil Smith argues:

> [For conservatives, t]he reality of US-sponsored repression or exploitation is either denied or excused as an exception to the norm, or else it is justified as a pragmatic necessity for the defeat of nefarious enemies: the American dream is cordoned off from reality. Liberals, by contrast, traditionally fold the contradiction into a narrative of realities versus ideals and focus on a moral parsing of specific events and episodes, sorting apart the regrettable failings of the ideal, the causes thereof and their implications. Wishing the contradiction into either the realm of human nature or that of philosophical inevitability, the liberal response too protects the ideal.[62]

This chapter has offered two contrasting forms of geopolitical narrative. The kind of narrative invoked for British and Canadian nationalist superheroes tend to rely on the fantastic as a means of asserting geopolitical relevance in a complex world. For Canadian heroes (and their readers), maintaining parallel equality with the United States was particularly important—hence the steady stream of affirmations of Canadian technological prowess and superheroic might in *Nelvana of the Northern Lights*, *Captain Canuck*, and *Alpha Flight*. For the United Kingdom, emphasizing the continued relevance of the empire (or commonwealth) was key; the notion of the United Kingdom as a paternal "first-among-equals" could be discerned in narratives of Captain Britain and *The Invaders*, particularly those relating to Africa. While British heroes' moral authority came to be associated with a rejection of imperialism, the paternal centrality of the United Kingdom was reinscribed through the creation of the Captain Britain Corps itself, which produced the entire multiverse as a British protectorate.

In *Captain America*, however, a different geopolitical narrative has been emphasized. Since 1964, Captain America has disavowed war and killing in an explicit attempt to distance the hero from his wartime roots. Therefore, even as the United States has become most central to the geopolitical order, its superhero embodiment has tried to downplay the role of force in producing that centrality. Instead, American power and authority is seen to result from the attractive power of American values and leadership. This serial narrative works to hide power relations that call national innocence into question.

# Alternate Worlds

What if Captain America had objected to the atomic bomb? This is the premise of a 1997 story line that reimagines the history of the hero along these lines. His principled objection to the atomic bomb led to his brainwashing by the American government, which had an interest in keeping him in action:

> **President Clinton**: What did he rebel against? A mission? Some dirty job you wanted him to do?
>
> **Nick Fury**: No. The bomb. He thought it wasn't right. It wasn't fair. It wasn't . . .
>
> **President Clinton**: American?
>
> **Nick Fury**: He said that a war fought with honor would end with disgrace if this bomb was used. He felt that the war in Asia would end soon anyway. On our side we felt that every day the war was shortened by, saved American lives in combat.[1]

Captain America is still frozen, in this timeline not in an iceberg but instead in suspended animation, from which the U.S. government periodically awakens him so that he can be brainwashed and sent into combat—in Korea he fought as Captain Battle, in Vietnam as Captain Strike. However, each time this is done he ends up in a similar crisis of morality; forced to choose between his morals and his orders, he chooses his morals and is put back into suspended animation. Eventually he discovers what is going on and rebels entirely, hitting the road to learn "what America is" (see the theme of mobility highlighted in Chapter 6).

This counterfactual history upends the continuity of the character, turning him into a tool of American foreign policy rather than the icon of the American Dream, as he is understood in "regular" continuity. Yet the story still manages to highlight Captain America's moral center, and the conflict between him and the U.S. government is framed as a liberal one, of ideals versus practicality (as described in Chapter 7). The story line therefore manages to interrogate recent American history through this liberal lens, exposing American foreign policy to a critical gaze while holding the essential goodness of America intact in the person of Captain America. In this story line, after leaving government service, Captain America founds his superhero team (the Avengers), battles racists, changes his uniform to something more familiar to the readers, and in general things end up as they do in "our" timeline. The metalesson seems to be that all roads lead to "our" present, and therefore American hegemony is given a teleological veneer.

This story line is an example of the kinds of work that the inclusion of reality-warping border crossings, whether produced through time travel or interdimensional portals, can do for national narratives. Transporting "conventional" national narratives into counterfactual histories and alternate worlds enables nationalism to be renarrated in ways that extend and deepen the characteristics deemed essential to the national identity in question. This chapter begins by linking the doubled narratives of superhero and nation (outlined in Chapters 4 and 5) with extant literature on science fiction and fantasy. It then shifts to an empirical engagement with narratives of time travel, interdimensional warping, and alternate continuities (what James Kneale, drawing on Tolkien, refers to as "secondary worlds")[2] involving Captain Britain and Captain America.[3] These narratives offer both reinforcement of primary themes found throughout these heroes' continuities and also opportunities to narrate political alternatives that may or may not be more politically progressive.

## Escaping Continuity

The existence of superheroes alone marks the genre as fantastic and unreal. Yet the departures from our familiar, commonplace world certainly do not stop there, as has hopefully already been evident. Unbelievable technological might is matched by both unimaginable moral uprightness and inhuman moral failings. Individuals plot to rule the world; others struggle to pay their bills while saving the world at night. While these superheroes and supervillains are clearly marked out from our world, they nevertheless are meant to exist within it, as indicated by the material landscapes they inhabit, the famous people they meet, and the sociopolitical systems they protect or threaten. It is from this overlap that the narratives draw their tension; if New York is destroyed in the comic book, this has meaning because the reader *knows* what New York is in her or his world. James Kneale and Rob Kitchin argue that science fiction (a genre that shares both origins and features with superhero comics) is "less a thing than a gap: between science and fiction, between the reader's reality and the world of the fiction, between the possible and the impossible."[4] They cite Rosemary Jackson as arguing that the fantasy genre has "refused to observe unities of time, space and character, doing away with chronology, three-dimensionality and with rigid distinctions between animate and inanimate objects, self and other, life and death."[5] Certainly superhero comics have often been accused of putting a barrier between life and death that is permeable at best.[6] This chapter, however, focuses on the chronology and three-dimensionality of Jackson's genre description.

Superhero narratives, like science fiction stories, are preoccupied with the maintenance of plausibility in the face of the fantastic. This usually takes the form of concern over continuity. Richard Reynolds argues that there are three different kinds of continuity. Serial continuity refers to the backstory of events that are known to have happened previously and are materialized in readers' personal archives. Hierarchical continuity refers to the comparison of various superheroes' powers, which are meant to be relatively consistent in comparison to other superheroes.

> Serial continuity, which is diachronic (it develops over time), and hierarchical continuity, which is synchronic (the state of affairs at a given moment), combine to produce structural continuity, which is, in short, the entire contents of the DC or Marvel universes.[7]

Reynolds also makes the point that structural continuity includes the extratextual events that are incorporated in the text (e.g., the Pearl Harbor attack that is referenced in *Captain America Comics* yet does not actually appear within the comic). Fans of comics are famous for their militant policing of continuity; therefore, what is plausible in comics is produced through a complex negotiation by audiences of the texts produced by writers and artists. Events in continuity, or attempts to escape continuity, must meet exacting, detailed readings by fans with significant cultural capital; of course, these particular audiences are also particularly open to events that would not seem plausible to many non–comics readers. Their contribution to authorship of these tales should not be underestimated.

Superhero continuity has links to Bhabha's national narrations, as outlined in Chapters 4 and 5. Both constructs struggle to provide coherence to their subjects, providing the illusion of consistency and singularity to what is ultimately an exponentially expanding set of narrative elements composed by countless authors. Of course, by escaping continuity, both kinds of narrative (superhero and national, or in the case of this book, a singular narrative enfolding both) enable "subversive critiques of worlds and world building, anti-worlds rather than worlds proper."[8] Superhero narratives often escape continuity via the narrative strategies of time travel or interdimensional travel, which, while distinct, nevertheless have in common the ability to envision geographies that simultaneously are and are not. "Here, [science fiction] becomes a useful cognitive space, opening up sites from which to contemplate material and discursive geographies and the production of geographical knowledges and imaginations."[9]

Time travel highlights the contingency of the present through multiple narrative strategies. Often the protagonist is responding to a horrible present or a prophecy of doom; in order to prevent this terrifying eventuality, the hero must either travel back in time to fix the present or fix the present to prevent the future from coming true (the latter involves time travel only through precognition or prophecy, but the narratives are ultimately more similar than different). Alternatively the hero may be thrust into the past, and there must prevent the disturbance of any causal relations that may undo the "real" present to which he or she wishes to return. As Barney Warf argues, "Alternative history 'pushes the envelope' of our sense of how histories and geographies are made, examining the ways in which multiple potential temporal and spatial trajectories of change exist simultaneously at different conjunctures."[10] The plurality of realities widens our ontological horizons, such that everything that could go differently, has—and the world that could have been, is. Warf continues: "Possible worlds are not parts of the actual one we inhabit, but alternatives to it. Which worlds are real and which are ersatz is a matter of actualization; *all* worlds are actualized somewhere, i.e., within different spatio-temporal co-ordinates."[11]

Narratives of interdimensional travel, then, are different from stories of travel through outer space or other forms of "escape" from our world. This tradition allows the narrative to explore alternative, yet equally "real," narrations of history, geography, and identity. Such exploration is a welcome antidote to teleological understandings of history, which are innately conservative: "Successful stories, such as the USA, generally snuff out consideration of paths not taken; after all, once they become wealthy and powerful, it is inconceivable for the past to have unfolded in any other way."[12] However, while "history is always written by the winners," it does not follow that narratives of alternative worlds are necessarily postcolonial or progressive. These narratives, especially in the medium of comic books, are themselves inescapably linked to prevailing discourses made available through corporate capitalism and discourses of nationalism as any other narrative; while the stories may be otherworldly, they are nevertheless bound to this world's political economy.[13] Thus, tales of time travel and alternative dimensions in nationalist superhero comics still tend to operate within the parameters set by national narratives, although they use the platform of time and interdimensional travel to highlight the uniqueness and fragility of *this* world's polities.

## Alter-nation

Time and interdimensional travel have functioned to different ends in narratives of Captain Britain and Captain America. Given Captain America's lengthier publishing history and centrality to the Marvel continuity, time and interdimensional travel have been used more extensively to explore his character. However, as shown in Chapters 6 and 7, Captain Britain is more intrinsically linked to these modes of alternative continuity. The high density within the British Isles of interdimensional links between the various worlds of the multiverse was explained as being productive of British geopolitical centrality within the tales of Captain Britain. Beyond Avalon and Otherworld, however, there is the further intersection between this earth and many others. Each earth is protected by a member of the Captain Britain Corps, each of whom reflects the contingent history of that timeline. Typically very little is explained about these histories, as the name and appearance of each Captain only hint at how the national narrative has unfolded differently. For instance, the rise of fascism in Britain is seen to result in the Lord High Justicer (a Judge Dredd look-alike), while the ascendancy of the Welsh and French at various points in history produced alternate timelines in which Captain Cymru and Chevalier Bretagne emerge as the kingdom's protector. Earlier divergences from "our" timeline result in presents that are even more difficult to understand. The lack (or defeat) of the Norman invasion seemingly produced Cap'n Saxonia, while the lack (or defeat) of mammals produced Britanicus Rex, the heroic defender of a Britain populated by sentient dinosaurs.[14]

However, sometimes one of these alternative earths becomes more central to the overarching narrative than these passing glimpses of secondary worlds. For instance, in 1985 a mercenary group known as Technet chased a renegade Captain known as Kaptain Briton to "our" dimension. An identical twin to Captain Britain, Kaptain Briton defeated him in combat and then passed himself off as Captain Britain in order to avoid his bounty hunters. Captain Britain, unconscious, is sent back to Kaptain Briton's dimension, which is a cruel world full of sadism and depravity; the classical visual motifs and the dialogue imply that the center of Roman power shifted to the British Isles. Empress Sat-yr-nin announces:

> People of the Empire of True Briton. Today is a day of great glory. Not only have our warwomen been victorious in the Antarctic Strife Zone . . . but also Kaptain Briton, hero of the Empire, has returned from missions on far off worlds to bring more honour to this glittering day. Let the slaughter commence.[15]

The depravity of this dimension is visible in the behavior of both the Empress Sat-yr-nin, who seduces Captain Britain with special incense, and by Kaptain Briton, who while impersonating Captain Britain in "our" dimension, attempts to rape the hero's sister. The implication is that the moral corruption of Rome has continued until the present day, highlighting the moral superiority of "our" world.

A similar story line unfolds in 1989 when Excalibur is taken to a parallel England where modern technology has developed alongside everyday usage of magic. The kingdom is ruled by the Queen Mother, and when the young prince falls in love with Excalibur member Kitty Pryde, the Queen Mother imprisons her and plans a royal wedding. Eventually saved by Excalibur, Kitty Pryde chastises the Queen Mother for her behavior: "The England I know—the realm Captain Britain's proud to represent—is grounded firm [sic] in the rights of the individual! Not the Queen—nor her government—is supposed to be above the law!"[16] Yet another world is protected by a Captain Britain Corps member known as Crusader X, and the world's geopolitics appears to be frozen in the Victorian era, with Prussia a threat to the British Empire and the American superhero Iron Man plotting to assassinate the empire's rulers until he is stopped by the teamwork of Crusader X and Captain Britain. As these examples indicate, alternative worlds revealed through interdimensional portals tend to highlight the politico-moral superiority of "our" world while highlighting the contingency of that outcome.

Time travel narratives similarly advocate a centrality to "our" present over other possibilities. Several *Excalibur* story lines involve time travel into our dystopic future, including a 1993 story that takes Excalibur forward to 2013. In this future, the Knights of Pendragon (including Union Jack) were killed trying to resist the imposition of rule by titanic American robots known as the Sentinels. Excalibur successfully liberates the Britain of 2013, but when traveling back through time Captain Britain disappears. When he reappears in 1994, he is no longer Captain Britain but the gruff and taciturn Britanic: "No normal mind could have coped with the bombardment of events from my time journey so I had to stop being 'normal'—stop being Captain Britain, or even Brian Braddock—and become Britanic."[17] During this time Britanic saw a new future for Britain, in which the Sentinels took over the United States and a secret British agency called Black Air made a deal to maintain British sovereignty by pursuing the Sentinels' agenda on their behalf. With this vision of the future in mind, he eventually shed his gravitas-laden persona of Britanic and fought with the rest of Excalibur in "our" present against the fascist Black Air, which was currently metastasizing within the British political system.

Time travel also featured in the pages of *New Excalibur* when the team traveled back in time because Camelot had been destroyed before its time, thus upending the present. It should be noted that this plot formulation establishes one reality as paramount to the others, and therefore more "real." This change to the past, readers discover, is caused by the invasion of space dragons[18] that conquered Camelot at what should have been its peak and therefore upset the time stream. The privileging of the present is perpetuated by the revelation that libidinous team member Pete Wisdom became intoxicated with mead and tried to seduce Guinevere; after his failure, Lancelot remained behind to comfort Guinevere, thus sparking their own famous illicit romance. This implies not only that New Excalibur had to travel back in time to set the present aright but also that this event was indeed already part of the present timeline.[19] Kneale defines this narrative tactic as a "second-order counterfactual"; it allows "an alternative history to return to the track taken in our world, effectively suggesting that events are so strongly determined that a diversion will eventually be cancelled out."[20]

As seen in the preceding example, time travel and interdimensional portals are central to the narration both of Captain Britain and the British nation.

While a near-infinitude of alternative Britains are alluded to in both narrative and image, the alternatives explored in more depth tend to privilege "our" Britain in politico-moral terms. Similarly, time travel story lines either highlight "our" present as something normatively to be defended or, somewhat contrarily, as something predestined. A final example serves as a bridge to a discussion of time travel and interdimensional portals in *Captain America*.

In 1989 Excalibur investigates the arrival in Britain of several artifacts and people who seem to come from an alternate reality in which Nazi Germany won World War II. Among these transplants is a Nazi version of Excalibur, complete with a Hauptmann Englande and an emaciated ghostly version of Jewish team member Kitty Pryde. They plot to conquer this world and establish a new Nazi hegemony; however, Excalibur captures them and they are deported back to their own dimension. The fascination with alternative histories in which the Nazis won World War II, common in the realm of counterfactual history and literature, is also popular within the realm of nationalist superheroes. The American iteration of this plot device was published in 2003–2004, only instead of the victorious Nazis invading "our" space/time, it is Captain America who changes theirs *and* ours—to produce the present with which we are familiar.

The story line begins with Captain America being fished out of the North Atlantic, not by his soon-to-be-friends in the Avengers as our continuity would have it, but by Nazis. In this timeline, following Captain America's disappearance in 1945, the war went badly for the Allies, culminating in an atomic bomb being dropped on Detroit and an eventual U.S. surrender. New York has been renamed New Berlin, and the Red Skull has established authoritarian rule over the United States. Captain America escapes and joins the Resistance, which is populated by other familiar superheroic figures. The Red Skull plans to use a new time/space transporter to send his Nazi armies into other places and times so that his reach can extend everywhere and for all eternity. Captain America is recaptured but only after seizing control of the airwaves to deliver a revolutionary message to the watching American public. The American people rise up, and in innumerable local skirmishes the Nazis are overthrown. Captain America is freed by the Resistance, and he battles the Red Skull; their melee disrupts the time/space transporter, causing energy to flash into the time stream, upsetting the established timeline. Both Captain America and the Red Skull tumble into the time portal—suddenly it is 1964 and Captain America is being pulled out of the North Atlantic again, this time by the Avengers. While it is unclear from the narrative whether this was how "our" continuity became such, or whether this was an alternate world whose history was made parallel to events on "our" earth, the moral appears to be the same: American resistance to totalitarianism remained ambient yet latent until the spark of revolution was provided by Captain America himself, the icon of the American Dream.

However, in *Captain America* not all stories of alternative worlds serve this same purpose. Another variety of story line works to illustrate the moral fiber of Captain America as beyond that of even other superheroes. For instance, a 1991 story line celebrated Captain America's fiftieth anniversary by having the hero chase a scythe-wielding villain down an alley; however, the villain uses his scythe to open a rift in time. Captain America chases him through the rift, only to meet Johnny Appleseed on the other side. In turn he meets Pecos Bill, John Henry, Paul Bunyan, and Uncle Sam. Indeed, this is the legendary America, the place where the American Dream becomes a reality:

> **Captain America**: I call myself Captain America. I'm lost. I don't know what I'm doing here. I don't even know where I am.
> **Paul Bunyan**: You're in the Heart of America, Captain.
> **Captain America**: I know, but it's not the same America as the one in my world.
> **Paul Bunyan**: I'll betcha it's a better America than the one you come from, Captain—an unspoilt America where all things are possible.[21]

Eventually Captain America finds the scythe-wielding Father Time, who tells him that he is an Elder of the Universe whose life's pursuit is to travel the universe commemorating significant events. Because it is his fiftieth anniversary, it is Captain America's time to become a legend. The hero, however, refuses to stop struggling to make the "real" America more like the "legendary" America. His moxie is appreciated by Uncle Sam, observing from the sidelines: "That's the spirit, Captain! Never say die! Show that sanctimonious so-and-so the way a real American goes out fighting! Give 'em what for, my most valiant of sons!"[22] This story would be easy to dismiss as an "anniversary" issue, but the theme of Captain America as a patriotic icon at the grandest scale appears elsewhere several times.

Therefore, time travel has been used in the pages of *Captain America* to expand the role of the hero transhistorically, offering him a sense of cosmic import and gravitas. For the remainder of this chapter, however, our attention shifts to two tales of alternate worlds offered in the wake of September 11, 2001, that featured Captain America while incorporating the entire Marvel Universe of characters. Both of these stories, *1602* and *The Ultimates*, narrate particular relationships between America and Europe that are relevant in the post-9/11 context.

## 1602

One notable attempt to tinker with the Marvel Universe continuity came when the publisher asked science fiction writer Neil Gaiman to produce a story making use of the Marvel characters. Writing the story in the wake of the September 11, 2001, attacks, however, made any high-profile project with superheroes potentially complicated: "No planes. No skyscrapers. No bombs. No guns. I didn't want it to be a war story, and I didn't want to write a story in which might made right—or in which might made anything."[23] Having spent some time in Venice, however, Gaiman would later write that "the past seemed very close to me" and that he wanted to write a story that tapped into the "playfulness" of the Marvel comics he read as an adolescent, which captured "a world borning."[24] I argue that this confluence of the past and the future, central to the narrative of *1602*, is spatialized by a narrative shift from Europe to America with the character of Captain America looming large in each.

The narrative of *1602* is sparked in the titular year by the arrival of Captain America from a dystopian future in which American democracy has deteriorated into an authoritarian state. There/then, with only scattered memories of the future from which he came, Steve Rogers was adopted by a Native American tribe. When the English resettled Roanoke and subsequently began to starve (again), Steve Rogers intervened to save them, having adopted the Native name and identity of Rojhaz. In particular he became the bodyguard and protector of Virginia Dare, the first European baby born in America: "She was a baby then. But I knew what she was. What she represented. What she *meant*. My America . . . I knew I had to protect her. To guard her. To fight for her, if I had to. I wasn't going to let her die. I failed before. I wasn't going to fail again."[25]

In the narrative this is not a fresh start just for Captain America but for all humanity, as Europe is torn asunder by political competition and greed. The arrival of Captain America from the future somehow engenders the premature rise of superpowered individuals in the general population, with each an historical cognate of a modern Marvel superhero. The villainous Magneto rises to become the High Inquisitor of the Spanish Inquisition (who selectively persecutes mutants who cannot pass as human while helping the others escape), while Nick Fury and Dr. Strange work for Elizabeth I of England. Dr. Doom rules over the eastern European state of Latveria (then as now), having imprisoned the Fantastic Four several years earlier, and the Mighty Thor is an aging Knight Templar.[26] These superheroes and villains alter the timeline in various ways, through both the aforementioned survival of Roanoke and other changes, such as the premature death of Elizabeth I and ascendancy of James I (who plotted her demise with the aid of "Count" Doom). There are also superficial background differences that indicate this timeline was never "our" own, such as the existence of dinosaur-like creatures in America. The most significant change, however, is visible in the weather; terrible thunderstorms devoid of rain began on the East Coast of North America with the arrival of Captain America from the future (fifteen years before the "present" of the story). In the intervening years these storms have spread across North America and are now global in scope, causing great unease among populations and rivalry among the states of Europe as they jockey to control magical objects that they hope will save them from Armageddon.

This political rivalry animates a narrative of continuous betrayal and violence, the results of which are the already mentioned fall of Elizabeth I and the subsequent rise of James I, as well as a papal crackdown on Magneto's faux inquisition. These events remove the last refuges for the superpowered in Europe, causing them to converge on America. It is perhaps notable that the ship on which most of the heroes arrive is called the *Eagle's Shadow*, and that its destination is Roanoke. Once they have arrived in Roanoke, there is recognition that the strange storms signal the impending collapse of not only this dimension but also all others. As James Fleming argues:

> In effect, *1602* charts the intersection of two contrary realities, specifically the textual/historical reality of early-modern England and the fantastic/textual reality of the postmodern Marvel superhero age. Despite their shared spatial and temporal zone, these two worlds are represented by Gaiman as being utterly incommensurable with each other, to the extent that they risk fully negating each other once they are combined.[27]

The heroes recognize that the only way to save their reality is to cast Rojhaz back through the dimensional portal. However, Rojhaz refuses to go, his hope for America now embodied in Virginia Dare and the Roanoke community. Ultimately he is betrayed by Nick Fury and carried unconscious through the portal to the future.

With the temporal rift healed, the denouement of the narrative hints at Gaiman's "world borning." Mr. Fantastic and Charles Xavier plot the shape of the Roanoke colony:

> **Mr. Fantastic**: My own suggestion [. . .] would be to declare the colony independent of England. Your people [the X-Men] can guard the coast. [King] James is a long way away; he lacks the coffers or the will to prosecute a war so far from home.
>
> **Charles Xavier**: And will you be their King, Reed?
>
> **Mr. Fantastic**: I do not believe that there will be any more call for Kings or for Queens. I shall propose to Master Dare [Virginia's father, the governor] that we make the colony a place where people—people of *all* shapes and talents—can prosper . . .[28]

Thus, transplanting Captain America into the past not only brought superheroes into the world that much sooner but also created an independent America almost two hundred years earlier than otherwise would have occurred. Indeed, by the end of the story things have come to resemble "our" world to a remarkable degree; Bruce Banner (the Hulk) and Peter Parker (Spider-Man) have gained their powers (after being normal humans for the whole story), Charles Xavier is setting up his school for mutants, and so on. Gaiman's eschewal of geopolitics following the September 11, 2001, attacks nevertheless ends up being tacitly geopolitical. His tale of time travel produces a binary geography of corruption and innocence, persecution and tolerance, Europe and America. The avoidance of 9/11 simply casts the narrative in the mold of earlier discourses of preimperial American exceptionalism rather than present-day rhetoric of Pax Americana.[29]

## The Ultimates

Another major attempt by Marvel to explore secondary worlds in the wake of the September 11, 2001, attacks came through the publication of *The Ultimates*, the first volume of which was released in 2002 and the second in 2004.[30] Written by Mark Millar, *The Ultimates* tells the story of familiar superheroes in the present day but immerses them in a completely different continuity. The world is immediately recognizable as our own but with some key differences obvious at the start. The story opens with Captain America, battling against the Nazis in World War II; however, his uniform is more militaristic than in "our" continuity, and Bucky is not his sidekick but an army photographer who follows him around for propaganda purposes. Further, we discover that in this continuity the Nazis allied themselves with aliens who are committed to ruling the universe and who still exist as sleeper cells within U.S. government and society in the present.

The opening sequence of *The Ultimates* is reminiscent of the wartime adventures of Captain America from regular continuity, with a more realistic uniform.[31] This Captain America carries a gun and has protective gear (beyond his shield), army boots, and a hypermasculine attitude toward warfare (Figure 8.1). Unlike "our" continuity, however, he is not found in his iceberg until 2002, and then by the U.S. government (rather than by his future teammates in the Avengers). Therefore, this Captain America is still very much a product of his experiences in wartime, not having gone through the identity politics that marked the 1960s–1990s. It is perhaps his hypermasculinity that has attracted the attention of critics who have drawn a (sometimes tacit) connection to American foreign policy in the 2000s: "simultaneously extraordinary and impotent."[32] Indeed, he kicks a defenseless Bruce Banner in the teeth after he has gone on a rampage as the Hulk, beats up a teammate after discovering he has been physically abusive to his wife, and shows no remorse in killing his enemies. While "our" Captain America has been used to draw a narrative line of America from the New Deal of the 1940s through the liberalism and multiculturalism of recent decades, "Ultimate" Captain America constructs an alternative narrative—from the wartime grit of the 1940s directly to the "moral clarity" of the post-9/11 moment.

The overarching narrative of the first volume of *The Ultimates* is concerned with the production by the United States (via the spy agency, SHIELD) of a team of superheroes intended to work for the government. In a reversal of *1602*, this story line does not feature premature superheroism but rather delayed onset. The loss of Captain America in 1945 was a setback for the United States in the race among states to produce their own super-soldiers. In this continuity,

Figure 8.1: Captain America demonstrating in *The Ultimates* that he missed out on the identity politics of the late twentieth century, by expressing a masculinity displaced from the 1940s. (Copyright © 2012 Marvel Characters, Inc. Used with permission.)

the Avengers never came together of their own accord to protect the world (as occurred in 1963 in regular continuity)—however, the same heroes are brought together by SHIELD to be the instruments of foreign policy in 2002, with the discovery of Captain America the final piece of the puzzle:

> **President G. W. Bush**: Is he as strong as you expected, General?
> **General Nick Fury**: Stronger, sir.
> **President Bush**: Is he smart?
> **General Nick Fury**: Tactically off the scale, Mister President. There's genuinely nobody in existence I'd rather have leading this team when they're out on the field. Add this Thunder God guy to the mix plus all the other Super-Soldiers Banner can create from Cap's blood and I don't see anyone acting up for a while. Do you, sir?
> **President Bush**: No, I don't, General Fury. No, I don't.[33]

However, the creation of the Ultimates as the most overt extension of the U.S. Superhero Defense Initiative (SDI) is paralleled by the creation of the European Defense Initiative (EDI), which operates out of Brussels (under the aegis of the European Union) and includes Captain Britain (still Brian Braddock), Captain Spain, Captain France, and Captain Italy (others are alluded to but never named). The distinction between America and Europe is initially established by Sir James Braddock, head of the EDI, upon Brian's mention to Captain America that he had hung a poster of Captain America in his Edinburgh dormitory room: "Other boys it was John Lennon and Che Guevara, my son it was the ultimate icon of military imperialism. Brian Braddock, ladies and gentlemen, Captain Britain. The only man under seventy-five who'd agree to wear a Union Jack on his chest."[34] This rhetorical distancing of the European project from the hegemonic purpose of the Ultimates is only partially successful; the EDI is after all a counterweight to the Ultimates, a product of the same logic of power and violence. In fact, in controversial moments in the second volume, the EDI fights alongside the Ultimates. A more successful voice for European political difference comes from Thor, the Norse thunder god.

While in "regular" continuity Thor is a full-fledged member of the Avengers, in *The Ultimates* he keeps his distance, never formally joining the team. He is first encountered by the reader leading a camp of his followers in Norway. However, he leads them not in religious terms but in political ones—he is anti-imperialist and, as such, fights alongside the Ultimates only when he feels the cause is worth the violence:

> **Bruce Banner**: The Ultimates isn't an army, Mister. They're a team of superheroes we assembled to take care of the post-human problems the armed forces can't handle anymore.
> **Thor**: Oh, it matters not whether you are wearing capes or combat boots, little man. You are all just thugs in uniform who will smash

> any threat to a corrupt status quo. Go back to your paymasters and
> tell them that the Son of Odin is not interested in working for a
> military-industrial complex who engineers wars and murders in-
> nocents. Your talk might be of super-villains now, but it is only a
> matter of time before you are sent to kill for oil or free trade.[35]

While it would be easy to see Thor as a caricature of the anti-Bush protesters so
common during the U.S./U.K. invasion and occupation of Iraq, this dismissal
would miss the larger political critique offered by the character within the narrative of *The Ultimates*.

Thor claims to be sent by his divine father, Odin, to purify the earth and
awaken humanity to the danger they pose to themselves: "Take a look around
you, Captain . . . your world is being bled dry while your people grow dull-
eyed and hypnotized by reality TV and Playstation 2. I'm here to wake you all
up again before mankind sleepwalks their way into oblivion."[36] The conflict
between the Ultimates and Thor remains latent until the second volume, in
which Captain America is deployed to Iraq to free hostages despite General
Nick Fury's public promises that the Ultimates would be used only for domestic
defense. Thor's public distancing of himself from the team leads to tension, but
even here there is wary respect between Captain America and Thor, with Thor
intervening during one confrontation to stop his followers when they begin to
pour beer on Captain America.

However, Thor's half-brother Loki, the trickster God of Mischief, works behind the scenes to convince the Ultimates that Thor is not the real Norse God
of Thunder, but simply a mental patient with a God complex who has stolen
super-soldier technology that gives him his powers. When Italian police beat
protesters who object to the creation of European super-soldiers, Thor angrily
intervenes, leading the Ultimates to think he has finally become a threat to
state-centric authority. The subsequent scene in which the Ultimates and the
EDI confront Thor in Norway is drawn to evoke Christ's betrayal (see Figure 8.2; the issue in which they battle is even titled "The Passion"): "I came
here to save the world and all you've done is try to crucify me."[37] Once they
have taken his belt (the source of his powers) away from him, he calls out to his
father, Odin, like Jesus on the cross.

Thor's warnings about the Ultimates come to fruition shortly thereafter,
when the team and the EDI are dispatched to an unnamed Middle Eastern
country to relieve them of their nuclear weapons. The occupation is dehu-
manizing and radicalizes a young man. This deployment of "people of mass
destruction" rallies countries who fear that they may be next; two months
later that same radicalized young man has been turned into an Islamic super-
soldier, and he leads a team of superheroes known as the Liberators. Two of
the Liberators are from China, while North Korea, Syria, and Russia each field
one team member. One month after that, the Liberators, with an army behind
them, occupy the United States after luring the Ultimates away on a wild-goose

Figure 8.2: Thor—sent by his divine father to save the earth—betrayed and suffering. (Copyright © 2012 Marvel Characters, Inc. Used with permission.)

chase. However, the rhetoric employed is startlingly different from that of most supervillains in comic book narratives: "I didn't come here for revenge, Loki. I volunteered to lead this international collective because America's plans simply had to be curtailed. The world is a safer place now this new Roman Empire has been restrained."[38]

Of course, the Ultimates come back to free the United States from its occupation, and Captain America faces off against the Islamic super-soldier:

Captain America: Name first.
Islamic super-soldier: What?
Captain America: I like to know a man's name before I put him in the ground.
Islamic super-soldier: I am simply Abdul al-Rahman and I was a farmhand in the northwest province of Azerbaijan, Captain. I'm afraid I have no interest in these super hero codenames. Don't you think it's a little immature to indulge in such childish conventions?[39]

Even here, Millar seems to be highlighting the moral high ground that the Liberators occupy; the remainder of their battle is devoid of the usual comic book banter but instead emphasizes the physicality of their struggle. When it is apparent that Captain America is going to win, al-Rahman allows his colleagues to restrain Captain America: "I wanted a fair fight, I really did. But you can't expect me to walk away with nothing, sir. Not after everything you did to the people I loved. I take no pleasure in what comes next. I only do this to wake your people up."[40] This "dirty trick" flips their moral emplotment in the fight, and al-Rahman's indication that he is going to behead the defenseless Captain America aligns the scene with the visual culture of beheadings such as that of journalist Daniel Pearl, which dominated media discourse following the invasion of Afghanistan and Iraq.[41] The battle concludes with Captain America being freed by the other Ultimates and again seizing the advantage in combat. Al-Rahman becomes verbose only when he is at Captain America's mercy:

Al-Rahman: Well, Captain, what now, eh? One of your John Wayne quips? Is this where you crack a joke? Is this where you finish me with a witty barb? My God! Do you even appreciate why we did this thing? [*Stabbed through chest by Captain America.*]
Captain America: No jokes, Abdul.[42]

The moral ambiguity of this final battle between the two super-soldiers is palpable, and even Captain America is moved by the circumstances. Confronting General Nick Fury afterward, he announces the resignation of the Ultimates from the government payroll, arguing that sending them overseas had been a mistake that stirred up hate against America.

To conclude, the gap between "our" continuity and that of *The Ultimates* is narrowed by the end of the second volume, with the team becoming more like the Avengers in regard to their political independence from the state and their more cosmopolitan perspective on violence, legitimacy, and authority. Like *1602*, the initial corruption of "regular" continuity is resolved in favor of a new continuity that is different from, but roughly parallel to, "ours." Also like *1602*, the spatial binary of America and Europe is held intact, although with the opposite valences. While in *1602* America heralds a new start for humanity, in *The Ultimates* it is Europe, as embodied by Thor, that offers a chance of messianic redemption for us all.

## Conclusions

James Kneale argues that reading

> fictions geographically might mean examining texts for evidence of sites of multiplicity, heterogeneity, or agonistic encounter. And if counterfactual fictions can be read in this way then they might be utopian, encouraging a kind of creative re-enchantment of the relationship between history and the present.[43]

Judging the preceding evidence by this rubric, it can be inferred that despite the potential for radical critique usually attributed to stories of time travel and alternate worlds, within these comics the tendency is instead for them to reinforce the superiority, or the inevitability, of the present time-space. The enchantment of time travel and dimension-hopping paradoxically leads to the disenchantment of our own space-time. This is true not only with regard to the geographies of these alternate worlds (i.e., throughout the multiverse there is no dimension without a Britain, even if those Britains vary among themselves) but also in terms of the heroes' characterization. Generally speaking, the heroes and villains in our dimension or timeline remain so in other worlds, foreclosing another narrative opportunity for representing political change and antistate or antinationalist alternatives. Even when political critique is offered, as in the character of Thor within *The Ultimates*, it does so by reifying the America/Europe binary that is ensconced in superhero culture from *Captain America Comics #1* to *Marvel 1602*.[44] It may be, however, that this conservatism is not traceable specifically to structural effects like the tyranny of the serial, or to individual writers' and artists' agency; it may simply be the result of the inertia and logic of narrativity itself, as Neil Gaiman asserts in this dialogue from *Marvel 1602*:

> **Human Torch:** So, what are these fundamental principles, if they are not atoms?

**Mr. Fantastic:** Stories. And they give me hope. We are a boatful of monsters and miracles, hoping that, somehow, we can survive a world in which all hands are against us. A world which, by all evidence, will end extremely soon. Yet I posit we are in a universe which favours stories. A universe in which no story can ever truly end; in which there can be only continuances. If we *are* in such a universe, as I hope, then we may have a chance.

[. . .]

**The Thing:** Reed—you spoke of transmutations. Can you restore to me my humanity? I have been a monster too long.

**Mr. Fantastic:** In truth, I do not know, my friend. The natural sciences say yes, a cure is possible. But the laws of story would suggest that no cure can last very long, Benjamin. For in the end, alas, you are so much more interesting and satisfying as you are.[45]

# Parody and Subversion

Blacksnake: Get me a car and an escort to Yankeeland! Or you're gonna
   have one less bitch— [. . .]
Captain Confederacy: Your kind never learns.
Blacksnake: I ain't 'fraid o' you! You're gonna die now!
Captain Confederacy: Violence only hurts your people's cause! [*Defeats Blacksnake.*] Someday colored people may be ready to be equal
   citizens of the Confederacy. But that right must first be earned.[1]

his dialogue, in the opening scene of *Captain Confederacy*, shows how easily the nationalist superhero subgenre can be parodied and turned upside
down. Suddenly the generic conventions are exposed in a new way: the
patriotism of Captain America morphs into ethnic hierarchy, the vigilantism of
Captain Britain becomes indistinguishable from that of the Ku Klux Klan, and
Captain Canuck's preservation of Canadian sovereignty turns out to be the imposition of a political order on those who want no part of it. *Captain America*
anti-fan Andrew Aldridge wrote to the editor to complain about the politics
built into the nationalist superhero genre:

Maybe I don't have a strong stomach, but every time I glance at this
title, nausea creeps over me and I flee from it. [. . .] We are living in a
time when nothing is what it seems and yet this guy can see through it
all and decide what's evil. I also hate how he is portrayed as being truly
good, and represents America. Therefore, we're supposed to think that
America is truly good.[2]

Clearly, (presumably occasional) readers of *Captain America* do not all buy into
the comic's conceits, and one can encounter a counternarrative in that very
comic's letters-to-the-editor page. However, to carry on Aldridge's critique, this
chapter shifts from the book's earlier focus on mainstream nationalist superheroes to a look at parodies of the subgenre, emphasizing not only what they

say about the subgenre itself but also how parody can be deployed to critique the constellation of power, legitimacy, and violence that nationalist superheroes embody.

## Irony, Fantasy, and Genre Play

In this book, I treat nationalist superheroes as a subgenre, albeit one that is at least partially of my own construction. Nevertheless, while *nationalist superhero* is not a term in common usage, the subgenre is distinguishable from other types of superheroes through its development in the genre cycle. Chapter 1 deals with the foundation of the nationalist superhero subgenre and its crystallization in a particular time and place. The intervening chapters trace the dynamism within the subgenre's narratives and spatializations as various writers, artists, and readers have produced a range of differentiations within the subgenre, attempting to both cope with the spread of the nationalist superhero to new geographic contexts and deal with the onslaught of time. One sign of the maturation of a subgenre is the development of parody, as articulated in the work of Mikhail Bakhtin: "a form of imitation, but imitation characterized by ironic inversion, not always at the expense of the parodied text."[3] If textual parody relies on an understanding of the original text's details, then generic parody relies on a common understanding of the *generic* conventions. Therefore, the emergence of comics parodying the nationalist superhero subgenre anticipates a popular understanding of what makes this subgenre distinctive.

Tracing these parodies can, of course, indicate popular understanding of nationalist superheroes and their politics, but equally it speaks to the spatio-temporal and political context in which the parody is deployed. Some parodies serve as affectionate gestures that reinforce the positives of what is parodied; other parodies aim for subversion. The representation of the nationalist superhero genre offered in this book has highlighted the diversity of narratives that can be told/read within the nationalist superhero subgenre, and consequently my theoretical assumptions are opposed to an understanding of nationalist superheroes as pure ideology. Nevertheless, as Chapter 8, among others, illustrates, there is a tendency within nationalist superhero narratives to privilege the status quo; even in stories of other dimensions and time travel—what might be considered fantasy stories told within fantasy stories—social relations are generally returned to "the way things are." Rosemary Jackson argues that

> to attempt to defend fantasy as inherently transgressive would be a vast, over-simplifying and mistaken gesture. Those elements which have been designated "fantastic"—effecting a movement towards undifferentiation and a condition of entropy—have been constantly re-worked, re-written and re-covered to *serve* rather than *subvert* the dominant ideology.[4]

Nevertheless, even if they are drowned within the generic conservatism of the nationalist superhero, it is worth examining attempts to subvert the subgenre. *Subversion* is the key term here, rather than *critique*, because of subversion's interiority vis-à-vis its object. Stemming from the Latin *subvertere*, meaning "to overturn," *subversion* carries connotations of undermining and corruption.

With this in mind, it is worth looking at some of the attempts by various comics writers and artists to subvert an *assumed* ideology associated with nationalist superheroes; in other words, some comics producers' understandings of nationalist superheroes as ideological have inspired particular resistances that attempt to call into question the particular nationalisms often perceived to be integral to the nationalist superhero subgenre. This ideological reading of nationalist superheroes draws on their seeming *obviousness*. Being associated with the nation-state offers particular leverage for parodies of muscular, heroic nationalism. As writer Rob Williams argues: "Just the fact that our main character wears the flag—his actions speak for themselves. That's the appeal of stories featuring characters like Captain America, Captain Britain, Fighting American and others."[5]

As with parody, Bakhtin provides a point of reference here. Bakhtin's notion of carnival involves the overturning of hierarchies, including fantasies and facts.[6] These overturnings are themselves sources of pleasure, and consequently are often associated with the body, with fun, with suspension of disbelief. Given this, we can see that superheroes are already a form of carnival: popular entertainment for the masses that overprivileges physicality and exaggerates the body. It is often the villain who is the intellectual rather than the hero, and the intellectual's humiliation at the hands of the superhero is to be celebrated. In contrast to our everyday dependence on a complex and rationalized society and its systems, in superhero narratives it is society that relies on the individual.[7] Therefore, even as nationalist superheroes act in ways that are broadly conservative (as described in the preceding chapters), they do so through the mechanisms of carnival and the tactical inversion of certain hierarchies.

For nationalist superheroes, a secondary inversion—the carnival of the carnivalesque—allows for the speaking of the unspeakable and the breach of taken-for-granted generic assumptions. As Paul Adams argues regarding carnival, "An alternative time, space, and social order can be created that permits naturalized social hierarchies to be symbolically, socially, and psychologically dissolved."[8] Thus, subversion brings the possibility of separating the nationalism discursively attached to the individual hero from the understanding of power and authority embedded within the sub-genre itself, and turning them against one another. A range of writers and artists have engaged in this type of subversion, through a variety of narrative strategies. However, these subversions are invariably temporary—either intended for only a limited series or otherwise doomed by the market to brevity, perhaps because the carnival of the carnivalesque is one carnival too far for most readers.

Having set up the role of parody and subversion, this chapter now turns to four examples that illustrate critical engagements with the nationalist superhero subgenre. Before this, however, it is worth noting that there is a distinct geographical dimension to the deployment of parody and subversion in the examples sketched here. Despite being written by both American and British creators, these comics all use the American nationalist superhero as a point of departure in various ways. For some creators, the American nationalist superhero provides an avenue to criticize American foreign policy, while for others it is the politics of the subgenre itself that is being subverted. Sometimes it is both. In any event, the American nationalist superhero (rather than the British, for example) serves as a lens for critique, so much so that two of the four nationalist superheroes to be discussed are simply named "American." This centrality certainly has to do with the importance of the American market to superhero comic sales, but when details of the generic origin from Chapter 1 are juxtaposed with the comics discussed in this chapter, it becomes apparent that the subgenre itself is deeply rooted in the time-space of Americanism, whether as friendly parody or subversive critique.

## A Carnival of Nationalist Superheroes

### Cla$$war

British writer Rob Williams's take on the nationalist superhero subgenre, *Cla$$war*, was published between 2002 and 2004 in a six-issue limited series for Com.x, a small publisher. It was originally scheduled to be released in 2001, but its start was delayed because of the September 11, 2001, attacks. The project originated in Williams's interest in leftist critique of American foreign policy:

> At the turn of the century I was extremely interested in U.S. politics and foreign policy, reading works by [Noam] Chomsky etc., and wanted to tell a story that dealt with those issues. I've always been a superhero fan too. Combining the two seemed like fun.[9]

Williams combined the two through his construction of a superhero team, Enola Gay, which works for the U.S. government (a theme linking all the comics in this chapter). This team fought in the first war in Iraq, and also intervened in 1990s touchstone moments such as the L.A. riots and the Branch Davidian siege in Waco. The team's leader was the nationalist superhero of the team, known simply as American:

> He was meant to be a symbol of all that's perceived to be good about America—heroic, square-jawed, good looking. Of course, he's also a soldier who, for much of his life, blindly follows orders and, as [Enola

Gay teammate] Icon says of him "he's not that bright, is he?" The President also comments that "I've got a dog back home with more smarts." But he proves them wrong. He's got a conscience and a good heart.[10]

Indeed, the primary plotline involves American's rebellion from Enola Gay and the U.S. government. Having been given a dossier of information by Isaac, a leftist militant, American kidnaps a president who strongly resembles George W. Bush, carves "LIAR" onto the president's forehead with his laser vision, and broadcasts a message to the American people:

> A group of the rich and powerful, through multinational corporations, control you through television, advertising, alcohol, and other drugs—they send American children to foreign lands to die to make them richer. They assassinate those who would question the status quo. They smuggle drugs into poor areas so the lower classes turn their anger upon each other, instead of where it should be directed. How do I know these things? I . . . have done some of these heinous acts on their behalf. I have . . . killed for my country. I will *not* do so again. I believe in the foundations that America was built upon. I believe in truth and justice and democracy. I believe in the beauty of every individual. I have not turned my back upon our country. I am going to be fighting for America and its people . . . those who believe in the same ideas held sacred by our fore-fathers. You are being lied to, people of America. It's time to do something about it.[11]

Having said all this, American flies away to plot his next move.

As this speech indicates, *Cla$$war* is a critique of American politics rather than a critique of the United States itself or the superhero genre. Writer Rob Williams describes his position:

> *Cla$$war* definitely isn't an anti-American story. It's anti- certain aspects of US foreign policy and society, certainly, but I always saw it as having a hopeful tone. That there is something in America that is worth fighting for, once you get past the greed inherent in any capitalist society.[12]

Indeed, the politics of *Cla$$war* is essentially redemptive: the U.S. presidency is seen as enthralled to powerful and mysterious corporate interests, and noble U.S. soldiers are seen as pawns in a corporate game rather than instruments of legitimate national security. American's goal is to wake up the essentially good American people to what is being done in their name.

While American (along with the rest of Enola Gay) is a government-produced super-soldier (like Captain America), and this fact sets him apart from society, his propaganda value to the U.S. government is derived from his lack of specific attributes. Williams wanted to inscribe this doubleness in him to express the government's motivations:

> I wanted him, in terms of image, to be a kind of everyman, representing all Americans. That's what he was created and marketed to be. I always envisaged there being some kind of high-powered PR movement behind his initial reveal to the public.[13]

But, of course, beyond that is also the revolutionary potential of American; by making him as "normal" as possible, Williams also defuses the tension between a superhero exercising political power and democratic values. If American's superpowers give him the ability to intervene against that system in a way that others cannot, at least he arrived at his decision regarding the corruption of the U.S. system as any citizen could.

The fallout from American's televised assault on governmental corruption undercuts the president's popularity. The president's corporate backers ask him to invade the fictional Caribbean island state of Glenada under the pretense of overturning a rebellion against the government (presumably a reference to the 1982 U.S. invasion of Grenada). This government is described as being central to the U.S. military's importation of drugs into poor neighborhoods. Initially the president refuses: "Now look here, son. I am not about to send American troops to kill some poor brown people to justify the defense budget and earn your friends a few billion in weapon sales."[14] However, when it is intimated to the president (and the reader) that the corporate patrons of the presidency assassinated John F. Kennedy because he did not "play ball," the president orders the invasion. While American intervenes to hamper the military intervention, he refuses to kill American soldiers. He and his allies instead capture a CIA operative and tape his account of the U.S. government's relationship to the Glenadan drug trade, uploading it to the Internet in their effort to provide truth to the American people. When Enola Gay traps and kills American soldiers in their effort to lure American into decisive battle, the hero ends up on a suicide mission against his former teammates. However, just as American is about to be overcome, U.S. troops intervene to save him, having seen that he is fighting on their behalf. This action recovers the soldiers' essential heroism in the narrative despite their mission's being dictated by corporate America.

While all this is occurring, the president's corporate backers order him to fire a nuclear missile at Glenada, killing the remaining U.S. soldiers and almost one hundred thousand islanders in a last-ditch effort to stop American. However, American survives the blast, and in his rage he sinks an aircraft carrier, a cruiser, and the submarine from which the missile was launched. The series ends with American on the loose, the remaining nuclear-scorched members of Enola Gay radicalized by the way they were to be sacrificed, and the president considering his position vis-à-vis both the superheroes and posterity.

The final action sequences enact superheroic violence in which American's actions simultaneously offer the reader a sense of catharsis and justice and produce narrative dissonance. Those dying at his hands (3,500 U.S. sailors) are, in the comic's own terms, heroic individuals not unlike the soldiers on Glenada who, when presented with the evidence, saw American's cause as their own. *Cla$$war*'s ambivalence about superheroic violence is expressed by its writer, Rob Williams:

> I guess I was as influenced by Hollywood action movies as I was by the writings of Chomsky, Gore Vidal etc. In an ideal world you could change the course of a nation through pacifist action—Dr. King did— but this is also a superhero story, so physical conflict is part of the language. It's a contradiction, I'm sure, but I'd never claim to have all the answers.[15]

Indeed, the art in the comic book gives American an aura of nearly limitless power, latent in almost every image (Figure 9.1). *Cla$$war*, despite its anti-imperialist politics, seems unable to escape from the violent politics of the nationalist superhero genre itself. The destruction of the Washington Monument by one of the superheroes in the story's denouement hints at future conflict between the U.S. government and its former vassals.

In its oppositional stance it nevertheless engages with the very same understandings of power and legitimacy that undergird American exceptionalism: the American people are essentially good and lack access to only the hard truth that their government has become a corporate oligarchy. If it takes an unelected, superpowered patriot to reinstate a truly democratic republic, then so be it.

## Watchmen

Alan Moore and Dave Gibbons's *Watchmen*, a twelve-issue miniseries published by DC Comics in 1986, has probably been the subject of more analysis than any other comic in history.[16] This is for good reason; *Watchmen* not only demolished the superhero genre but also gave it new life. It did so by taking the history of the genre seriously and considering the implications of superheroes should they really exist. Geoff Klock describes Moore's approach:

> [*Watchmen*] begins questioning the assumptions of the superhero with its title, which lures the comic-savvy reader into assuming that it is the eponym of a superhero team around which the book revolves—not in fact the case. The last page of the work reveals that the title is actually taken from the [Roman satirist] Juvenal epigraph *Quis custodet ipsos custodes?* ("Who watches the watchmen?"), a phrase that occurs throughout the work in the form of graffiti. The statement contains a

Figure 9.1: *Cla$$war*. The art imbues American with a sense of latent power. (Courtesy of Com.x Ltd. Used with permission.)

kind of a priori destabilization of the assumptions that make superhero comics work: that heroes can simply look after a population without complications. The understanding that the police require police
officers ad infinitum questions whether the very foundations of superhero literature can in fact be maintained. *Watchmen* declares that
they cannot.[17]

By interrogating the assumed moral purity of superheroes and envisioning how
the world would have changed if superheroes really existed, Moore subverts
"our" superhero genre to expose the baldness of its accommodation to the status quo.

For example, *Watchmen* is set in 1985's New York, but neither the New
York nor the 1985 that we know. Rather, this is an alternate timeline in which
American superheroes won the war in Vietnam, enabling Richard Nixon to
amend the U.S. Constitution and remain in office until the present. Their deployment against the American people during a 1977 riot led to the official
censure of all costumed heroes; only two continue to explicitly work for the
U.S. government while the rest have mostly returned to civilian life. Both of
these superheroes fight in Vietnam, but only one is central to both the victory in that war and the present geopolitical order. Dr. Manhattan is a near-
omnipotent superhero whose existence serves as the ultimate defense against
Soviet attack but whose near-divinity erodes his identification with humanity over the course of the narrative. Dr. Manhattan's eventual departure from
earth upsets the Cold War balance of power and brings the world to the brink
of nuclear war. A second element of "realism" in *Watchmen* is the mediocrity of
the other heroes. Dr. Manhattan is the only hero with actual superpowers; all
the rest are mere costumed adventurers with a range of fetishes and dysfunc-
tions that inspire them to dress up and battle crime as vigilantes. This emotional and moral "realism"[18] is also traceable to the other superhero working for
the U.S. government alongside Dr. Manhattan—the Comedian.

Each of the heroes in *Watchmen* is a proxy for an established superhero
archetype in "our" universe. The Comedian, also known as Edward Blake, is a
stand-in for the nationalist superhero in Moore's alternate earth: "The Comedian, in one of Moore's more powerful tropes, is a kind of Captain America if
Captain America had gone to Vietnam."[19] Given the contortions that writers
went through to keep Captain America out of Vietnam (as described in Chapter 7), this is hardly a throwaway counterfactual. Geoff Klock describes the
work accomplished through the mere posing of the hypothetical:

> In relation to Captain America, Alan Moore's Comedian performs
> [Harold] Bloom's *clinamatic* swerve: "a corrective movement in [the lat-
> ter] poem, which implies that the precursor poem went accurately up to
> a certain point, but then should have swerved, precisely in the direction
> that the new poem moves." The Comedian is this swerve.[20]

When DC Comics (for whom Moore was working) bought the rights to the defunct superhero characters of Charlton Comics in 1985 (thereby inheriting a stable of heroes parallel to their own), Moore had the idea of using them to tell his "realist" tale of superheroes since DC would never let him use their own heroes for such a deconstructive effort. But DC also did not want to see the Charlton heroes "ruined" either, and so it was suggested that Moore should create his own heroes parallel to the Charlton heroes. Moore describes the process of inventing the Comedian this way:

> The Comedian was The Peacemaker [a Charlton hero whose tagline was "A man who loves peace so much he is willing to fight for it"] and we decided to make him slightly right-wing, patriotic, and we mixed in a little bit of [SHIELD director] Nick Fury into The Peacemaker make-up, and probably a bit of the standard Captain America patriotic hero-type. [. . . I] believe I took the name from Graham Greene's book, *The Comedians*. At that point, I'd done quite a bit of research upon various kinds of CIA and intelligence community dirty tricks, so Dave and I saw him as a kind of Gordon Liddy character, only a much bigger, tougher guy. [I]f Liddy had comic book muscles . . . and with Liddy es-pousing all that Nietzsche philosophy, and the bollocks of holding his hand in a candle flame and not feeling the pain, even though it's sear-ing. So yeah, bits of Liddy worked into The Comedian's make-up, those sort of barking-mad, right-wing adventurists.[21]

Richard Reynolds describes the Comedian as "in the tradition of the existen-tial men of action who come to realize themselves through violent conflict and death—such as William Holden in *The Wild Bunch* or Warren Oates in *Bring Me the Head of Alfredo Garcia*. More than just tough guys, these heroes or anti-heroes follow through the logic of their code, even if it leads to their own de-struction."[22]

Indeed, the Comedian appears in *Watchmen* only through flashbacks, as the primary plot of the narrative is the investigation by the other heroes of his defenestration from a skyscraper apartment—an end entirely appropriate to his life of violence. Like Captain America, the Comedian fought in World War II alongside other costumed heroes in a team known as the Minutemen, although he does not begin as a nationalist superhero. Rather, clad in a yellow and purple union suit with a Greek comedy mask as a belt buckle, Edward Blake embodied a certain antiheroic nihilism that would remain with him until the end. His attempted rape of a heroine known as the Silk Spectre con-tributed to the disintegration of the Minutemen.[23] Following this, he served with U.S. troops in the Pacific theater of World War II. When invited to join another superhero team in the 1960s (the Crimebusters), he scoffed at the idea that the country's problems (such as racial unrest and moral decline) could be fixed by superheroes.

By this time, the Comedian had abandoned his earlier costume for one that was more nationalist in design: black leather with American flag–styled sleeves and shoulder protection. The only remaining visual concession to his pseudonym was a yellow "happy face" button that he wore when on duty or off. Eschewing the liberal heroics of the other heroes, the Comedian went to work for the U.S. government, fighting in Vietnam even though he considered the war to be not for Vietnamese liberation, but rather for the enrichment of the few. He also fought the Sandinistas, ended the Iranian hostage crisis, and in general worked as a point man for American foreign policy. The Comedian's "joke" serves as one of the organizing themes of the entire miniseries, and it is existential in nature. The world is full of misery, largely inflicted on humans by other humans. The forces arrayed against society (and its heroes) are enormously powerful, and there is little hope. Given that hopelessness, the Comedian thrives on the violence that is part of his job, laughing at the license he is given to hurt and kill in the name of peace and prosperity.

While the Comedian necessarily does not play a central role in the contemporary events of *Watchmen*, his existential "joke" suffuses the entire narrative, which can be read as a critique of superhero politics and its inadequacy given the nature of the world's problems. In contrast to *Cla$$war*, *Watchmen* represents a world in which heroic violence is rarely, if ever, noble and in which the heroes are highly problematic as instruments of the status quo. The Comedian represents the withdrawal of nobility from the nationalist superhero. He is not morally bound to righteous action on behalf of his people; rather, his sanctioning by the U.S. government channels his violence toward state ends. In this way, *Watchmen* is allied with *Cla$$war* in its alignment of nationalist superheroes with state policy interests, but contradicts it through its pessimism.

## The American

Mark Verheiden's *The American* was a series published by Dark Horse Comics sporadically between 1987 and 1992. The story is slightly different from the other nationalist superhero comics discussed in this book in that the primary protagonist is not the superhero but rather a hard-drinking, morally absent reporter. This narrative element, along with the story's location in Los Angeles and its general tone, link *The American* not only to the nationalist superhero subgenre but also to the film noir tradition. Where *Watchmen* and *Cla$$war* embrace the superhero tradition even while twisting it, *The American* maintains a healthy cynicism appropriate to its noir context.[24]

*The American* produces this cynicism toward the nationalist superhero in its opening sequences. In a scene similar to many throughout the superhero subgenre, a group of terrorists have taken over a Beirut airport lounge, and a superhero named "the American," clad in a red, white, and blue costume with an eagle motif, attacks to save them. However, in this case the American is supported by a government-sponsored team that installs special effects and cameras throughout the airport lounge to both give the impression that the American has superpowers and document the rescue for later dissemination to the news media. When the American is killed during the rescue attempt, the footage is edited to show otherwise, and another soldier-actor is sent on the next mission to provide the illusion of invulnerability. That American (henceforth "the Last American" to identify him vis-à-vis both his predecessors and his namesake from *Cla$$war*), however, had been childhood friends with the preceding one, and he rebels when confronted with the government's disavowal of the previous dead "superheroes." He joins forces with Dennis Hough, the reporter and main protagonist, to expose the government's American squad as a fraud. This story line is fulfilled by the end of issue #4, with the Last American seemingly emergent as a "real" nationalist superhero after (nearly) single-handedly exposing the government program and severing his ties to the seemingly corrupt governmental structures.

During these early issues, *The American* introduces a metatextual reference through the existence within the story of a clichéd nationalist superhero comic book about the hero, which disseminates the character's mythology to young people. The comic book version of the American has an origin story similar to that of Captain America (although set in the 1950s) and a nemesis who looks like the Red Skull but is called "the Bones."[25] Indeed, the soldier-actors who have recently played the American are drawn to the part because if they survive, they are entitled to a share of the merchandising proceeds, a fact that indirectly leads to the death of the American in the Beirut airport scene. This element of the story not only calls into question the idealism of the nationalist superhero but also follows in the tradition of *Watchmen* by highlighting the gaping chasm between the comic book narratives and what superheroes would be like in "reality" by literally juxtaposing the comic book exploits of the fictive American with the corruption of the "real" one.

However, following the conclusion of the initial story arc, *The American* veers off into new territory, working toward a more character-driven story following the deterioration of both Hough and the Last American. Of interest for our purposes is the erosion of the Last American's sense of self. When the Last American interrupts a convenience store robbery, his military training kicks in and he ends up killing the defenseless getaway driver. Hough considers the impact of being the Last American on his otherwise nameless friend:

> Even knowing his military background, it never occurred to me that the American was anything more than a jock with a glandular problem. The American didn't need a gun. He *was* the gun. And those punks pulled the trigger. Trouble was, the American was more than some fancy tooled chunk of iron. He had to live with all this.[26]

Indeed, the Last American struggles to come to grips with his relationship to society. A significant portion of the American people see the Last American as

a traitor who weakened the country by exposing the American squad; nevertheless, he continues to wear his costume everywhere, unable to find an identity outside of his superheroism:

> Maybe I believed it myself. When I look in the mirror, I don't see a
> man. I see the American. [. . .] I broke ranks with the American squad
> because I couldn't live with the human truth of modern war. People are
> numbers. People are casualties. People are disposable. And, by the same
> logic, so were we.[27]

Subsequent struggles of the Last American to carve out an identity outside of superheroism lead him to (a thinly veiled) Scientology. The story arc
begins as a heroic rescue tale, with Hough and Candice (the Last American's
girlfriend) going undercover to bring the Last American home. During his period of isolation after arriving at the compound, the Last American connects
his personal struggles to the national narrative:

> The American used to stand for something—I was the embodiment of
> America's ideals. I believed—we all believed. It was all a lie. We have
> new heroes now. [Iran/Contra scandal figures] North, Poindexter,
> Keating. We pretend nothing's changed. "America is strong, America
> is good, America is right—" My God. Sometimes we believe that, too. I
> just can't pretend anymore.[28]

Following this realization, the cult deems him ready for full inclusion and they
shower him with love.

The Last American, Hough, and Candice are thrust into a conflict between
the cult members and the nearby town. The reader realizes that Hough and
Candice have been struggling mightily to save the Last American from the only
people who genuinely accept him as an individual rather than as a superhero—
the cult even names him Adam, the only nonsuperheroic name he has in the
entire run of the comic. In the final action sequences Candice is wounded,
leading the Last American to rage against the xenophobic townspeople, only
to be rejected by the cult afterward for his violence. In the denouement, Hough
gains a moral compass through his relationship with the Last American, and
the Last American himself finds peace and a sense of identity through his relationship with Candice, whom he helped recover from her bullet wounds.

*The American* offers a pointed critique of the U.S. government as well as
the nationalist superhero subgenre itself. Unlike *Cla$$war*, the series generally
avoids criticizing specific U.S. policies, but in general the U.S. government is
seen as corrupt, self-serving, and unconcerned with the value of human life.
Its creation of the American squad speaks to the government's willingness to
deceive the American people, but whereas *Cla$$war* implies that justice will
emerge from the lifting of the American people's ignorance, *The American*

indicates that such whistle-blowing is disparaged by the American people, who prefer to live in ignorance. This thread is tied to the comic's critique of American exceptionalism; it is the Last American's realization that the United States is not special that leads him to call into question everything for which he has lived. Finally, whereas *Cla$$war* left the politics of superheroic violence largely unexamined, *The American* brings them to the fore. Virtually every instance of the Last American's deployment of violence is seen as highly problematic, and the hero endlessly wrestles with the consequences of his actions. In the end, his rampage against the townspeople (the narrative double of American's sinking of the U.S. warships in *Cla$$war*) leads directly to his rejection by the cult. The only resolution to his sense of alienation and endless identity crisis is found when he rejects metanarratives entirely and is content to just take care of Candice. While the denouement's dependence on heteronormative assumptions of masculinity and the redemptive power of "the right woman" (itself a kind of metanarrative) is certainly problematic, it provides a refreshing contrast to the usual superheroic conventions of perpetual vigilance and violence.

## Captain Confederacy

The final example of nationalist superhero subversion takes a page from the alternate earths of Chapter 8. Will Shetterly and Vince Stone's *Captain Confederacy* was published sporadically between 1986 and 1992, first with SteelDragon Press and later with Epic Comics. The counterfactual narrative of the comic diverts from "our" earth through the victory of the Confederacy in the U.S. Civil War and the subsequent fragmentation of the union. Per Barney Warf's admonition that good counterfactual history requires a genuinely possible change in the timeline,[29] Shetterly (who outlined his vision through the letters-to-the-editor pages) makes his historical diversion the inability of Union troops to discover Robert E. Lee's battle plans for Antietam. With the war over in 1862, the Confederate States of America (CSA) managed to expand into the Caribbean and Central America and abolished slavery in the 1880s through democratic action. Nevertheless, it remains a deeply racist society. Will Shetterly says that the common "what if the South had won the Civil War?" counterfactual led inexorably to a consideration of its impact on the nationalist superhero: "I was thinking about nationalistic superheroes in general and Captain America in particular, and I realized that if the South had seceded, Captain America would be a white man with a bullwhip. I grew up in the South, where an alternate South is always present, with its rebel flags and gray uniforms."[30]

However, this change in our timeline led inexorably to second-order changes; the Union army's refusal to depart from New Orleans led to the eventual creation of the Louisiana Free State as an African American–led state. The CSA's inability to deal with this enclave of the Other led to dissatisfaction in Texas, which seceded peacefully but remains a sympathetic ally of the CSA (as Louisiana maintains ties with the United States). The settlements of Utah (and surrounding areas) similarly managed their own self-governance in defiance of U.S. ideas of manifest destiny, creating a Mormon theocracy. With no link to the West Coast, the United States never gained any traction in the Pacific, and so the nominally independent California fell under the influence of the Japanese Empire. Oregon and Washington eventually joined with British Columbia, which itself seceded from British North America and became the independent state of Pacifica. Intriguingly, this world never experienced World War II; therefore, Japan and Germany remain global imperial powers.

Taking this fragmented North America as a starting point, Shetterly and Stone produced two large story arcs, each of which subverts an element of the nationalist superhero. In the first story line, we are introduced to Jeremy Gray, an actor hired to play Captain Confederacy in propaganda news footage of his exploits. He is joined by his deeply racist partner, Miss Dixie, and his opposite numbers, Aaron and Kate. Aaron and Kate are two African American actors who play a coterie of masked African American villains, such as Blacksnake (quoted at the beginning of this chapter). As in the Captain America narrative, the heroes' (and villains') superpowers come from the application of an "Ultimate Potential" serum, and also as in *Captain America* (but predating *Truth: Red, White, and Black* by more than a decade), the serum was tested on black bodies before being finally applied to a white body. When Kate and Aaron rebel against their role in the media charade, they are both shot by government agents. Kate survives, but the loss of his friend Aaron radicalizes Captain Confederacy and leads him to defect with her, and they join a ragtag team of U.S., Louisianan, and Japanese agents, and together they plan to use the public persona of Captain Confederacy to expose the Confederate government's deceit.

Jeremy Gray and Kate become romantically involved in the interim, and their media campaign to undermine the racist regime culminates in a compromise with the CSA president that they hope will bring racial healing to the Confederacy: the African American Kate is announced as the new Captain Confederacy while the white Jeremy Gray is installed as her sidekick, Kid Dixie. In this fashion, both the racial and gendered assumptions of the nationalist superhero are challenged but with the explicit goal of mediating a new national narrative via a new embodied form. By foregrounding the role of the nationalist superhero as a media celebrity used to legitimate regimes, Shetterly parodies two of the key assumptions associated with the nationalist superhero: "Two improbable things about superheroes had interested me: the gaudy costumes, and how easy it is for them to find evil to thwart. Both made more sense if superheroes were propaganda tools."[31]

The second story arc shifts from the domestic to the international, with the new Captain Confederacy and Kid Dixie heading to a meeting of nationalist superheroes in Louisiana. These include Germany's Iron Falcon, Texas's Lone Star, Mexico's El Brujo, the Mormon Dr. Deseret, California's multicultural team of Spirits, Japan's Solar Samurai, and the U.S. Union Maid. The plot revolves around the murder of Lone Star and the subsequent framing of Captain Confederacy and Kid Dixie. After much action and adventure it is revealed that this was an attempt to drive a wedge between erstwhile allies Texas and the Confederate States, perpetrated by the shadowy North American Union Foundation (NAUF), which sponsored the conference and works toward a postnationalist, unified North America (similar, although not identical, to "our" United States—indeed, it is hinted that the NAUF is a front for U.S. policy objectives). By sparking a war between Texas and the CSA that would weaken both, the United States could sweep in and reincorporate both. When the nationalist heroes recognize how they are being used, they band together to maintain peace (and consequently the territorially fragmented status quo).

Just as in the Marvel Universe, there is the realist assumption that each country has its own nationalist superhero (e.g., Sabra, the Arabian Knight) who looks out for his or her nation-state's interests, yet these counterfactual nationalist superheroes have no problem with seeing their mutual interest in the status quo as a cause to rally around. Iron Falcon even defies her "national interest" to help the other heroes and is killed by her government handler for doing so. Interestingly, this narrative contrasts with the alternate earths described in Chapter 8 in that it perpetuates the difference on which the counterfactual is founded; in working to maintain the status quo (a facet of superheroism that is here left uninterrogated), *Captain Confederacy* paradoxically works to preserve what, to the reader, is a completely foreign geopolitical order (a fragmented North America in which each country is a "minor power" on the global stage).

If this story line can be understood as perpetuating the subgenre's conservative streak, it cannot be accused of maintaining the subgenre's gendered and racial norms. The development of Kate's character as the new Captain Confederacy locates a black female body as the superheroic embodiment of a deeply racist society (she and Kid Dixie are hassled repeatedly by the Knights of Old Dixie, a group resembling the Ku Klux Klan). This has the effect of normalizing the Confederacy among the other states at the conference, and the racism of the CSA is downplayed, presumably as a result of the redemptive actions of the heroes in the first story line.

**Louisianan reporter:** Is it hard being the first person of color who's a national costumed hero?

**Captain Confederacy:** Wasn't the first Captain Confederacy beige?

**Reporter:** You're making a joke?

**Captain Confederacy:** I think it's important to know who we exclude. No one is literally white or black. We're all people of color.

**Reporter:** You say that wearing a flag that's the symbol of slavery and oppression to many of our people.

**Captain Confederacy:** Oh? Slavery in the CSA ended in the 1870s. It lasted much longer in nations like Brazil and Cuba. [. . .] Robert E. Lee and other opponents of slavery fought under this flag. It's just the flag of a nation, and that nation has changed.[32]

This sense of optimism regarding the ability of a few heroic individuals to hasten the Confederacy's development in race relations takes the embodied form of Captain Confederacy and Kid Dixie's unborn child; indeed, throughout the entire second story line, Kate is heavily pregnant. "I wanted to show that the society had changed as dramatically as possible, so a black woman was the right choice for a hero, and the child was meant to be the synthesis of the past and present."[33]

For the most part the new, female Captain Confederacy engages in little action, instead opting for nonviolent action and puzzle solving as a means to resolving problems, as in this confrontation between the heroes and the Knights of Old Dixie:

> **Knight**: You that Kid Dixie, huh? The C.S.A.'s very own miscegenational [sic] superhero. Pass me by, Kid Dixie.
> **Captain Confederacy, to Kid Dixie**: Don't get all macho, white boy.
> **Knight**: That's right, white boy. Do what the black bitch tells—
> **Kid Dixie**: Shush. [Puts finger across knight's mouth.]
> **Captain Confederacy**: We'll wait. Police will be along soon enough.[34]

Of course, the particulars of the Captain Confederacy narrative are highly relevant; the traditional masculinism of the neo-Confederate identity and the dominant scripting of the neo-Confederate movement as backward and worthy of derision may give the authors' decisions to shift from a traditional, masculine hero to a pregnant female hero a somewhat spiteful, emasculating dimension.[35] In other words, it may be possible to imagine a nationalist superhero this way only if the nationalism itself is deemed beyond the pale. Further, the pregnancy of the new Captain Confederacy feminizes her as the object of other heroes' protection, especially her lover, Kid Dixie. When physical conflict inevitably breaks out, Kid Dixie's masculinity is allowed to reemerge in emphatically phallic style (Figure 9.2).

The subversion of the nationalist superhero is here undoubtedly linked to the authors' disdain for southern nationalism in its more racist forms. While this portrayal of the Confederacy may have resonated with many readers, it obviously disconnected with the geographical imaginations of neo-Confederates. One such reader wrote in to express his disdain:

> "Captain Confederacy" is a vile piece of pornographic trash which slanders the heroic American Southland and white people everywhere. [. . .] Your ludicrous plot, self-hate (assuming you are white), and Negro-worship would disgust any reasonable person acquainted with the facts, not only of Southern, but world, history. The leaders of the slave-owning South, the post-Reconstructionist redeemers, and the architects of the Jim Crow regimes, have been the only American political figures to deal with the Negro honestly and to recognize him as he is:

Figure 9.2: Kid Dixie's narrative emplotment as the source of phallic masculinity, which is not entirely subordinated by the pregnant Captain Confederacy's cool head and aversion to violence. (Courtesy of Will Shetterly. Used with permission.)

an obviously inferior sub-species of homo sapiens. [. . .] If your reply to one of the pathetic letters from your readers is truthful, you were born and lived for some time in the South, although you now defile a Yankee state with your pestiferous presence. I certainly hope you don't fancy yourself a Southerner in any way, shape, or form.[36]

Clearly, from this reader's perspective *Captain Confederacy* lacks any ambiguity, and indeed the comic is clearly antiracist in intent. Nevertheless, it engages in subtle ambiguity with regard to its portrayal of the South. Southern nationalism, when rooted in racism, is undeniably portrayed in a negative light. Still, the South itself is seen as potentially progressive, especially as embodied in the two main characters, Jeremy and Kate. While in the first story line the media deployment of Captain Confederacy to bolster white supremacy is itself the conspiracy to be exposed, in the second story line Captain Confederacy and Kid Dixie's media-friendly embodiment of a postracial Confederacy is seen as leading to positive social change (in regard to both gender and race). Together both story lines imagine the counterfactual South as a sovereign space no less legitimate than the United States of "our" world, neither inherently regressive nor without its own social issues to resolve.

## Conclusions

The carnivalesque allows for subversion of genre expectations through the breach of convention. The four comics discussed in this chapter have all subverted varying aspects of the nationalist superhero, enabling the tracing of generic expectations through their violation. Further, these comics have engaged in critique, of either the nationalist superhero genre's politics or the genre's "real world" equivalent: U.S. foreign policy. *Cla$$war* thrilled in the generic conventions with regard to the expectations of righteous violence but turned that violence against what is described as a crassly capitalist, imperialist foreign policy. In this way, the nationalist superhero is deployed to enable critique of the disconnect between the American people and the U.S. state. *Watchmen* introduces "realism" to the nationalist superhero genre, which has the effect of souring *Cla$$war*'s exultant violence. Indeed, the withdrawal of heroic nobility from the nationalist superhero is rooted in the Comedian's visceral pleasure in (sometimes sexual) violence, thereby framing nationalism and state power as a license for nihilistic violence and occasionally misogyny.

*The American* follows *Watchmen*'s commitment to realism, also highlighting the disconnect between heroic action and heroic motivation (in this case, capitalism rather than misanthropy). However, *The American* also illustrates the impact of a life of violence on not only its victims but also the hero himself, who is forced to live at the margins of society as a result of his emplotment within the military-industrial-media-entertainment complex.[37] With this emplotment, *The American* also highlights the role of nationalist superheroes as media objects, playing metatextually with the nationalist superhero subgenre as a whole. If *The American* is a comic book within a comic book, based on actors performing to reify state power, then what is *Captain America? Captain Confederacy* pushes this emphasis on mediation still further, also seeing the nationalist superhero as a prop for unsavory political regimes. However, *Captain Confederacy* is yet more subversive as it shows the nationalist superhero as a mechanism for legitimating a counterfactual state: one that does not exist in our world. In embodying a fictitious state, Captain Confederacy foregrounds the role of the nationalist superhero in the discursive production of geopolitical imaginations. Further, it is only in this alternative earth, and when aligned with a highly problematic nationalism, that a comics writer and artist have created the space to have a nationalist superhero (Kate, the later Captain Confederacy) who genuinely eschews violence where possible and embraces a model of feminine heroism.

Of course, the examples in this chapter are not representative of all the work parodying the nationalist superhero subgenre, and the lines between the subgenre and its parodies are not always so clear. At times the subgenre can seem to slide into an ironic parody of itself. For instance, the Greek demigod Hercules had this to say about Captain America: "On Olympus, we measure wisdom against Athena . . . speed against Hermes . . . power against Zeus. But we measure courage . . . against Captain America."[38] Irony is, of course, nothing intrinsic to the text but is something brought to it by the reader, and so identifying which comic is "real" and which is parody is perhaps futile.

It is perhaps telling, however, that a raft of satirical parodies of the nationalist superhero have historically emerged from Canada, in contrast to the more "serious" parodies described earlier, which are all Anglo-American. As examples, we can turn to Captain Canada and Capitaine Kébec. Captain Canada was published in two issues of *Fuddle Duddle* comics in 1972; the hero is a man who ingests the bog of the Canadian Arctic, which has been imbued with power by a meteor from outer space. Captain Canada is assisted by his sidekick, Beaver Boy, who is more sophisticated than the hero himself. Indeed, Captain Canada mistakes peaceful protesters for communists and attacks them and later is duped by anarchists into carrying explosives into the Canadian Parliament. In the latter, Beaver Boy plays a key role, as his own cynicism over Canadian politics boils over. Capitaine Kébec followed shortly thereafter, being published in 1973–1974 in *Les Aventures du Capitaine Kébec and L'Illustré,* and again briefly in 1984's *Titanic.* Capitaine Kébec is actually a string of heroes who have purportedly held the title from the 1920s until the present, although the hero's origin story is of decidedly 1970s origin: some drugs, meditation, and the experience of nature. This satire draws on a diminution of the stakes associated with nationalist superhero adventure; for instance, Capitaine Kébec's first nemesis is Frogueman, who fires pea soup from a gun.

All this recalls the comment by John Bell, paraphrasing the period between the Canadian World War II heroes and that heralded by the birth of Captain Canuck:

> One measure of the U.S. domination of the comics medium during the fifties and sixties is that when Canadian superheroes finally did return during the 1969–1974 period, the first characters were buffoons. It was as if Canadian comics artists and writers recognized the absence of Canadian heroes, but could not quite—after a twenty-year diet of foreign comics—bring themselves to take such figures seriously.[39]

The American birth of the nationalist superhero genre and its interconnection with developments in international politics since that origin story have been revealed in this chapter, and indeed throughout the book, as a generic predisposition from which it is difficult to escape. American political hegemony has emphasized a generic formula for nationalist superheroes that equates righteous violence with the superhero/superpower and constructs villains as "rogue states" that cannot be dealt with through normal (geo)political action. American economic hegemony in the comic book publishing world has subordinated British and Canadian superhero comics to American models of nationalism, authority, and righteous violence. While alternatives exist, both in "mainstream" nationalist superhero comics like some iterations of Captain Britain and in parodies like *The American*, these are necessarily fringe, short-lived, or eventually pulled back into the "mainstream" norms as a result of market forces and the cultural logic that produces those forces. Further, given the way nationalist superhero comics already verge on parody to begin with, the double carnival (what I have called here the carnival of the carnivalesque) of nationalist superhero parody may squeeze the last vestiges of fun and pleasure out of a subgenre that is already rooted in exaggeration and fantasy.

Nevertheless, these superhero "carnivals" provide some space for tactical resistance to hegemonic discourses of superheroic violence.[40] Similarly, readers imbue these texts with their own subjectivities, bringing to bear their own understandings of key superhero terms such as "justice" and "righteousness," as well as more ironic readings. Collectively, the attempts by various writers and artists to rework the nationalist superhero as it moves through space and time, and the audience power brought to bear in the interpretive process and in subsequent cultural production (fan websites, fan fiction, etc.), work to prevent any final closure on the meaning of the nationalist superhero.[41]

# Afterword

To close this book, this afterword begins by recapitulating the empirical findings of this study, considering the chapters as pairs that together take up a particular facet of the nationalist superhero. Subsequently, two themes that cut across all the chapters are considered in some depth: hegemony and authorship.

## The Never-Ending Story

Throughout this book, and in previous papers I have written, I have referred to the superheroes discussed in this book as "nationalist" rather than the slightly more popular descriptor of heroes like Captain America as "national" superheroes. The latter is, admittedly, a slightly less awkward construction. However, the awkwardness of its construction is one of the things I like about *nationalist superheroes*; it calls attention to the difference between something that is "national" and something that is "nationalist." If something is national, it is simply associated with a particular nation: in this vein we might consider beer as the national drink of Germany, and St. George as the national saint of England. Identifying a superhero as nationalist, however, implies a relationship in which the superhero *actively* cultivates a particular vision of the nation-state and its role in the world. Documenting how the nationalist superhero contributes to our popular discourses of nations, states, and international affairs has been the primary focus of this book. Four themes have been developed in some depth: body, story, space, and anomaly.

The nationalist superhero's body has emerged as a crucial contributor to discourses of the nation-state in a range of ways. The superhero's body serves as a tangible sign of the unity of the nation, even as it simultaneously serves as a reminder of the state's protection of that nation. This embodiment compresses the demographic diversity of the nation into a singularly gendered and raced body. Writers and artists generally attempt to moderate this representational violence through a range of narrative strategies, including the incorporation of "ethnic" sidekicks and partners. However, if the superhero's whiteness has been the object of well-meaning (if sometimes ham-handed) liberal reformism by writers and artists, the superhero's masculinity has been less well interrogated. In fact, often the danger that the masculine superhero/state repels is itself a descent into feminine softness, perhaps best witnessed in the Femizonia story line from Chapter 2, in which Superia dipped Captain America into a chemical bath that would turn him into a woman. Heading off such feminization is fundamental to a genre of storytelling in which the superheroic body is meant to act, to punish, and to be punished. Given the role of the superheroic body as an embodiment of the nation-state, this generic structure also has implications for the perception of the nation-state's role in the world. Like the nationalist superhero, the nation-state is perceived as a "man of action," with all that implies.

The second theme taken up by this book is another parallel between the nationalist superhero and the nation: their existence as stories. Both the nation and its superhero can be understood as serial narratives that unfold over time, each with origins, cyclical patterns that maintain the status quo, and linear shifts that maintain the narratives' relevance to current events. These narratives are policed by volunteer armies of fans, who invest heavily in the maintenance of continuity.[1] A key part of maintaining these fans of the story is the ambiguity of the narratives themselves. A wide array of Americans, with differing political views, believe that Captain America speaks for them because they interpret the hero's actions as conforming to their ideal of America.[2] By providing an attractive pole for an increasingly fragmented political community, superheroes like Captain Britain and Captain Canuck interpellate readers as national subjects. This effect is hardly effortless, though, as change must be constantly effected without the appearance of abandoning the past. This phenomenon is perhaps most notable in the use of the Red Skull to give solidity to all that which is deemed un-American in a range of times: Nazism, communism, reckless individualism, racism, extremist corporate capitalism. By changing the meaning of Captain America's nemesis, the creative staff effectively change the meaning of the hero as well, but without having to resort to a rejection of past iterations. Captain America provides a seemingly stable presence that pivots to combat the new aims of the Red Skull.

The third theme developed here is that of space. While space is, of course, inherent to the entire book, an effort was made to ground the preceding narratives in particular territories that were themselves enmeshed in a particular set of global relationships. This took the form initially of a range of visual techniques used to distinguish "our" space from "theirs," as shown in the analysis of World War II covers from *Captain America Comics*. Later, as superheroes became more supernatural in their origins, national territory was naturalized in the superheroes' bodies. Not only did these bodies stand in for those of the body politic, itself a form of naturalization, but their superpowers were often also mapped onto national territories. Even Captain America, who has no such supernatural link, can be seen as deriving his commitment and moral power from his routine touring of the American territory.

These territories were themselves located in particular constellations of power and importance by the narrative development of each hero. For non-hegemonic powers (Canada and the United Kingdom), the importance of the hero's nation-state had to be pumped up to match the importance of the hero. A range of techniques effected this change, from the elevation of Captain Britain to be the foremost of the Captain Britain Corps, the transdimensional enforcers of order, to simply setting the *Captain Canuck* narrative in a future dominated by Canadian power. In *Captain America*, however, the dominant geopolitical vision is of the United States as just another country, like all the others. Sovereignty is valued as an ideal, but the universalism of American values trumps it; the hero continuously intervenes (reluctantly) in other countries, seeing the ends as always justifying the means. These comics therefore not only produce territorial understandings of the nation-state; they narrate a range of relationships among those territorial states.

The final theme of this book has been that of anomaly. By "anomaly" I mean that continuity is bypassed or that the generic conventions are subverted; what formerly had been taken for granted can be no longer. Narrative devices from science fiction such as time travel or interdimensional leaps have often been described as a method of critiquing the status quo of "our" world. However, in nationalist superhero comics, such techniques tend to portray these alternative worlds as dystopian rather than utopian. Invariably "our" world is highlighted as being preferable to whatever else might be created. The portrayal of alternative worlds only reiterates the value of the status quo.

More successful have been attempts in noncanonical comics to parody and subvert the genre conventions of the nationalist superhero. These conventions stem from the genre's creation in New York during World War II, in a historical moment in which patriotism was unironic, fascism was seen as a potential source of strength for weak democracies, and the nation-state was under existential threat. The contemporary generic values of the nationalist superhero are not, of course, determined by this origin, but nevertheless they are still extant in the more taken-for-granted aspects of the stories. Attempts to directly contradict these values, such as *Captain Confederacy*, can be powerful criticisms of not only the nationalist superhero genre but also the imagined realm of international affairs that the genre conjures into being.

These four themes together demonstrate the contrapuntal interplay between our readings of nationalist superhero comics and our imaginings of the way the realm of international affairs is constituted and operates. There is, of course, no singular imagination of how international affairs work, and I am not claiming that the imagination informed by nationalist superheroes predominates in any particular time or place. Rather, just as nationalist superheroes are a genre of storytelling, they illustrate a school of thought about international relations. They are a discourse that can be called on by politicians, pundits, and everyday people to make sense of the world around us and our role in it.

## Hegemony and the Globalizing Superhero

Even as this book has examined the geopolitics of the nationalist superhero subgenre, it has also traced the subgenre's movement across national borders into new contexts. This movement is fundamentally an act of translation, an effort to transplant something indigenous to one milieu into another milieu. Such an event is always pregnant with power, even if it appears banal at first glance. In the case of the nationalist superhero, it is surely relevant that the idea being transplanted is American and is in fact in many ways the quintessential symbol of American power (see again the painting *Massacre in Haditha*). Nevertheless, I want to be clear in distancing this project from any crude notions of American imperialism. Rather, the evidence points to the complex processes through which hegemony is worked out.

John Agnew describes hegemony as "the enrollment of others in the exercise of your power by convincing, cajoling, and coercing them that they should want what you want."[3] Considering the nationalist superhero in this lens is useful in that it decenters state power in favor of a broader approach that considers power as diffuse, polycentric, and relational. Some of the heroes described in this book were created explicitly as attempts to gain or expand a U.S. corporate foothold in new markets (e.g., Captain Britain, Alpha Flight). Others are indigenous attempts to produce a "local" version of the American superhero (e.g., Nelvana of the Northern Lights, Captain Canuck). Both reflect the adoption of the idea of the nationalist superhero as commonsensical in contexts generally far removed both in space and time from the subgenre's New York origins in World War II.

Nevertheless, just as in Antonio Gramsci's original formulation of hegemony, we cannot consider this a one-way process of domination.[4] Rather, to the extent that hegemony can be claimed in any given case, it entails the compromise of some elements of the hegemon's culture and practices. This compromise can be witnessed in the examples found in this book across multiple dimensions. Considering the horizontal (in a Cartesian sense) migration of the subgenre across state borders, this book has documented many cases in which the American model for the nationalist superhero has been intentionally modified by publishers to suit the national narratives of Britain and Canada, such as the association of Captain Britain with magic, or Captain Canuck's original lack of superpowers. Therefore, it is hard to argue that the nationalist superhero subgenre has been imposed wholesale on other societies through domination. Equally, the vertical dimension of this hegemony, in which comic book producers attempt to convey particular political messages to audiences, has been shown to be equally contingent. Audiences, for comic book production companies, are meant to be catered to; quite simply, if they do not like the comic being produced, the comic will fold shortly thereafter. While this is true of all commercial popular culture, comics have always been particularly susceptible to being canceled, often with no notice at all. The webs of power connecting producers and audience members in these countries are complex and multifaceted.

These webs of power are, of course, mediated by the market. This simple observation helps focus our understanding of the way in which hegemony operates. Of course, part of the America-centric hegemony is exactly this elevation of the market as global arbiter; thus, even the relative market marginalization of American superhero comics in the United Kingdom can be understood as a victory of sorts for America-centric hegemony writ large. More often, of course, we have seen that the arbitration of the market has tended to favor American nationalist superheroes: recall, for instance, that the golden era of Canadian nationalist superheroes occurred during World War II, when American imports were prohibited. Further, the marginalization of later British and Canadian superheroes resulted from their integration within the larger United States–centric Marvel Universe. *Captain Britain and MI13* writer Paul Cornell describes the role of British publishing marginality in the cancellation of his comic:

> Paul Cornell: One of the things I wanted to put over with the title was we kept saying this is not "that British book." One of the biggest faults [of my run] was to not get out of Britain and to the States as soon as possible. Again, if I hadn't done "Hell Comes to Birmingham" [a story line set in the British Midlands] . . .
>
> Me: Was that the turning point?
>
> Paul Cornell: Yes, because we lost a lot of our sales in the second [story] arc, as soon as we were out of *Secret Invasion* [a Marvel Comics crossover story line that began the comic's run]. [. . .] Because people don't buy British titles. I asked [a British] audience, "Would you buy *Captain Belgium*?" It's true. This is why the history of Captain Britain is so marginal throughout—because you need *Excalibur* connecting back to the X-Men with lots of recognizable mutant characters throughout to get a good run going.[5]

From this it is clear that the size of the U.S. comics market makes it the indispensible arbiter of what will be published, even in regard to other countries' nationalist superheroes.

However, this hegemony is not purely economic. Instead, it stretches forth in politico-cultural terms. The idea of nationalist superheroes for countries other than the United States emerges not only from a corporate need to expand into new markets. It also reflects the reciprocal desire by British and Canadian comic fans to participate in the prime modernity on offer by the hegemon.[6] Even when the specific nature of this modernity is being "localized" in the ways already mentioned, it nevertheless does so within the generic frame of the nationalist superhero. One of the reasons for this ready adoption

is that the nationalist superhero reflects an idea ensconced in international society during the American postwar hegemony: the treatment of nation-states
as theoretically equal within an international system predicated on liberal values, as perhaps best illustrated by the establishment of the United Nations.
Indeed, it was this assumption of equality that made *Captain Britain* fans so
excited about the first meeting of Brian Braddock and Steve Rogers. Carried
to its extreme, the idea that every state has its own hero was satirized in the
recent children's cartoon *Super Hero Squad*, in which Captain America led
the All-Captains Squad into battle, including the pint-sized Captain Liechtenstein ("tiny but economically prosperous!"). As funny as this is, it points to
the way in which the liberal assumption glosses over the vast inequalities in
power among these states; Captain Liechtenstein is a figure of comic fun (he
fights with a hovering snowboard and ski poles), and even the Captain Canada
of the early 1970s was an attempt to mock the power and pretension of the
American archetype. As described in the chapter on geopolitical orders, the
American narration of the international realm paradoxically denies American
hegemony as a technique of maintaining it. All of this illustrates not that the
international phenomenon of the nationalist superhero is the result of American hegemony, but rather that this phenomenon is part of the process through
which American hegemony works.

## Authorship Reconsidered

Finally, it is worth returning to the question of authorship in regard to these
stories; authorship is a theme that has emerged at various points in this book
that considers the role of agency in producing narrative. A relatively naïve perspective sees geopolitical discourse as the result of elite decisions, intended to
justify and enable policy decisions.[7] Clearly the case with nationalist superhero
comics is far more complicated than this. Here, as in the preceding discussion of hegemony, the evidence points to the diffuse and polycentric nature of
power. Rather than the (highly naïve) perspective of nationalist superheroes as
state-sponsored propaganda, or the (somewhat naïve) perspective of nationalist superheroes as corporate propaganda on behalf of the state, we see instead
nothing so much as the fragmentation of agency and authorship.

Authorship of the comics themselves during the Depression and World
War II drew on a Taylorist model, emphasizing assembly line production and
formulaic writing, done by freelance companies providing content to publishers. One person would write plots and design characters, which would then be
drawn by an artist, which would then be colored in by a third worker. Finally,
a fourth worker would insert the text. This method of production encouraged
geographic centralization, as art school graduates took on freelance work on
the assembly line to tide them over during the Depression until their "real" ca-
reers took off with something more respectable.[8] The fragmentation of creative
agency left the publishers with all the rights to the characters they published.

Indeed, some authorship can be seen to be embedded in the publishers. In the 1950s, production was brought in-house to force a diversification in the comics being produced in hopes of staving off declining sales. This led to the creation of "house styles" as publishers sought to differentiate themselves from each other, leading to creative staff accommodating the artistic and writing styles with which publishers sought to brand themselves. This emphasis of publisher-specific production processes remained even after superheroes made their big comeback in the 1960s and the market consolidated under DC Comics and Marvel Comics. Within these publisher-established processes, the relative power of creative staff has changed over time. According to *Captain America* writer Steve Englehart, "in the 1970s, the writers were top dogs. Artists became ascendant in the late 1980s."[9] This fragmentation of agency and authorship among writers, artists, and editors produces unpredictable outcomes. For instance, in the 1970s, as discussed earlier, Englehart wanted to write Captain America as adopting a new pacifist stance but was prevented from doing so by his editors. When *Captain America* made news in 2010 for implying that the conservative Tea Party movement was racist,[10] Marvel Comics blamed the characterization on a nameless letterer who exceeded his or her remit. Just because a writer, artist, and editor have their names on a comic does not mean that they are all responsible for the choices within.

However, the question of a comic's authorship is not limited to the people who make it. Linked to the rise of the "star" system in the American comics industry, in which elite writers and artists bring their fans with them when they change projects (or even companies), is the decentralization of comic book creative activity. During the first half century of superhero comics production, the "bullpen" (where assembly line production took place) was produced not only because of the need for workers to hand paper back and forth to one another as it was produced but also because it represented the power of the publisher within such a Taylorist system. However, shifts in corporate strategy and distribution within the comic book industry during the 1980s and 1990s toward subculture marketing have weakened the centralizing tendencies of comic book publishing. As Glen Norcliffe and Olivero Rendace argue:

> Since [the 1980s], comics have been increasingly addressed to specific submarkets, with artists using know-how, specialized skills, and their own contact networks to assess the interests of readers. In this latter interpersonal world, a great deal of reflexivity is found between producers and consumers who are in frequent communication, especially during the comic convention season.[11]

Thus, the question of authorship must actively deal with the role of the audience as supplier of raw ideas through informal networks that incorporate production staff. This means that the consumer is already present within the process of authoring, either as a concrete contributor or as an idea in the mind of the writer/artist of what the audience will pay for, tolerate, and so on. This phenomenon cannot be overstated, given the self-appointed role of the audience as the "keeper of continuity." *Captain Britain* writer Paul Cornell complained about just this phenomenon, arguing that the crowd-sourced knowledge of fandom nevertheless sometimes gets it wrong: "What gets me is that even having pinned all this [continuity] down, the [Internet] message boards like to think of themselves as the keepers of continuity—and so you've got it wrong even if you haven't."[12]

What all this fragmentation hints at is the idea that the superheroes themselves are immanent characters, emergent from these practices of production and consumption. Never under the control of any one author at all, superheroes appear to take on a life of their own, as noted by famed comics writer Grant Morrison:

> Actually, it's as if [Superman's] more real than we are. We writers come and go, generations of artists leave their interpretations, and yet something persists, something that is always Superman. We have to adapt to his rules if we enter his world. We can never change him too much, or we lose what he is.[13]

If we take up again the method of doubling used throughout this book, Morrison's claim about the superhero can also be taken as a claim about the discourse of the nation-state and its geopolitics. The nation-state emerges through diffuse discursive practices that reify, naturalize, and make claims about it. Even those supposedly "authoring" the state's policies (the president, prime minister, etc.), as with the writer, artist, or editor of a superhero comic, can only nudge around the edges of characterization that is acceptable to the masses. This is as much a statement of the limits of policy making in a democratic society as it is a statement of the limits of elites' political imagination. Discourse is as much about what is said as what cannot be said, and as much about what is thought as what cannot be thought.

This understanding of diffuse authorship not only implicates all readers (and potential readers) of nationalist superhero comics in the emergent shape of the narratives but also produces us all as authors of our national narratives, and hence of our states and their policies. Of course, the nationalist superhero and its narration of states and the international realm is only one genre of popular geopolitical discourse, and it is neither always applicable nor relevant to a given geopolitical event. Nevertheless, what all the near-infinite genres of popular geopolitical discourse have in common is exactly this element of diffuse author-ity and responsibility. Each of these discourses overlaps with some of the others in certain aspects, but each overlaps with *all* the others through its ineluctable connection to our individual practices. In this way it might be said that we *all* have superpowers, to shape the spaces of the world in ways both large and small.

# Notes

CHAPTER 1

1. It should be noted that Picasso's painting was itself a revisioning of Goya's *The Third of May 1808*. The artists' recycling of one another's images can be understood as a commentary on the cyclical nature of violence.

2. For a detailed exegesis of the inside/outside boundary, see Walker 2010.

3. Tanya Tier, "Massacre in Haditha—the Story behind the Painting," unpublished document available from the artist.

4. For an example of psychology research that uses superheroes as a proxy for "social support for authoritarianism," see Peterson and Gerstein 2005.

5. For an example of a work that positions superheroes in these ways, see Costello 2009.

6. Critical geopolitics is a poststructuralist project generally themed around the production of space in discourses of global politics. See D. Campbell 1992; Dalby 1991; and Ó Tuathail 1996. On state-centrism, see Sparke 2005; and P. Taylor 1996.

7. But see Billig 1995.

8. Sparke 2005, xii.

9. Lopes 2009.

10. Tilly 2002, 211.

11. Barthes 1977; Foucault 1984; Bourdieu 1993.

12. Wright 2001; Lopes 2009.

13. Matton 2000; Stevens 2011.

14. See Jackson and Mandaville 2006.

15. Astro Boy, the Mighty Morphin Power Rangers, and Voltron were known as Atom Boy, Super Sentai, and Beast King GoLion, respectively. On differences among comic book heroic archetypes around the world, see Allison 2006; Lunning 2008; McLain 2009; and Lofficier and Lofficier 2004.

16. Coogan 2006.

17. Ibid., 47.

18. Reynolds 1992, 7.

19. Coogan's chapter, "The Definition of a Superhero," actually has a judicial-sounding subheading titled "Ruling In and Ruling Out."

20. Fingeroth 2004.

21. For an alternative narrative of Superman in which he fights for the Soviet Union, see Millar and Johnson 2003.

22. Larry Porter, quoted in Jurgens and Kubert 2000, 22.

23. R. Williams 2009.

24. Thomas 2009; Burke 2005; Skidmore and Skidmore 1983.

25. Reynolds 1992.

26. Morson and Emerson 1990, 290–293.

27. Ro 2004.

28. Wolf-Meyer 2003.

29. Epigraph to Chabon 2001. See also Jones 2004.

30. Ro 2004, 13.

31. Wright 2001, 35–36.

32. Lockhart 2003; Madsen 1998; Spanos 2008.

33. Jewett and Lawrence 2003.

34. Richard Reynolds describes it this way: "A new kind of popular hero had emerged: the self-reliant individualist who stands aloof from many of the humdrum concerns of society, yet is able to operate according to his own code of honour, to take on the world on his own terms, and win." Reynolds 1992, 18.

35. J. Campbell (1949) 2008.

36. As to what influenced Lucas in his creation of the prequel trilogy, I defer to toxicology reports.

37. Jewett and Lawrence 2003, 29.

38. Pease 2009, 24.

39. Scot Myers, quoted in Waid and Garney 1998b.

40. N. Smith 2004.

41. While the United States was not involved in the establishment of the ICC, the court has clear antecedents in the efforts of the United States to constitute the international sphere as a realm with norms and expectations analogous to those of the domestic sphere. Further, the United States has supported the creation of special courts to try individuals for war crimes and human rights abuses in postwar Germany, Rwanda, and Yugoslavia.

42. BBC 2002.

43. Ó Tuathail 2005, 370. See also Carter and Dodds 2011.

44. For more on the role of emplotment in narrative, see Entrikin 1991.

45. Brubaker and Perkins 2006b, 13–14.

46. Sparke 2005; P. Taylor 1996.

47. Hoffman 2001.

48. Enloe 2004.

49. For example, negotiating the relationship between the British state and so-called have-a-go-heroes who seek to stop antisocial behavior was a continual issue under the last Labour government.

50. Bainbridge 2007, 460. Bainbridge traces the relationship between superheroes and governmental authority in depth, although his framing of justice as premodern/modern/postmodern is overly teleological. For more on the importance of embodiment in understanding nationalist superheroes, see Chapters 2 and 3.

51. Chomsky 2000.

52. Jurgens and Layton 2002, 58.

53. Cornell 2009.

54. Superman even appeared in a release of Canada Post stamps meant to commemorate Canadian superheroes.

55. Reynolds 1992, 18.

56. David Gordon-MacDonald, quoted in DeMatteis and Zeck 1982b, 23.

57. The dominance of Marvel's comics in this book (vis-à-vis their rival DC Comics) is attributable to the engagement with "real-world" locations in the Marvel Universe. For instance, whereas DC situates their heroes in cities such as Gotham or Metropolis, Marvel's heroes are ensconced in New York City. This makes Marvel's heroes more likely to meet the explicitly nationalist criteria for inclusion in this research sample.

58. Carpenter 2005.

59. Hillborough soon collapsed. See Bell 1992.

60. Ibid., 3.

61. It is worth noting that this is not the more famous *Iron Man* later published by Marvel Comics.

62. *Triumph-Adventure Comics* was initially published by Hillborough Studios but was later published by Bell Features in the wake of Hillborough's collapse. The title of the comic was later shortened to *Triumph Comics*.

63. The Group of Seven was a collection of Canadian landscape painters in the 1920s that were heavily influenced by European impressionism.

64. Bell 1992, 5.

65. See Sim 1973.

66. Bell 1992, 7.

67. Ibid.

68. Ibid., 20.

69. Dittmer and Larsen 2007; Edwardson 2003.

70. Byrne 2008.

71. Bell 1992.

72. Biggles's real name was James Bigglesworth. See A. Kirby 2000.

73. Gravett and Stanbury 2006.

74. It was during this time that famed writer Alan Moore took his turn with the hero.

75. McDermott 2009.

76. Morganthou 1960.

77. The former does not exist per se, but see Sparke 2000; the latter can be seen at http://www.captaineuro.com (accessed June 6, 2010).


CHAPTER 2

1. Gruenwald and Hoover 1995, 26.

2. Daniel Bigelow, quoted in Gruenwald and Carrasco 1994, 31.

3. Bukatman 2003, 31.

4. Singer 2008, 280. See also M. Brown 2006.

5. Among the superheroes analyzed in this research, the only women are Nelvana of the Northern Lights and a variety of women who fight as part of nationalist superhero teams (such as Alpha Flight and the Knights of Pendragon). Certainly the most famous nationalist superheroes—those who bear the name of their country, such as Captain America and Captain Britain—are all men.

6. Rasmussen and Brown 2005.

7. Bell 1992, 7.

8. It should be noted that this also occurs through the deployment of nonhuman bodies as metonyms for the active state and passive nation. For instance, in the United States the bald eagle often displaces the state as a protector figure, while the buffalo stand in as a symbol of the nation as in need of protection.

9. Saldanha 2008, 323.

10. Hobbes 1994, 138.

11. Vincent 1987.

12. Anderson 1991; Billig 1995; Gagen 2004.

13. Gagen 2004, 434.

14. For an excellent discussion of the relationship between the nationalistic uniform of the hero and masculinity in Captain America novels, see DuBose 2009.

15. Enloe 2004; Weber 1999, 2005; Sylvester 2002; Peterson 1992.

16. Dalby 1994, 598. Dalby reflects on the work of Enloe 1990.

17. For more on the work done through the deployment of that hyphen, as referenced in Chapter 1, see Sparke 2005.

18. Jewett and Lawrence 2003.

19. For more on this, see Jeffords 1994. A related notion of "armored bodies" is offered by Bukatman 2003.

20. On the spatiality of the western, see Goss 2004. On secret agents and geopolitics, see Dodds 2003, 2005, 2006, 2010.

21. Dittmer 2009.

22. Emad 2006, 982. Emad is drawing on Domosh and Seager 2001.

23. Bukatman 2003, 66.

24. DeMatteis 2009.

25. Englehart 2009.

26. B. Williams, quoted in Friedrich, Lieber, Wilson, Budiansky, and Kida 1977b, 17.

27. Alascia 1945a, 25.

28. Betty Ross is sometimes written in postwar issues as "Betsy Ross," and when Captain America returned to print in the 1960s, she was seemingly retconned into the character of Peggy Carter (although there seem to be some key distinctions between the two characters).

29. In this stereotypical love triangle the woman is attracted to the superhero persona, with whom the purposely boring alter ego cannot compete. In a later retcon it is established that Golden Girl is not here teamed up with Steve Rogers but with a replacement Captain America, Jeff Mace (the Patriot).

30. Shores and Alascia 1948, 20.

31. The Liberty Legion primarily appeared in the pages of *The Invaders* but was later trialed as a stand-alone super-team in *Marvel Premiere*. They were never given their own comic book.

32. Thomas, Buckler, and Ayers 1975, 10.

33. Madrid 2009, 17. This is a visual cliché to which Alan Moore paid homage in his *Watchmen* (1986) series via the character Silk Spectre.

34. The name Sabra comes from the Israeli term for the New Jews created in Palestine. The term compares these settlers to the cactus—tough and prickly on the outside but delicate and sweet on the inside. It should be noted that Israel maintains compulsory military service for both young men and young women, which may contribute to the characterization of Sabra.

35. For an excellent treatment of the gendered superhero body, see A. Taylor 2007.

36. For the work that aligning geopolitical identities with feminist and homophilic values can do, see Puar 2007.

37. Gage and Perkins 2006b, 13.

38. It should be noted again that this draws on the particular state context of Israel, in which women are conscripted into combat roles. See Sasson-Levy 2003.

39. For an interesting discussion of fascism's relationship to women and its expression in Jack Kirby's art, see Fischer 2003.

40. Emad 2006; Robinson 2004; Reynolds 1992.

41. Anonymous, quoted in Gruenwald and Levins 1992b, 31.

42. Englehart and Colletta 1974, 27.

43. Rodney Boyce, Daniel Braun, and Ed Brubaker, quoted in Brubaker and Perkins 2006a, 30.

44. Pierre Comtois, quoted in Brubaker and Epting 2006b, 30.

45. Bukatman 2003; Dutton 1995; Neale 1993.

46. J. Kirby 1976, 11.

47. By my calculation, Captain America, taking into account his age at the time of embarking on his career and the time spent frozen in an iceberg, lost his virginity at age forty-two (in *Captain America #290*).

48. DeMatteis and Frenz 1984, 2–3.

49. Dallan Baumgarten, Brian and Amy Cottrell, and Ed Brubaker, quoted in Brubaker and Epting 2006a, 30.

50. The recent decision to retcon Spider-Man's marriage into oblivion is another indication of the difficulty comics writers have telling genre stories about domesticated masculinity.

51. T. M. Maple, quoted in Delano and Davis 1985d, 20.

52. Ian Watson, quoted in Davis, Lobdell, and Madureira 1992, 31.

53. Jeff Kozzi, quoted in Ellis and Jones 1996a, 22.

54. Without evidence, I assume that the new spellings of Nelvana and Koliak were done to slip past copyright law; *Alpha Flight* was published by Marvel Comics, while *Nelvana of the Northern Lights* was published by Hillborough Studios.

55. For an interesting take on this phenomenon using queer theory, see Schott 2010.

56. Lee and Romita 1971b, 7.

57. Lee, Romita, and Buscema 1969, 17.

58. Lee and Colan 1970b, 9.

59. Englehart and Buscema 1972, 17.

60. J. Kirby 1977a, 3.

61. DeMatteis and Neary 1984c, 16.

62. Gruenwald and Lim 1990b, 14.

63. Battleaxe is actually armed with a labrys, a symbol of the lesbian community. For this insight I am grateful to Steven Flusty.

64. This is an event that does not recur anywhere in Captain America continuity and that, along with references to the possibility of nonconsensual sex perpetrated by the women on the defeated men, lends credence to the idea that this domination of Captain America by feminine power is seen as not only a threat but also a source of sexual fantasy.

65. Gruenwald and Levins 1991b, 8.

66. The feminist potential of this damsel-saves-hero narrative is diffused by having Captain America and Paladin dress up in women's clothing as camouflage after they are freed. This "drag show" undercuts the heroism and turns the finale into a farce.

67. Gruenwald and Hoover 1994, 29.
68. Mark Burrier, quoted in Gruenwald and Hoover 1995, 31.
69. Scott McLean, quoted in Waid and Garney 1995, 30.
70. Jurgens 2001a, 9.
71. Jennifer Cole, quoted in Jurgens 2001c, 31.
72. W. Smith 1980; Bassin 1987.
73. James Fish, quoted in Lee and Romita 1971a, 31.

CHAPTER 3

1. Liefield and Loeb 1997, 11–12.
2. It should be noted here that a well-established concept within the social sciences is that race is a social construction in which biology forms at least part of the basis for ethnic differentiation. This chapter, however, focuses on popular conceptions of race and its embodied nature and thus frequently discusses race as if it existed. This is in no way meant to be an endorsement of this view. In addition, it is undoubtedly true that there are *many* masculinities and femininities and that, therefore, it is inaccurate to claim that there are only two genders; however, for the purpose of the argument here, I use the simpler form.
3. Grabham 2009, 69.
4. Ibid., 69–70; Ahmed 2007.
5. Carpenter 2005, 58.
6. Quoted in ibid., 59.
7. Englehart 1974, 19.
8. King 2009, 218.
9. Ibid., 217.
10. J. Brown 1999, 28.
11. Scott 2006, 300.
12. Black Panther is T'Challa, the king of Wakanda, a technologically advanced state in Africa. Nama 2009, 142.
13. Scott 2006, 303–304.
14. This confluence of race, gender, and power may also speak to the dearth of black supervillains in both comic books and other media. See Cunningham 2010. On the possibility of racial progressivism in media, see hooks 1999.
15. Grabham 2009, 72. On metaphors of racial and ethnic purity, see Anthias and Yuval-Davis 1992; Stepan 1991; Weitz 2003; and D. Campbell 1998.
16. *Captain America Comics* was first published ten months before the entry of the United States into World War II, but while the war was already ongoing in Europe, the North Atlantic, and in East Asia. For more on wartime comics, see Murray 2000.
17. Bressey 2008.
18. Dingle, n.d., 2.
19. Dittmer 2007a. During World War II, both the American and British armed forces incorporated ethnic "others," although usually within segregated (U.S.) or colony-based (U.K.) units. The discourse of a "war between races," therefore, is notable not only for perpetuating racialism (e.g., "white versus yellow") but also for selectively forgetting various racial groups within the polity.
20. Shores 1943, 33.
21. It is, of course, fascinating to see the deployment of the term *concentration camp* by Americans to describe American policy before public knowledge of the Holocaust.

22. In this story, the Japanese are in disguise as Mexicans, which perhaps gives some insight into the level of sophistication attributable to the treatment of racial others. I certainly would not want to endorse the notion that racial types should be well known by everyone, but the fact that in *Captain America Comics* Japanese agents are effectively disguised as American Indians, Pacific Islanders, a Hindu god, an Indian fakir, a Sikh prophet, and the aforementioned Mexicans during the war indicates a narrative emphasis on Japanese trickery over Japanese phenotype.

23. Even if interned Japanese Americans were aware of their representation within popular culture, there was little capacity to object given their relegation to bare life. While there is evidence that comic books were available within the camps, the historical record is clear that the U.S. government was willing to intervene to prevent images of camp life from circulating outside the camp. On both points, see Gordon and Okihiro 2006.

24. Thomas and Robbins 1978, 31.

25. They were known as Golden Girl and the Human Top, respectively. This Golden Girl is unrelated to the actual World War II heroine.

26. Burgoyne 2010.

27. McWilliams 2009.

28. Friedrich and Buscema 1972, 13.

29. Friedrich and Romita 1971, 17, 23.

30. Lee and Colan 1970c, 20.

31. Alascia 1945b, 15.

32. Tyner 2004.

33. Dittmer 2007b.

34. Jurgens 2001c, 20–21.

35. This is true both before the September 11, 2001, attacks and afterward. See Dittmer 2005.

36. Friedrich and Romita 1971, 22.

37. Mercer 1994, 142.

38. Friedrich and Romita 1971, 11.

39. Lee and Romita 1971a, 6.

40. The Falcon has described Captain America in just these terms. He tells the story (via flashback) of when he confronted Captain America with the fact that they had recently been catching only black criminals, which was playing into the hands of white supremacist groups in the area, who conflated race and crime. Captain America claimed to have not noticed the pattern. "Of course he hadn't noticed. As corny as it sounds, Steve's mind didn't work that way. The only colors he saw were red, white, and blue." Waid and Hamner 1999, 6.

41. *Truth* editor Axel Alonso explicitly saw the story as a way of narrating America through a tale of Captain America's embodiment. "I thought it would be a really interesting way to use the character to tell a larger story, a chapter of American history. [We used] *Captain America* as a metaphor for America itself." Carpenter 2005, 54.

42. Weinstein 2006, 971.

43. Ibid.

44. Carpenter 2005.

45. Grabham 2009, 72.

46. Race is, of course, a fluid concept; for instance, at one point it was common to consider the Irish as nonwhite. Similarly, the Celtic histories of Wales, Scotland, and Ireland could be seen as racialized. Here, however, I am limiting the discussion to the

introduction of people of color into national discourse and the rise of multiculturalism as a narration of Britishness. This, of course, comes well after the actual existence of people of color within the United Kingdom and is certainly not meant to dismiss these early histories.

47. It should be noted in the context of this chapter that the Black Knight is not, in fact, black.

48. Cornell and Olliffe 2008, 15.

49. Cornell 2009.

50. Ibid.

51. Ibid.

52. Material on Canadian national superheroes and race in this chapter originally appeared in Dittmer and Larsen 2007, 2010.

53. Dingle, n.d., 2.

54. Lee and Avison 1942a, 14.

55. How the heroes are going to save a base that is under attack when they cannot even fend off a bear is a question left unanswered.

56. Comely 1975a, 10.

57. Byrne 1985b, 24.

58. Gittings 1998.

59. DeMatteis and Neary 1984a, 18.

60. Bill Ford, quoted in DeMatteis and Neary 1984d, 23.

61. Tripp Reade, quoted in ibid.

62. DeMatteis and Neary 1984e, 2.

63. Ibid., 20.


CHAPTER 4

1. Ellis and Jones 1996b, 5–6.

2. Bhabha 1994, 159. For a critique of Bhabha's understanding of space, see Sparke 2005.

3. Bhabha 1994, 142.

4. Said 1983, 145.

5. Schlereth 1994.

6. Burgoyne 2010, 121.

7. Locke 2005, 26.

8. Ibid., 32.

9. It is interesting to note that Captain America's costume is always referred to as a "uniform" despite his being the only person who wears it. It is clearly not meant to help him homogenize within a large group, but to stand out. I assume this is meant to convey the seriousness and formality of his role as American nationalist superhero and his links to the U.S. military.

10. Dittmer 2005.

11. Cornell 2009.

12. This shift is at least partly attributable to the institution of the industry-policing Comics Code in the 1950s, which governed the kind of behaviors that could be demonstrated in comic books. However, the Comics Code should not be seen as a structure that restricts the ways in which Captain America's origin can be narrated, but as part and parcel of the changing American attitudes toward power, violence, and authority that the writers and artists of Captain America were trying to narrate.

13. Marvel Comics had by this time long abandoned the Comics Code and was free to portray this event as they wanted. Again, though, I would argue that they could abandon the code because American attitudes toward superheroes and violence had shifted; this is not about structure and agency so much as their co-constitution. I should also note that the 2009 origin is not actually a retelling of the origin, but a reliving, as Captain America in this story line was adrift through time and reliving key moments. This could be understood, then, as not a renarration but a retcon; however, I do not think the distinction matters here.

14. For details on the evolution of the 1964 retcon, see Dittmer 2007b. Also see Weiner 2009.

15. This solution raises the question of why the U.S. Army would release a false story of Captain America's origin that nevertheless gave away the hero's real identity. It is perhaps best not to question these things too closely.

16. Jesse Ojeda, quoted in Brubaker and Epting 2006c, 30.

17. This Red Skull is not *the* Red Skull. The character of the Red Skull is discussed extensively in Chapters 2 and 5.

18. Kennan 1947.

19. In 1980 the change would be explained away by saying that Reinstein was Erskine's pseudonym, meant to protect him from the Nazis—to no avail, apparently.

20. Nicieza and Maguire 1991, 17.

21. Vaughan and Harris 1999, 20.

22. The writers have some fun here, having the young Steve Rogers contradict his later persona by uttering phrases such as "I'm not very good at speech-making" and "So confident. So paternal. So darned paternal! I'll never be like that . . ." Nicieza and Maguire 1991, 22, 40.

23. Gruenwald and Lim 1990a, 13.

24. Gruenwald and Lim 1990c, 23.

25. Ali Kokmen, quoted in Gruenwald and Levins 1992a, 31.

26. Kent Lowther and Howard Kidd, quoted in Gruenwald and Levins 1991a, 31.

27. This comparison of Captain Canuck's origins was originally published in Dittmer and Larsen 2007.

28. Comely 1975a, 3. Readers interested in this topic should see the 2010 Wikileaks revelations regarding U.S. strategic evaluation of Canada, as well as Evenden 2009.

29. Comely 1975b, 23. This origin resonates with notions of "frontier masculinity"; see Nonnekes 2008.

30. John Deyarmond, quoted in Comely 1975c, 17–18.

31. John Toews, quoted in Comely 1975b, 23.

32. Jim Bell, quoted in Comely and Freeman 1980, 20.

33. This story line coincides with the 1995 referendum on Quebecois secession.

34. Langlois and Langlois 2004, 3.

35. Langlois 2009.

36. At varying times Guardian is named Vindicator. For simplicity's sake I am standardizing the name throughout as Guardian.

37. Byrne's claim to have created Guardian during this time period insulates him from criticism that he copied Richard Comely's vision of a Canadian nationalist superhero from *Captain Canuck*.

38. Mantlo and Brigman 1987, 3.

39. Locke 2005, 26.

40. Jones 2004.

41. Locke 2005, 42.
42. To be fair, this is not a point that Locke is either making or contradicting. He is purely concerned with the incorporation of superheroes into debates over the role of science in modernity.
43. Parts of this argument were made in Dittmer 2011.
44. At varying times Merlin's name is spelled *Merlyn*. I have standardized it here for simplicity.
45. Claremont and Trimpe 1976b, 2–3.
46. Keith Sparrow, quoted in Friedrich and Trimpe 1976, 16.
47. *Captain Britain* eventually became *Super Spider-Man and Captain Britain* and then was canceled in 1977. Captain Britain teamed up with Spider-Man in *Marvel Team-Up* in 1978 and then appeared as a secondary character in the Black Knight comic strip found in *Hulk Comic* in 1979. In the early 1980s Captain Britain appeared in *Marvel Superheroes, The Daredevils,* and *The Mighty World of Marvel,* before returning in his own title.
48. For more on *Watchmen,* see Chapter 9. See Klock 2002.
49. Delano and Davis 1985a, 9.
50. Damian Spencer, quoted in Delano and Davis 1985c, 26.
51. Cornell 2009.
52. Ellis and Jones 1996a, 8.
53. Tony Ingram, quoted in Raab and Larroca 1997, 23.
54. Claremont and Huan 2007, 12–13.
55. Cornell and Kirk 2008a, 20–21.
56. Cornell 2009.
57. Claremont and Byrne 1978, 3.
58. Cornell 2009.

CHAPTER 5

1. Byrne and Stern 1981, 22.
2. American-published comics are released monthly, while early British-produced comics used in this study were published weekly; later they became monthly like American comics. The Canadian-published comics in this study tend to be published irregularly given their precarious financial position.
3. This argument has some resonance with the arguments detailed in Hobsbawm and Ranger 1983.
4. I make this argument in more detail in Dittmer 2007c.
5. Bhabha 1994, 158.
6. Another aspect of this is the occasional numbering of an issue as "zero" if it is a prologue or prequel to a series about to begin.
7. DeMatteis 2009.
8. Huntington 1996.
9. Tilly 2002, xiii (emphasis added).
10. Englehart 2009. The New Deal refers to the policies of President Franklin D. Roosevelt and can be seen as a watershed in the emergence of a liberal consensus until the 1970s.
11. Thomas and Robbins 1976, 10.
12. *The Invaders* did draw on the short-lived World War II *All-Winners Comics,* but the stories of that comic are a collection of individual adventures by the team's members

rather than those of a modern superhero team. Similarly, the first Union Jack is described as being a member of Freedom's Five, an international team of allied superheroes fighting during World War I against the Central Powers. This is more than just a playful anachronism; it is the colonization of history with present-day understandings of power, authority, and nationalism embodied by superheroes.

13. Bhabha 1990, 1.

14. Raab and Cassaday 1999, 8.

15. Tim Rogerson, quoted in Friedrich, Lieber, Wilson, Budiansky, and Kida 1977a, 20.

16. Cornell 2009.

17. Steven Chapman, quoted in Abnett, Tomlinson, and Erskine 1991c, 26.

18. Gage and Perkins 2006, 20.

19. Mitchell 2000.

20. Claremont and Trimpe 1976b, 9.

21. Ibid., 3.

22. Baron 2003; Trushell 2004.

23. Claremont and Davis 1987, 46.

24. Claremont and Cummings 2006, 22.

25. Abnett, Tomlinson, and Erskine 1991b, 15.

26. Ibid., 5.

27. The Green Knight is also known as the Green Man and can be found in pub names all over England.

28. *Sir Gawain* 2006.

29. Ellen Foley, quoted in Abnett, Tomlinson, and Erskine 1991a, 27.

30. Abnett, Tomlinson, and Erskine 1991b, 21–22.

31. It should be noted that *Knights of Pendragon* was printed on "Scangloss" paper, which was purportedly more environmentally friendly.

32. Hixson 2008; Weber 2005.

33. Jurgens and Scott 2000, 14.

34. Lt. Delvin Williams, quoted in Jurgens 2001b, 32.

35. DeMatteis and Zeck 1981a, 6.

36. Rashid Roby, quoted in Waid and Kubert 1998, 23.

37. Terkel 1997.

38. One reader wrote in to *Captain America* with the following: "Cap stands for America, so I prefer stories that go against America. Terrorist organizations, mad Russian generals, Nazis, Arab antagonists, as well as good American supervillains with a reason to exist should be the types of villains Cap faces." This kind of laundry list of the un-American provides an excellent snapshot of this individual's geopolitical imagination at the time. Larry Porter, quoted in Gruenwald, Levins, and Bulanadi 1993, 31.

39. It is worth noting that the first appearance of the Red Skull, in *Captain America Comics #1*, is apparently a different character from the subsequent appearances of the Red Skull. In this original appearance he is an American titan of industry, Mr. Maxon; at some subsequent point, without explanation, this continuity is ignored and the Red Skull becomes the character later identified as Johan Schmidt.

40. Romita 1953, 15. It should be noted that this Red Skull is later retconned into being an imposter, Albert Malik.

41. Ian Jull, quoted in Lee and Colan 1970a, 24.

42. Although Dean Leto did write in to say that he "never really went for the Nazi hate this country gets into every few years. It's sort of disgusting!" Quoted in Thomas, Robbins, and Springer 1977, 19.

43. Lee and Kirby 1966, 20.

44. Lee and Kirby 1968, 17–18.

45. Lee and Buscema 1969, 4.

46. DeMatteis and Zeck 1981b, 23.

47. It is perhaps best not to ask too many questions about the science here.

48. Stern and Byrne 1981, 8.

49. The Red Skull would also save Captain America's life in 1996 when the hero was in medical distress.

50. Gruenwald and Dwyer 1989, 41.

51. Ibid., 7.

52. Brubaker and Epting 2008, 1–2.

53. Herb 2004.


CHAPTER 6

1. Claremont and Olliffe 2007, 14.

2. Murphy 1996. For more on the relationship between territory and sovereignty, see Elden 2009.

3. Haines 2009.

4. Appadurai 1996, 35.

5. Raento 2006; Raento and Brunn 2000, 2005.

6. Fall 2010, 142.

7. Paasi 2003, 113.

8. Olwig 2008, 59. See also Daniels 1994.

9. Bell 1992.

10. Fall 2010, 146.

11. Material on Flag-Smasher was first published in Dittmer 2007c.

12. Gruenwald and Neary 1985, 3.

13. Flag-Smasher follows up his high-profile attack on the UN by attacking a flag factory. With this kind of strategic planning, it seems unlikely that Flag-Smasher will unify the world through force anytime soon.

14. Gruenwald and Neary 1985, 22.

15. Quoted in Gruenwald and Neary 1986b, 23.

16. Gruenwald and Dwyer 1988, 15.

17. *Subtle* is here used in a relative sense.

18. Herb 2004.

19. Byrne 1984a, 2.

20. Mantlo and Mignola 1985, 20.

21. Giddens 1985.

22. Cornell and Kirk 2008e, 2–3.

23. The geopolitical sophistication of this story line is fairly advanced for a comic book that begins with Dracula on the moon.

24. This character originated (in a more lively form) in Marvel's *Tomb of Dracula* from the 1970s. He was purportedly the son of Mina and Jonathan Harker from Bram Stoker's *Dracula*.

25. For a discussion of the multiple spatialities of British airspace, see A. Williams 2011.

26. Material on post-9/11 *Captain America* story lines was first published in Dittmer 2005.

27. Rieber and Cassaday 2002a, 1.

28. Ibid., 2–3.

29. For more on American exceptionalism and interventionism/isolationism, see Pfaff 2009.

30. Rieber and Cassaday 2002a, 4 (emphasis added).

31. Readers learn later in the story line that Centerville is the location of a factory for American land mines, which is why al-Tariq chose it.

32. This is so for a variety of reasons; a production-focused explanation is that comics writers and artists traditionally live in New York City and write about what they know. Alternatively, a narrative focus would emphasize that the urban context heightens the danger caused by superheroes and makes it more likely that a superhero could maintain a double life.

33. Rieber and Cassaday 2002b, 3.

34. This material was first published in Dittmer and Larsen 2010.

35. Grace 2001; Jansson 2003.

36. Bell 1992, 7.

37. Robert Service, quoted in Byrne 1984a, 1.

38. Cornell 2009.

39. Peter Martin, quoted in Friedrich and Trimpe 1977b, 16.

40. Claremont and Trimpe 1976a, 7.

41. Higgins and Lim 1990, 19.

42. The relationship of Captain Britain to Captain UK is explained in Chapter 7. Davis 1991b, 16.

43. Cornell and Kirk 2008a, 10.

44. Cornell and Kirk 2008b, 8.

45. Cornell and Kirk 2008d, 10.

46. Cornell and Kirk 2008c, 20.

47. Cornell and Kirk 2008d, 14.

48. Englehart and Buscema 1974a, 32.

49. Englehart and Buscema 1974b, 18.

50. Bob Rodi, quoted in Warner and Robbins 1975, 19.

51. Lopes 2009.

52. Gruenwald and Neary 1985, 14.

53. Herb 2004, 159.

54. Häkli 2001.

55. Fall 2006, 665.


CHAPTER 7

1. Waid and Garney 1998a, 29.

2. N. Smith 2005, 12.

3. For a sophisticated take on this approach, see Agnew and Corbridge 1995.

4. For example, see Haass 2008.

5. Dalby 2003, 2008; Ó Tuathail 1996.

6. Dodds 2003, 2005.

7. Power and Crampton 2005.

8. Canadian belief in their technological excellence vis-à-vis American and other military industrial complexes can be seen in the controversy over the 1958 cancellation of the Avro CF-105 Arrow, a jet interceptor on the verge of production for the Royal

Canadian Air Force. The cancellation, which occurred amid increasing cooperation between the United States and Canada in hemispheric defense, gutted the Canadian aerospace industry and led its talent to decamp for NASA. The eventual purchase of American fighters to perform the function of the Avro Arrow helped lead to the fall of the Diefenbaker government. This topic is still controversial today; see Gainor 2007; Campagna 2010; and Dow 1997.

9. Comely 1975a, 3.
10. Comely 1975b, 31.
11. Byrne 1983, 5.
12. Joshua Latten, quoted in Mantlo and Mignola 1986, 24.
13. Byrne 1984b, 2.
14. Byrne 1985a, 23.
15. The Hulk was created when Dr. Bruce Banner was accidentally bombarded by gamma rays, which cause him to morph into the incredibly strong, unstoppable green Hulk whenever he is angry.
16. Byrne 1983, 1.
17. Mantlo and Ross 1987, 16.
18. Mantlo and Lee 1988, 23.
19. Dittmer 2011.
20. Friedrich and Trimpe 1977a, 1.
21. Budiansky, Lawrence, and Wilson 1977, 4.
22. T. M. Maple, quoted in Davis 1985, 29.
23. Lobdell and Kolins 1992, 22.
24. Lobdell and Kolins 1993, 17.
25. Newsinger 1986.
26. Thomas and Robbins 1977, 10.
27. Ibid., 27, 30.
28. Al Schroeder, quoted in Glut and Kupperberg 1978, 23.
29. H. S. Williams, quoted in Thomas, Glut, Kupperberg, and Heck 1979, 19.
30. Davis 1993, 10.
31. Ibid., 25.
32. Davis 1991a, 3.
33. This is a point I first make in Dittmer 2011.
34. Gerber, Buscema, Esposito, and Tartaglione 1978, 27, 30.
35. N. Smith 2005, 43.
36. Lee and Avison 1942b, 46.
37. Lee and Colan 1970d, 4, 19. King Irabia's awestruck attachment to the United States was paralleled in 2004 by a group of women who had been sold into sexual slavery within the United States and then later saved by Captain America and the FBI. Despite their horrific experience and their imminent deportation, they are all eager to return to the United States.
38. "I represent the American dream! A dream that has precious little to do with borders, boundaries, and the kind of blind hatred your ilk espouses!" DeMatteis and Zeck 1982a, 24.
39. Lee and Avison 1942c, 44.
40. The story is told in flashback, so there is little evidence of the actual timing of the events.
41. Steven Bennett, quoted in McKenzie, Fleisher, Buscema, and Perlin 1979, 31. It should be noted that Bennett seems to be using "war" as a proxy for "conflict."

42. Nyberg 1998.

43. Lee and Rico 1942, 44.

44. Also, at this point the industry-regulating Comics Code was fully implemented and murder by heroes was impermissible.

45. Nils Osmar, quoted in Lee and Colan 1970e, 24.

46. Lee and Colan 1971, 15.

47. Englehart 2009.

48. Why Cox had to be a conscientious objector when he never would have been called to fight given his disability is never explained. It would seem that Englehart wrote Cox as someone who had previously fought in order to avoid interpretation of his pacifism as cowardice.

49. Englehart and Buscema 1973, 7.

50. Ibid., 18.

51. DeMatteis and Neary 1984b, 10.

52. DeMatteis 2009.

53. Gruenwald and Neary 1986c, 22.

54. First quotation from "Steve and Ben" and second from Jesse Guzman. Both quotations and subsequent editor's reply found in Gruenwald and Neary 1987, 23.

55. Garney and Waid 1998, 17.

56. See also Cunningham 2009.

57. J. Kirby 1977b, 10.

58. Larry Lisowski, quoted in J. Kirby 1977c, 15.

59. J. Kirby 1977b, 15.

60. Gruenwald and Neary 1986a, 8.

61. Jurgens 2001b, 5.

62. N. Smith 2005, 13.


CHAPTER 8

1. Robinson and Phillips 1997, 14.

2. Kneale 2003, 40.

3. Time travel and interdimensional travel are plot devices typically used by creators to break out of a restrictive continuity. Unfortunately, the Canadian superheroes analyzed in this study never established a substantial enough continuity to allow for this strategy to be deemed useful.

4. Kneale and Kitchin 2002, 4.

5. R. Jackson 1981, 1–2; cited in Kneale and Kitchin 2002, 4.

6. There used to be a saying in the superhero comics world that nobody is ever *really* dead except Spider-Man's Uncle Ben and Captain America's partner Bucky. That wisdom was thrown out the door when Bucky was brought back to life in 2005 after being "dead" for forty-one years. Perhaps it is time to start a "life pool" for Uncle Ben.

7. Reynolds 1992, 41.

8. McHale 1987, 33.

9. Kneale and Kitchin 2002, 9.

10. Warf 2002, 21.

11. Ibid., 28.

12. Ibid., 25.

13. For a more optimistic reading, see Fenton 2008.

14. It is worth noting that Steve Rogers appears as "Captain Colonies" in *Excalibur #44*.

15. Delano and Davis 1985b, 9.

16. Claremont and Davis 1989, 24.

17. Lobdell, Cooper, Junior, and Abrams 1994, 4.

18. I know, I know.

19. Alternatively, the "real" present and the "new" present were simply two different paths to the same historical eventuality. It is impossible to distinguish this from the
evidence of the story line.

20. Kneale 2010, 301. It should be noted that Camelot is a literary tradition and the
events of Arthurian mythology did not take place "in our world," strictly speaking.

21. Gruenwald and Lim 1991, 17.

22. Ibid., 26.

23. Gaiman 2003, 201.

24. Ibid.

25. Gaiman and Kubert 2004b.

26. Names in this part of the chapter have been standardized to the "contemporary"
Marvel names so as to avoid confusion.

27. Gaiman and Kubert 2004b, 3.

28. Ibid., 35.

29. Madsen 1998; Lockhart 2003; Spanos 2008; Pease 2009.

30. There has been a third volume (with perhaps more to come), but this analysis
focuses on the narratives envisioned for *The Ultimates* by its initial writer, Mark Millar.

31. I use the term "realistic" here with full awareness of its relativity.

32. Sutliff 2009, 122. See also Stevens 2007.

33. Millar and Hitch 2002a, 21.

34. Millar and Hitch 2005a, 14.

35. Millar and Hitch 2002b, 10–11.

36. Millar and Hitch 2002c, 14.

37. Millar and Hitch 2005b, 14.

38. Millar and Hitch 2006a, 26.

39. Millar and Hitch 2006b, 4.

40. Ibid., 28–29.

41. Tait 2008.

42. Millar and Hitch 2006b, 30–31.

43. Kneale 2010, 300.

44. "As the ruthless war-mongers of Europe focus their eyes on a peace-loving
America . . . the youth of our country heed the call to arm for defense[.] . . . But great as
the danger of foreign attack . . . is the threat of invasion from within . . . the dreaded fifth
column." Simon and Kirby 1940, 1.

45. Gaiman and Kubert 2004a, 19.

## CHAPTER 9

1. Shetterly and Stone 1986, 1–3.

2. Andrew Aldridge, quoted in Gruenwald and Levins 1992c, 31.

3. Hutcheon 1989, 87–88.

4. R. Jackson 1981, 175.

5. R. Williams 2009.

6. Bakhtin 2009.

7. I am grateful to Paul Adams for making this apparent to me. See also Fiske 1988.

8. Adams 2009., 172.

9. R. Williams 2009.

10. Ibid.

11. Williams, Hairsine, and Foreman 2009, 34.

12. R. Williams 2009.

13. Ibid.

14. Williams, Hairsine, and Foreman 2009, 55.

15. R. Williams 2009.

16. For example, see Hughes 2006; Wolf-Meyer 2003; Barnes 2009; and Venezia 2010.

17. Klock 2002, 62.

18. Of course, *realism* here means "real in comparison to the superhero genre as usually told." *Watchmen* contains many anti-realist plot devices (Dr. Manhattan is the most obvious, but notably also the teleportation of a "space squid" into the heart of New York City).

19. Klock 2002, 66.

20. Ibid., 67. The interior quotation is Harold Bloom's definition of *clinamen* from Bloom 1973, 14.

21. Moore and Cooke 2000.

22. Reynolds 1992, 106–107.

23. The nationalist superhero in the Minutemen was Dollar Bill, a red, white, and blue hero with a dollar sign on his chest. Apropos of Moore's "realism," Dollar Bill was sponsored by a local bank that designed his costume to maximize visibility; Dollar Bill was killed when his cape got caught in a revolving door when trying to stop a bank robbery, shot dead in ignominious fashion.

24. For more on cynicism and noir, see Naremore 2008.

25. The "real world" version of the Bones was captured long ago, installed in an isolation chamber and subjected to indoctrination. He emerges at a key point in the story line, more patriotic and pure than either the government's forces or those of Hough and the Last American. He is promptly killed for standing up for that in which he believes.

26. Verheiden and Miehm 1988, 13.

27. Ibid., 17–18.

28. Verheiden and Marrinan 1992, 8.

29. Warf 2002.

30. Shetterly 2011.

31. Ibid.

32. Shetterly and Stone 1991b, 13–14. See also Leib 2004.

33. Shetterly 2011.

34. Shetterly and Stone 1991a, 21–22.

35. McPherson 2003; Jansson 2003.

36. Quoted in Shetterly and Stone 1987.

37. Der Derian 2001.

38. Waid and Garney 1995, 13.

39. Bell 1992, 20.

40. de Certeau 1984.

41. Bratich 2005, 2008; Jenkins 1992.

AFTERWORD

1. Dittmer and Dodds 2008, 437–457.
2. Dittmer, forthcoming.
3. Agnew 2005, 1–2.
4. Gramsci 1992.
5. Cornell 2009.
6. P. Taylor 1999.
7. Müller 2008.
8. Wright 2001. Comics icon Stan Lee (whose name is Stan Lieber) adopted his pseudonym in hopes of preserving his real name for a forthcoming career in journalism. See Ro 2004.
9. Englehart 2009.
10. Dittmer, forthcoming.
11. Norcliffe and Rendace 2003, 247.
12. Cornell 2009.
13. Morrison 2011, 14.

# References

*Comic books are cited by the author(s) and title of the main story; pages in the note citations that fall outside the reference list page range refer to letters to the editor that appear outside the main story.*

Abnett, D., J. Tomlinson, and G. Erskine. 1991a. "Revelations." In *The Knights of Pendragon #7*, ed. S. White, 1–27. London: Marvel UK.

———. 1991b. "Nightfall ('The Wounded Land' Part 4 of 6)." In *The Knights of Pendragon #10*, ed. S. White, 1–22. London: Marvel UK.

———. 1991c. "The Last War." In *The Knights of Pendragon #18*, ed. S. White, 1–26. London: Marvel Comics.

Adams, P. 2009. *Geographies of Media and Communication: A Critical Introduction.* Hoboken, NJ: Wiley-Blackwell.

Agnew, J. 2005. *Hegemony: The New Shape of Global Power.* Philadelphia: Temple University Press.

Agnew, J., and S. Corbridge. 1995. *Mastering Space: Hegemony, Territory and International Political Economy.* London: Routledge.

Ahmed, S. 2007. "A Phenomenology of Whiteness." *Feminist Theory* 8:149–168.

Alascia, V. 1945a. "Diavolo and His Symphony of Death." In *Captain America Comics #49*, ed. S. Lee, 23–37. New York: Timely Comics.

———. 1945b. "The League of Hate." In *Captain America Comics #49*, ed. S. Lee, 1–15. New York: Timely Comics.

Allison, A. 2006. *Millennial Monsters: Japanese Toys and the Global Imagination.* Berkeley: University of California Press.

Anderson, B. 1991. *Imagined Communities: Reflections on the Origin and Spread of Nationalism.* London: Verso.

Anthias, F., and N. Yuval-Davis. 1992. *Racialized Boundaries: Race, Nation, Gender, Colour and Class and the Anti-racist Struggle.* London: Routledge.

Appadurai, A. 1996. *Modernity at Large: Cultural Dimensions of Globalization.* Minneapolis: University of Minnesota Press.

Bainbridge, J. 2007. "'This Is *the Authority*: This Planet Is under Our Protection'—An Exegesis of Superheroes' Interrogations of Law." *Law, Culture and the Humanities* 3:455–476.

Bakhtin, M. 2009. *Rabelais and His World.* Bloomington: Indiana University Press.

Barnes, D. 2009. "Time in the Gutter: Temporal Structures in *Watchmen*." *KronoScope* 9:51–60.

Baron, L. 2003. "X-Men as J Men: The Jewish Subtext of a Comic Book Movie." *Shofar* 22:44–52.

Barthes, R. 1977. "The Death of the Author." In *Image-Music-Text*, trans. S. Heath, ed. R. Barthes, 142–148. New York: Hill and Wang.

Bassin, M. 1987. "Imperialism and the Nation State in Friedrich Ratzel's Political Geography." *Progress in Human Geography* 11:473–495.

BBC. 2002. "US Renounces World Court Treaty." Available at http://news.bbc.co.uk/1/hi/world/americas/1970312.stm.

Bell, J. 1992. *Guardians of the North: The National Superhero in Canadian Comic-book Art.* Ottawa: National Archives of Canada.

Bhabha, H. 1990. "Introduction: Narrating the Nation." In *Nation and Narration*, ed. H. Bhabha, 1–7. New York: Routledge.

———. 1994. "DissemiNation: Time, Narrative and the Margins of the Modern Nation." In *The Location of Culture*, ed. H. Bhabha, 139–170. London: Routledge.

Billig, M. 1995. *Banal Nationalism.* Thousand Oaks, CA: Sage.

Bloom, H. 1973. *The Anxiety of Influence.* Oxford: Oxford University Press.

Bourdieu, P. 1993. *The Field of Cultural Production.* New York: Columbia University Press.

Bratich, J. 2005. "Amassing the Multitude: Revisiting Early Audience Studies." *Communication Theory* 15:242–265.

———. 2008. "Activating the Multitude: Audience Powers and Cultural Studies." In *New Directions in American Reception Study*, ed. P. Goldstein and J. Machor. Oxford: Oxford University Press.

Bressey, C. 2008. "It's Only Political Correctness—Race and Racism in British History." In *New Geographies of Race and Racism*, ed. C. Bressey and C. Dwyer, 29–40. Aldershot, UK: Ashgate.

Brown, J. 1999. "Comic Book Masculinity and the New Black Superhero." *African American Review* 33:25–42.

Brown, M. 2006. "A Geographer Reads Geography Club: Spatial Metaphor and Metonym in Textual/Sexual Space." *Cultural Geographies* 13:313–339.

Brubaker, E., and S. Epting. 2006a. "Twenty-First Century Blitz, Part 1 of 4." In *Captain America vol. 5, #18*, ed. J. Quesada, 1–32. New York: Marvel Comics.

———. 2006b. "Twenty-First Century Blitz, Part 2 of 4." In *Captain America vol. 5, #19*, ed. J. Quesada, 1–32. New York: Marvel Comics.

———. 2006c. "The Winter Soldier Conclusion." In *Captain America vol. 5, #14*, ed. T. Brevoort, 1–32. New York: Marvel Comics.

———. 2008. "The Burden of Dreams, Part 4." In *Captain America vol. 3, #34*, ed. T. Brevoort, 1–22. New York: Marvel Comics.

Brubaker, E., and M. Perkins. 2006a. "Collision Courses, Part 2 of 2." In *Captain America vol. 5, #17*, ed. J. Quesada, 1–32. New York: Marvel Comics.

———. 2006b. "The Drums of War." In *Captain America vol. 5, #22*, ed. T. Brevoort, 1–22. New York: Marvel Entertainment.

Budiansky, B., J. Lawrence, and R. Wilson. 1977. "When Hero Turns Villain." In *Captain Britain #38*, ed. L. Lieber, 1–7. London: Marvel UK.

Bukatman, S. 2003. *Matters of Gravity: Special Effects and Supermen in the 20th Century.* Durham, NC: Duke University Press.

Burgoyne, R. 2010. *Film Nation: Hollywood Looks at U.S. History.* Minneapolis: University of Minnesota Press.

Burke, A. 2005. "Against the New Internationalism." *Ethics and International Affairs* 19:73–89.

Byrne, J. 1983. "Shadows of the Past." In *Alpha Flight #2*, ed. D. O'Neil, 1–17. New York: Marvel Comics.

———. 1984a. "Biology Class." In *Alpha Flight #14*, ed. D. O'Neil, 1–22. New York: Marvel Comics.

———. 1984b. "Dreams Die Hard." In *Alpha Flight #17*, ed. D. O'Neil, 1–22. New York: Marvel Comics.

———. 1985a. "How Long Will a Man Lie in the Earth 'Ere He Rot?" In *Alpha Flight #18*, ed. D. O'Neil, 1–32. New York: Marvel Comics.

———. 1985b. "Night of the Beast." In *Alpha Flight #23*, ed. J. Shooter, 1–31. New York: Marvel Comics.

———. 2008. "Frequently Asked Questions: Questions about Comic Book Projects." Available at http://www.byrnerobotics.com/FAQ/listing.asp?ID=2&T1=Questions+about+Comic+Book+Projects#119.

Byrne, J., and R. Stern. 1981. "Blood on the Moors." In *Captain America #254*, ed. J. Salicrup, 1–22. New York: Marvel Comics.

Campagna, P. 2010. *Storms of Controversy: The Secret Avro Arrow Files Revealed.* Toronto: Dundurn Press.

Campbell, D. 1992. *Writing Security: United States Foreign Policy and the Politics of Identity.* Minneapolis: University of Minnesota Press.

———. 1998. *National Deconstruction: Violence, Identity, and Justice in Bosnia.* Minneapolis: University of Minnesota Press.

Campbell, J. (1949) 2008. *The Hero with a Thousand Faces.* San Francisco: New World Library.

Carpenter, S. 2005. "Truth Be Told: Authorship and the Creation of the Black Captain America." In *Comics as Philosophy*, ed. J. McLaughlin, 46–62. Jackson: University Press of Mississippi.

Carter, S., and K. Dodds. 2011. "Hollywood and the 'War on Terror': Genre-Geopolitics and 'Jacksonianism' in *The Kingdom*." *Environment and Planning D: Society and Space* 29:98–113.

Chabon, M. 2001. *The Amazing Adventures of Kavalier and Clay.* New York: Picador.

Chomsky, N. 2000. *Rogue States: The Rule of Force in World Affairs.* New York: South End Press.

Claremont, C., and J. Byrne. 1978. "Introducing, Captain Britain." In *Marvel Team-up #65*, ed. A. Goodwin, 1–22. New York: Marvel Comics.

Claremont, C., and S. Cummings. 2006. "Howling Mad!" In *New Excalibur #5*, ed. M. Marts, 1–22. New York: Marvel Comics.

Claremont, C., and A. Davis. 1987. *Excalibur Special Edition: The Sword Is Drawn.* New York: Marvel Comics.

———. 1989. "The Marriage of True Minds." In *Excalibur #13*, ed. T. Kavanaugh, 1–31. New York: Marvel Comics.

Claremont, C., and J. Huan. 2007. "Two Captains, One Destiny . . ." In *New Excalibur #24*, ed. N. Lowe and A. Schmidt, 1–22. New York: Marvel Comics.

Claremont, C., and P. Olliffe. 2007. "Turn Back the Clock." In *New Excalibur #22*, ed. N. Lowe and A. Schmidt, 1–31. New York: Marvel Comics.

Claremont, C., and H. Trimpe. 1976a. "The Origin of Captain Britain." In *Captain Britain #1*, ed. L. Lieber, 1–8. London: Marvel UK.

———. 1976b. "From the Holocaust—A Hero!" In *Captain Britain #2*, ed. L. Lieber, 1–9. London: Marvel UK.

Comely, R. 1975a. "Arctic Standoff." In *Captain Canuck #1*, ed. R. Comely, 1–24. Winnipeg, Canada: Comely Comix.

——— 1975b. "The Brain Machine." In *Captain Canuck #2*, ed. R. Comely, 1–14. Winnipeg, Canada: Comely Comix.

——— 1975c. "The Canadian Connection." In *Captain Canuck #3*, ed. R. Comely, 1–14. Winnipeg, Canada: Comely Comix.

Comely, R., and G. Freeman. 1980. "The Cold Vacuum of Space . . ." In *Captain Canuck #9*, ed. G. Freeman, 1–18. Calgary, Canada: CKR Productions.

Coogan, P. 2006. *Superhero: The Secret Origin of a Genre.* Austin, TX: MonkeyBrain Books.

Cornell, P. 2009. Interview with author. Oxford.

Cornell, P., and L. Kirk. 2008a. "The Guns of Avalon, Part 1." In *Captain Britain and MI13 #1*, ed. N. Lowe, 1–22. New York: Marvel Comics.

———. 2008b. "The Guns of Avalon, Part 2." In *Captain Britain and MI13 #2*, ed. N. Lowe, 1–32. New York: Marvel Comics.

———. 2008c. "The Guns of Avalon, Part 3." In *Captain Britain and MI13, #3*, ed. N. Lowe, 1–32. New York: Marvel Comics.

———. 2008d. "The Guns of Avalon, Conclusion." In *Captain Britain and MI13 #4*, ed. N. Lowe, 1–32. New York: Marvel Comics.

———. 2008e. "Vampire State Prologue." In *Captain Britain and MI13 #10*, ed. N. Lowe, 1–22. New York: Marvel Comics.

Cornell, P., and P. Olliffe. 2008. "Hell Comes to Birmingham, Prologue." In *Captain Britain and MI13 #5*, ed. N. Lowe, 1–22. New York: Marvel Comics.

Costello, M. 2009. *Secret Identity Crisis: Comic Books and the Unmasking of Cold War America.* London: Continuum.

Cunningham, P. 2009. "Stevie's Got a Gun: Captain America and His Problematic Use of Lethal Force." In *Captain America and the Struggle of the Superhero: Critical Essays*, ed. R. Weiner, 176–189. Jefferson, NC: McFarland.

———. 2010. "The Absence of Black Supervillains in Mainstream Comics." *Journal of Graphic Novels and Comics* 1:51–62.

Dalby, S. 1991. "Critical Geopolitics: Discourse, Difference, and Dissent." *Environment and Planning D: Society and Space* 9:261–283.

———. 1994. "Gender and Critical Geopolitics—Reading Security Discourse in the New-World Disorder." *Environment and Planning D: Society and Space* 12:595–612.

———. 2003. "Calling 911: Geopolitics, Security and America's New War." *Geopolitics* 8:61–86.

———. 2008. "Imperialism, Domination, Culture: The Continued Relevance of Critical Geopolitics." *Geopolitics* 13:413–436.

Daniels, S. 1994. *Fields of Vision: Landscape Imagery and National Identity in England and the United States.* Cambridge, UK: Polity Press.

Davis, A. 1985. "Should Auld Acquaintance . . ." In *Captain Britain Monthly #14*, ed. I. Rimmer, 3–15. London: Marvel UK.

———. 1991a. "Witless for the Prosecution." In *Excalibur #44*, ed. T. Kavanagh, 1–32. New York: Marvel Comics.

———. 1991b. "Nightcrawler's Technet." In *Excalibur #45*, ed. T. Kavanagh, 1–22. New York: Marvel Comics.

———. 1993. "White Lies, Dark Truths." In *Excalibur #65*, ed. T. Kavanagh, 1–32. New York: Marvel Comics.

Davis, A., S. Lobdell, and J. Madureira. 1992. "For Whom the Bell Trolls!" In *Excalibur #57*, ed. T. Kavanaugh, 1–30. New York: Marvel Comics.

de Certeau, M. 1984. *The Practice of Everyday Life*. Berkeley: University of California Press.

Delano, J., and A. Davis. 1985a. "Myth, Memory, and Legend." In *Captain Britain #1*, ed. I. Rimmer, 1–12. London: Marvel UK.

———. 1985b. "A Long Way from Home." In *Captain Britain #6*, ed. I. Rimmer, 1–11. London: Marvel UK.

———. 1985c. "Winds of Change." In *Captain Britain #9*, ed. I. Rimmer, 1–11. London: Marvel UK.

———. 1985d. "The House of Baba Yaga." In *Captain Britain #11*, ed. I. Rimmer, 4–13. London: Marvel UK.

DeMatteis, J. M. 2009. E-mail interview with author.

DeMatteis, J. M., and R. Frenz. 1984. "Echoes." In *Captain America #290*, ed. M. Gruenwald, 1–22. New York: Marvel Comics.

DeMatteis, J. M., and P. Neary. 1984a. "An American Christmas." In *Captain America #292*, ed. M. Gruenwald, 1–23. New York: Marvel Comics.

———. 1984b. "Field of Vision." In *Captain America #293*, ed. M. Gruenwald, 1–30. New York: Marvel Comics.

———. 1984c. "The Centre Cannot Hold!" In *Captain America #295*, ed. J. Shooter, 1–22. New York: Marvel Comics.

———. 1984d. "Things Fall Apart!" In *Captain America #296*, ed. M. Gruenwald, 1–23. New York: Marvel Comics.

———. 1984e. "Das Ende!" In *Captain America #300*, ed. M. Gruenwald, 1–22. New York: Marvel Comics.

DeMatteis, J. M., and M. Zeck. 1981a. "Death of a Legend?" In *Captain America #262*, ed. J. Salicrup, 1–21. New York: Marvel Comics.

———. 1981b. "The Last Movie!" In *Captain America #263*, ed. J. Salicrup, 1–21. New York: Marvel Comics.

———. 1982a. "Peace on Earth—Goodwill to Man." In *Captain America #268*, ed. J. Salicrup, 1–32. New York: Marvel Comics.

———. 1982b. "Mean Streets." In *Captain America #272*, ed. M. Gruenwald, 1–23. New York: Marvel Comics.

Der Derian, J. 2001. *Virtuous War: Mapping the Military-Industrial-Media-Entertainment Network*. Boulder, CO: Westview Press.

Dingle, A. n.d. No title. In *Triumph Comics #16*, 1–12. Toronto: Bell Features.

Dittmer, J. 2005. "Captain America's Empire: Reflections on Identity, Popular Culture, and Post-9/11 Geopolitics." *Annals of the Association of American Geographers* 95:626–643.

———. 2007a. "'America Is Safe while Its Boys and Girls Believe in Its Creeds!': Captain America and American Identity prior to World War 2." *Environment and Planning D, Society and Space* 25:401–423.

———. 2007b. "Retconning America: Captain America in the Wake of WWII and the McCarthy Hearings." In *The Amazing Transforming Superhero! Essays on the*

*Revision of Characters in Comic Books, Film and Television*, ed. T. Wandtke, 33–51. Jefferson, NC: McFarland.

———. 2007c. "The Tyranny of the Serial: Popular Geopolitics, the Nation, and Comic Book Discourse." *Antipode* 39:247–268.

———. 2009. "Fighting for Home: Masculinity and the Constitution of the Domestic in the Pages of *Tales of Suspense* and *Captain America*." In *Heroes of Film, Comics and American Culture: Essays on Real and Fictional Defenders of Home*, ed. L. DeTora, 96–115. Jefferson, NC: McFarland.

———. 2011. "Captain Britain and the Narration of Nation." *Geographical Review* 101:71–87.

———. Forthcoming. "Captain America in the News: Changing Mediascapes and the Appropriation of a Superhero." *Journal of Graphic Novels and Comics* 3.

Dittmer, J., and K. Dodds. 2008. "Popular Geopolitics Past and Future: Fandom, Identities and Audiences." *Geopolitics* 13:437–457.

Dittmer, J., and S. Larsen. 2007. "Captain Canuck, Audience Response, and the Project of Canadian Nationalism." *Social and Cultural Geography* 8:735–753.

———. 2010. "Aboriginality and the Arctic North in Canadian Nationalist Superhero Comics, 1940–2004." *Historical Geography* 38:52–69.

Dodds, K. 2003. "Licensed to Stereotype: Geopolitics, James Bond and the Spectre of Balkanism." *Geopolitics* 8:125–156.

———. 2005. "Screening Geopolitics: James Bond and the Early Cold War Films (1962–1967)." *Geopolitics* 10:266–289.

———. 2006. "Popular Geopolitics and Audience Dispositions: James Bond and the Internet Movie Database (IMDb)." *Transactions of the Institute of British Geographers* 31:116–130.

———. 2010. "Jason Bourne: Gender, Geopolitics, and Contemporary Representations of National Security." *Journal of Popular Film and Television* 38:21–33.

Domosh, M., and J. Seager. 2001. *Putting Women in Place: Feminist Geographers Make Sense of the World.* New York: Guilford Press.

Dow, J. 1997. *The Arrow.* Toronto: James Lorimer.

DuBose, M. 2009. "The Man behind the Mask? Models of Masculinity and the Persona of Heroes in Captain America Prose Novels." In *Captain America and the Struggle of the Superhero: Critical Essays*, ed. R. Weiner, 204–214. Jefferson, NC: McFarland.

Dutton, K. 1995. *The Perfectible Body: The Western Ideal of Male Physical Development.* London: Continuum.

Edwardson, R. 2003. "The Many Lives of Captain Canuck: Nationalism, Culture, and the Creation of a Canadian Comic Book Superhero." *Journal of Popular Culture* 37:184–201.

Elden, S. 2009. *Terror and Territory.* Minneapolis: University of Minnesota Press.

Ellis, W., and C. Jones. 1996a. "Counterfire." In *Excalibur #97*, ed. S. Gaffney, 1–19. New York: Marvel Comics.

———. 1996b. "After the Bomb." In *Excalibur #102*, ed. J. Gardner and M. Idelson, 1–21. New York: Marvel Comics.

Emad, M. 2006. "Reading Wonder Woman's Body: Mythologies of Gender and Nation." *Journal of Popular Culture* 39:964–984.

Englehart, S. 1974. "Believe It or Not: The Banshee!" In *Captain America #172*, ed. R. Thomas, 1–32. New York: Marvel Comics.

———. 2009. E-mail interview with author.

Englehart, S., and J. Buscema. 1972. "Captain America—Hero or Hoax?" In *Captain America and the Falcon #153*, ed. R. Thomas, 1–20. New York: Marvel Comics.

———. 1973. "Beware of Serpents." In *Captain America and the Falcon #163*, ed. R. Thomas, 1–30. New York: Marvel Comics.

———. 1974a. ". . . Before the Dawn!" In *Captain America and the Falcon #175*, ed. R. Thomas, 1–32. New York: Marvel Comics.

———. 1974b. "The Coming of the Nomad." In *Captain America and the Falcon #180*, ed. R. Thomas, 1–32. New York: Marvel Comics.

Englehart, S., and V. Colletta. 1974. "J'Accuse!" In *Captain America and the Falcon #170*, ed. R. Thomas, 1–32. New York: Marvel Comics.

Enloe, C. 1990. *Bananas, Beaches and Bases: Making Feminist Sense of International Politics*. Berkeley: University of California Press.

———. 2004. *The Curious Feminist: Searching for Women in a New Age of Empire*. Berkeley: University of California Press.

Entrikin, J. N. 1991. *The Betweenness of Place: Towards a Geography of Modernity*. Baltimore: Johns Hopkins University Press.

Evenden, M. 2009. "Mobilizing Rivers: Hydro-Electricity, the State, and World War II in Canada." *Annals of the Association of American Geographers* 99:845–855.

Fall, J. 2006. "Embodied Geographies, Naturalised Boundaries, and Uncritical Geopolitics in *La Frontiere Invisible*." *Environment and Planning D: Society and Space* 24:653–669.

———. 2010. "Artificial States? On the Enduring Geographical Myth of Natural Borders." *Political Geography* 29:140–147.

Fenton, N. 2008. "Mediating Hope: New Media, Politics and Resistance." *International Journal of Cultural Studies* 11:230–248.

Fingeroth, D. 2004. *Superman on the Couch: What Superheroes Really Tell Us about Ourselves and Our Society*. London: Continuum.

Fischer, C. 2003. "Fantastic Fascism? Jack Kirby, Nazi Aesthetics, and Klaus Theweleit's *Male Fantasies*." *International Journal of Comic Art* 5:334–354.

Fiske, J. 1988. *Television Culture*. London: Routledge.

Foucault, M. 1984. "What Is an Author?" In *The Foucault Reader*, ed. P. Rabinow, 101–120. New York: Pantheon Books.

Friedrich, G., L. Lieber, R. Wilson, B. Budiansky, and F. Kida. 1977a. "In the Shadow of the Hawk!" In *Captain Britain Weekly #31*, ed. L. Lieber, 1–7. London: Marvel UK.

———. 1977b. "Only the Strong Survive!" In *Captain Britain #32*, ed. L. Lieber, 2–8. London: Marvel UK.

Friedrich, G., and J. Romita. 1971. "Power to the People." In *Captain America and the Falcon #143*, ed. S. Lee, 1–31. New York: Marvel Comics.

Friedrich, G., and H. Trimpe. 1976. "Burn, Witch, Burn!" In *Captain Britain #11*, ed. L. Lieber, 1–8. London: Marvel UK.

———. 1977a. "From the Ashes." In *Captain Britain #13*, ed. L. Lieber, 1–8. London: Marvel UK.

———. 1977b. "Once upon a Death Wish." In *Captain Britain #15*, ed. L. Lieber, 1–9. London: Marvel UK.

Gage, C., and M. Perkins. 2006a. "London Falling, Part 1: Enemies of the Crown." In *Union Jack vol. 2, #1*, ed. A. Schmidt, 1–22. New York: Marvel Comics.

———. 2006b. "London Falling, Part 2." In *Union Jack vol. 2, #2*, ed. A. Schmidt, 2–22. New York: Marvel Comics.

Gagen, E. 2004. "Making America Flesh: Physicality and Nationhood in Early Twentieth-Century Physical Education Reform." *Cultural Geographies* 11:417–442.

Gaiman, N. 2003. *Marvel 1602.* New York: Marvel Comics.

Gaiman, N., and A. Kubert. 2004a. "1602 Part Seven." In *Marvel 1602 #7*, ed. N. Lowe, 1–23. New York: Marvel Comics.

———. 2004b. "1602 Part Eight." In *Marvel 1602 #8*, ed. N. Lowe, 1–35. New York: Marvel Comics.

Gainor, C. 2007. *Who Killed the Avro Arrow?* Edmonton, Canada: Lone Pine.

Garney, R., and M. Waid. 1998. "Sentinel of Liberty." In *Captain America: Sentinel of Liberty #1*, ed. M. Idelson, 1–32. New York: Marvel Comics.

Gerber, S., S. Buscema, M. Esposito, and J. Tartaglione. 1978. "Devastation!" In *Captain America #225*, ed. R. Stern, 1–32. New York: Marvel Comics.

Giddens, A. 1985. *The Nation-state and Violence.* Cambridge, UK: Polity Press.

Gittings, C. 1998. "Imaging Canada: The Singing Mountie and Other Commodifications of Nation." *Canadian Journal of Communication* 23. Available at http://www.cjc-online.ca/index.php/journal/article/viewArticle/1062/968.

Glut, D., and A. Kupperberg. 1978. "Five against the Flying Death." In *The Invaders #30*, ed. R. Thomas, 1–32. New York: Marvel Comics.

Gordon, L., and G. Okihiro. 2006. *Impounded: Dorothea Lange and the Censored Images of Japanese American Internment.* New York: Norton.

Goss, J. 2004. "Unforgiven and the Spirit of the Laws: Despotism, Monarchy and Democratic Virtue in Clint Eastwood's Last Western." *Film and History CD-ROM Annual.*

Grabham, E. 2009. "'Flagging' the Skin: Corporeal Nationalism and the Properties of Belonging." *Body and Society* 15:63–82.

Grace, S. 2001. *Canada and the Idea of North.* Montreal: McGill-Queen's University Press.

Gramsci, A. 1992. *Prison Notebooks.* New York: Columbia University Press.

Gravett, P., and P. Stanbury. 2006. *Great British Comics.* London: Aurum Press.

Gruenwald, M., and D. Carrasco. 1994. "Baron Ground." In *Captain America #432*, ed. M. Rockwitz, 1–31. New York: Marvel Comics.

Gruenwald, M., and K. Dwyer. 1988. "Out of Commission." In *Captain America #348*, ed. R. Macchio, 1–22. New York: Marvel Comics.

———. 1989. "Seeing Red." In *Captain America #350*, ed. R. Macchio, 1–41. New York: Marvel Comics.

Gruenwald, M., and D. Hoover. 1994. "The Next Generation." In *Captain America #431*, ed. M. Rockwitz, 1–23. New York: Marvel Comics.

———. 1995. "Everybody Hurts Sometime." In *Captain America #436*, ed. M. Rockwitz, 1–31. New York: Marvel Comics.

Gruenwald, M., and R. Levins. 1991a. "Pageant of Power." In *Captain America #389*, ed. R. Macchio, 1–23. New York: Marvel Comics.

———. 1991b. "No Man's Land." In *Captain America #391*, ed. R. Macchio, 1–23. New York: Marvel Comics.

———. 1992a. "Trick or Treat." In *Captain America #396*, ed. R. Macchio, 1–23. New York: Marvel Comics.

———. 1992b. "Dances with Werewolves." In *Captain America #405*, ed. R. Macchio, 1–31. New York: Marvel Comics.

———. 1992c. "Diamonds Are for Vengeance." In *Captain America #410*, ed. M. Rockwitz, 1–31. New York: Marvel Comics.

Gruenwald, M., R. Levins, and D. Bulanadi. 1993. Untitled. In *Captain America #416*, ed. M. Rockwitz, 1–31. New York: Marvel Comics.

Gruenwald, M., and R. Lim. 1990a. "Sold on Ice!" In *Captain America #372*, ed. R. Macchio, 1–23. New York: Marvel Comics.

———. 1990b. "The Devil You Know." In *Captain America #375*, ed. R. Macchio, 1–23. New York: Marvel Comics.

———. 1990c. "Grand Stand Play!" In *Captain America #378*, ed. R. Macchio, 1–23. New York: Marvel Comics.

———. 1991. "I Am Legend." In *Captain America #383*, ed. R. Macchio, 1–26. New York: Marvel Comics.

Gruenwald, M., and P. Neary. 1985. "Deface the Nation." In *Captain America #312*, ed. M. Carlin, 1–22. New York: Marvel Comics.

———. 1986a. "Asylum." In *Captain America #314*, ed. M. Carlin, 1–30. New York: Marvel Comics.

———. 1986b. "Justice Is Served!" In *Captain America #318*, ed. M. Carlin, 1–23. New York: Marvel Comics.

———. 1986c. "Super-Patriot Is Here." In *Captain America #323*, ed. D. Daley, 1–30. New York: Marvel Comics.

———. 1987. "Clashing Symbols." In *Captain America #327*, ed. D. Daley, 1–23. New York: Marvel Comics.

Haass, R. 2008. "The Age of Nonpolarity: What Will Follow U.S. Dominance." *Foreign Affairs* 87:44–56.

Haines, S. 2009. "The Influence of Operation Allied Force on the Development of the *Jus ad Bellum*." *International Affairs* 85:477–490.

Häkli, J. 2001. "In the Territory of Knowledge: State-Centred Discourses and the Construction of Society." *Progress in Human Geography* 25:403–422.

Herb, G. 2004. "Double Vision: Territorial Strategies in the Construction of National Identities in Germany, 1949–1979." *Annals of the Association of American Geographers* 94:140–164.

Higgins, M., and R. Lim. 1990. "The Eye of the Beholder." In *Excalibur #20*, ed. T. Kavanaugh, 1–31. New York: Marvel Comics.

Hixson, W. 2008. *The Myth of American Diplomacy: National Identity and U.S. Foreign Policy*. New Haven, CT: Yale University Press.

Hobbes, T. 1994. *Leviathan: With Selected Variants from the Latin Edition of 1668*. Indianapolis, IN: Hackett.

Hobsbawm, E., and T. Ranger. 1983. *The Invention of Tradition*. Cambridge: Cambridge University Press.

Hoffman, J. 2001. *Gender and Sovereignty: Feminism, the State and International Relations*. Basingstoke, UK: Palgrave Macmillan.

hooks, b. 1999. *Black Looks: Race and Representation*. New York: South End Press.

Hughes, J. A. 2006. "'Who Watches the Watchmen?': Ideology and 'Real World' Superheroes." *Journal of Popular Culture* 39:546–557.

Huntington, S. 1996. *The Clash of Civilizations and the Remaking of the World Order*. New York: Simon and Schuster.

Hutcheon, L. 1989. "Bakhtin and Parody." In *Rethinking Bakhtin: Extensions and Challenges*, ed. G. Morson and C. Emerson, 87–103. Evanston, IL: Northwestern University Press.

Jackson, P. T., and P. Mandaville. 2006. "Glocal Hero: Harry Potter Abroad." In *Harry Potter and International Relations*, ed. D. Nexon and I. Neumann, 45–59. Lanham, MD: Rowman and Littlefield.

Jackson, R. 1981. *Fantasy: The Literature of Subversion*. London: Methuen.

Jansson, D. 2003. "Internal Orientalism in America: W. J. Cash's *The Mind of the South* and the Spatial Construction of American National Identity." *Political Geography* 22:293–316.

Jeffords, S. 1994. *Hard Bodies: Hollywood Masculinity in the Reagan Era*. Piscataway, NJ: Rutgers University Press.

Jenkins, H. 1992. *Textual Poachers: Television Fans and Participatory Culture*. London: Routledge.

Jewett, R., and J. S. Lawrence. 2003. *Captain America and the Crusade against Evil: The Dilemma of Zealous Nationalism*. Grand Rapids, MI: Eerdmans.

Jones, G. 2004. *Men of Tomorrow: Geeks, Gangsters, and the Birth of the Comic Book*. New York: Basic Books.

Jurgens, D. 2001a. "Brothers." In *Captain America vol. 3, #37*, ed. J. Quesada, 1–22. New York: Marvel Comics.

———. 2001b. "Fractured." In *Captain America vol. 3, #42*, ed. B. Chase, 1–32. New York: Marvel Comics.

———. 2001c. "America Lost, Part II of IV." In *Captain America vol. 3, #46*, ed. B. Chase, 1–31. New York: Marvel Comics.

Jurgens, D., and A. Kubert. 2000. "Grotesqueries." In *Captain America vol. 3, #28*, ed. B. Harras, 1–23. New York: Marvel Comics.

Jurgens, D., and B. Layton. 2002. "To the Core." In *Captain America vol. 3, #50*, ed. B. Chase and A. Lis, 44–58. New York: Marvel Comics.

Jurgens, D., and G. Scott. 2000. "Who Is . . . Protocide?!" In *Captain America 2000*, ed. B. Chase, 1–30. New York: Marvel Comics.

Kennan, G. 1947. "The Sources of Soviet Conduct." *Foreign Affairs* 25:566–582.

King, C. R. 2009. "Alter/native Heroes: Native Americans, Comic Books, and the Struggle for Self-Definition." *Cultural Studies ↔ Critical Methodologies* 9:214–223.

Kirby, A. 2000. "The Construction of Geopolitical Images: The World according to Biggles (and Other Fictional Characters)." In *Geopolitical Traditions: A Century of Geopolitical Thought*, ed. K. Dodds and D. Adkinson, 52–71. London: Routledge.

Kirby, J. 1976. "Captain America's Love Story." In *Captain America and the Falcon #198*, ed. J. Kirby, 1–17. New York: Marvel Comics.

———. 1977a. "Face to Face with the Swine!" In *Captain America and the Falcon #206*, ed. J. Kirby, 1–17. New York: Marvel Comics.

———. 1977b. "The Tiger and the Swine!" In *Captain America #207*, ed. J. Kirby. New York: Marvel Comics.

———. 1977c. "Nazi X!" In *Captain America #211*, ed. J. Kirby, 1–32. New York: Marvel Comics.

Klock, G. 2002. *How to Read Superhero Comics and Why*. New York: Continuum.

Kneale, J. 2003. "Secondary Worlds: Reading Novels as Geographical Research." In *Cultural Geography in Practice*, ed. A. Blunt, P. Gruffudd, J. May, M. Ogborn, and D. Pinder, 39–51. London: Edward Arnold.

———. 2010. "Counterfactualism, Utopia, and Historical Geography: Kim Stanley Robinson's *The Years of Rice and Salt*." *Journal of Historical Geography* 36:297–304.

Kneale, J., and R. Kitchin. 2002. "Lost in Space." In *Lost in Space: Geographies of Science Fiction*, ed. R. Kitchin and J. Kneale, 1–16. London: Continuum.

Langlois, R. 2009. E-mail interview with author.

Langlois, R., and D. Langlois. 2004. "Heart of Gold." In *Captain Canuck: Unholy War #1*, ed. R. Comely, 1–22. Brandon, Canada: Comely Comics and Rev Studios.

Lee, S., and A. Avison. 1942a. "The Horde of the Vulture!" In *Captain America Comics #14*, ed. S. Lee, 1–19. New York: Timely Comics.

———. 1942b. "The Fiend That Was the Fakir!" In *Captain America Comics #20*, ed. S. Lee, 34–49. New York: Timely Comics.

———. 1942c. "Satan and the Sorcerer's Secret." In *Captain America Comics #21*, ed. S. Lee, 29–44. New York: Timely Comics.

Lee, S., and J. Buscema. 1969. "Now Begins the Nightmare!" In *Captain America #115*, ed. S. Lee, 1–20. New York: Marvel Comics.

Lee, S., and G. Colan. 1970a. "The Coming of the Man-Brute!" In *Captain America #121*, ed. S. Lee, 1–24. New York: Marvel Comics.

———. 1970b. "Suprema, the Deadliest of the Species!" In *Captain America #123*, ed. S. Lee, 1–20. New York: Marvel Comics.

———. 1970c. "The Fate of the Falcon!" In *Captain America #126*, ed. S. Lee, 1–31. New York: Marvel Comics.

———. 1970d. "The Vengeance of the Red Skull." In *Captain America #129*, ed. S. Lee, 1–32. New York: Marvel Comics.

———. 1970e. "Bucky Reborn!" In *Captain America #131*, ed. S. Lee, 1–24. New York: Marvel Comics.

———. 1971. "The World Below." In *Captain America and the Falcon #136*, ed. S. Lee, 1–30. New York: Marvel Comics.

Lee, S., and J. Kirby. 1966. "He Who Holds the Cosmic Cube." In *Tales of Suspense #80*, ed. S. Lee, 13–22. New York: Marvel Comics.

———. 1968. "When Wakes the Sleeper!" In *Captain America #101*, ed. S. Lee, 1–20. New York: Marvel Comics.

Lee, S., and D. Rico. 1942. "The Mikado's Shell." In *Captain America Comics #18*, ed. S. Lee, 30–46. New York: Timely Comics.

Lee, S., and J. Romita. 1971a. "The Badge and the Betrayal." In *Captain America and the Falcon #139*, ed. S. Lee, 1–31. New York: Marvel Comics.

———. 1971b. "The Unholy Alliance." In *Captain America and the Falcon #141*, ed. S. Lee, 1–19. New York: Marvel Comics.

Lee, S., J. Romita, and J. Buscema. 1969. "The Man behind the Mask!" In *Captain America #114*, ed. S. Lee, 1–20. New York: Marvel Comics.

Leib, J. 2004. "Robert E. Lee, 'Race,' Representation, and Redevelopment along Richmond's Canal Walk." *Southeastern Geographer* 44:236–262.

Liefield, R., and J. Loeb. 1997. "Fire." In *Captain America vol. 2, #4*, ed. B. Harras, 1–22. New York: Marvel Comics.

Lobdell, S., C. Cooper, K. Junior, and P. Abrams. 1994. "Beginnings, Middles and Endings." In *Excalibur #81*, ed. S. Gaffney, 1–23. New York: Marvel Comics.

Lobdell, S., and S. Kolins. 1992. "Enter . . . the Panther." In *Excalibur #59*, ed. T. Kavanagh, 1–32. New York: Marvel Comics.

———. 1993. "Braddock of the Jungle." In *Excalibur #60*, ed. T. Kavanagh, 1–32. New York: Marvel Comics.

Locke, S. 2005. "Fantastically Reasonable: Ambivalence in the Representation of Science and Technology in Super-hero Comics." *Public Understanding of Science* 14:25–46.

Lockhart, C. 2003. *The Roots of American Exceptionalism: History, Institutions, and Culture.* New York: Palgrave Macmillan.

Lofficier, J.-M., and R. Lofficier. 2004. *Shadowmen 2: Heroes and Villains of French Comics.* Encino, CA: Black Coat Press.

Lopes, P. 2009. *Demanding Respect: The Evolution of the American Comic Book.* Philadelphia: Temple University Press.

Lunning, F. 2008. "Giant Robots and Superheroes: Manifestations of Divine Power, East and West: An Interview with Crispin Freeman." *Mechademia* 3:274–282.

Madrid, M. 2009. *The Supergirls: Fashion, Feminism, Fantasy, and the History of Comic Book Heroines.* Minneapolis, MN: Exterminating Angel Press.

Madsen, D. 1998. *American Exceptionalism.* Jackson: University Press of Mississippi.

Mantlo, B., and J. Brigman. 1987. "Specters!" In *Alpha Flight #52*, ed. C. Potts, 1–22. New York: Marvel Comics.

Mantlo, B., and J. Lee. 1988. "Warped!" In *Alpha Flight #56*, ed. C. Potts, 1–32. New York: Marvel Comics.

Mantlo, B., and M. Mignola. 1985. "Cut Bait and Run!" In *Alpha Flight #29*, ed. C. Potts, 1–22. New York: Marvel Comics.

———. 1986. "The Grateful Dead!" In *Alpha Flight #31*, ed. C. Potts, 1–31. New York: Marvel Comics.

Mantlo, B., and D. Ross. 1987. "Strike across the Border!" In *Alpha Flight #43*, ed. C. Potts, 1–32. New York: Marvel Comics.

Matton, A. 2000. "Reader Responses to Doug Murray's *The 'Nam*." *International Journal of Comic Art* 2:33–44.

McDermott, M. 2009. "The Invaders and the All-Star Squadron: Roy Thomas Revisits the Golden Age." In *Captain America and the Struggle of the Superhero: Critical Essays*, ed. R. Weiner, 36–52. Jefferson, NC: McFarland.

McHale, B. 1987. *Postmodern Fictions.* London: Routledge.

McKenzie, R., M. Fleisher, S. Buscema, and D. Perlin. 1979. "Death Dive!" In *Captain America #236*, ed. R. Stern, 1–31. New York: Marvel Comics.

McLain, K. 2009. *India's Immortal Comic Books: Gods, Kings, and Other Heroes.* Bloomington: Indiana University Press.

McPherson, T. 2003. *Reconstructing Dixie: Race, Gender, and Nostalgia in the Imagined South.* Durham, NC: Duke University Press.

McWilliams, O. 2009. "Not Just Another Racist Honkey: A History of Racial Representation in *Captain America* and Related Publications." In *Captain America and the Struggle of the Superhero: Critical Essays*, ed. R. Weiner, 66–78. Jefferson, NC: McFarland.

Mercer, K. 1994. *Welcome to the Jungle: New Positions in Black Cultural Studies.* London: Routledge.

Millar, M., and B. Hitch. 2002a. "21st Century Boy." In *The Ultimates vol. 1, #3*, ed. R. Macchio, 1–22. New York: Marvel Comics.

———. 2002b. "Thunder." In *The Ultimates vol. 1, #4*, ed. R. Macchio, 1–22. New York: Marvel Comics.

———. 2002c. "Giant-Man vs. The Wasp." In *The Ultimates vol. 1, #6*, ed. R. Macchio, 1–23. New York: Marvel Comics.

———. 2005a. "The Trial of the Hulk." In *The Ultimates vol. 2, #3*, ed. R. Macchio, 1–24. New York: Marvel Comics.

———. 2005b. "The Passion." In *The Ultimate vol. 2, #5*, ed. R. Macchio, 1–25. New York: Marvel Comics.

———. 2006a. "Grand Theft America." In *The Ultimates vol. 2, #9*, ed. R. Macchio, 1–29. New York: Marvel Comics.

———. 2006b. "America Strikes Back." In *The Ultimates vol. 2, #11*, ed. R. Macchio, 1–29. New York: Marvel Comics.

Millar, M., and D. Johnson. 2003. *Superman: Red Son.* New York: DC Comics.

Mitchell, R. 2000. *Myth and National Identity in Nineteenth-Century Britain: The Legends of King Arthur and Robin Hood.* Oxford: Oxford University Press.

Moore, A., and J. Cooke. 2000. "Toasting Absent Heroes: Alan Moore Discusses the Charlton-Watchmen Connection." *Comic Book Artist,* June 16. Available at http://twomorrows.com/comicbookartist/articles/09moore.html.

Morganthou, H. 1960. *Politics among Nations: The Struggle for Power and Peace.* New York: Knopf.

Morrison, G. 2011. *Supergods.* New York: Spiegel and Grau.

Morson, G., and C. Emerson. 1990. *Mikhail Bakhtin: The Creation of a Prosaics.* Stanford, CA: Stanford University Press.

Müller, M. 2008. "Reconsidering the Concept of Discourse for the Field of Critical Geopolitics: Towards Discourse as Language and Practice." *Political Geography* 27:322–338.

Murphy, A. 1996. "The Sovereign State as Political-Territorial Ideal." In *State Sovereignty as Social Construct,* ed. T. Biersteker and C. Weber, 81–120. Cambridge: Cambridge University Press.

Murray, C. 2000. "*Pop*aganda: Superhero Comics and Propaganda in World War II." In *Comics and Culture: Analytical and Theoretical Approaches to Comics,* ed. A. Magnussen and H. C. Christiansen, 141–156. Copenhagen: Museum Tusculanum Press.

Nama, A. 2009. "Brave, Black Worlds: Black Superheroes as Science Fiction Ciphers." *African Identities* 7:133–144.

Naremore, J. 2008. *More Than Night: Film Noir in Its Contexts.* Berkeley: University of California Press.

Neale, S. 1993. "Masculinity as Spectacle: Reflections on Men and Mainstream Cinema." In *Screening the Male: Exploring Masculinities in Hollywood Cinema,* ed. S. Cohan and I. R. Hark, 9–20. London: Routledge.

Newsinger, J. 1986. "Lord Greystoke and Darkest Africa: The Politics of the Tarzan Stories." *Race and Class* 28:59–71.

Nicieza, F., and K. Maguire. 1991. "First Flight of the Eagle." In *The Adventures of Captain America #1,* ed. M. Rockwitz, 1–46. New York: Marvel Comics.

Nonnekes, P. 2008. *Northern Love: An Exploration of Canadian Masculinity.* Edmonton, Canada: Athabasca University Press.

Norcliffe, G., and O. Rendace. 2003. "New Geographies of Comic Book Production in North America: The New Artisan, Distancing, and the Periodic Social Economy." *Economic Geography* 79:241–263.

Nyberg, A. K. 1998. *Seal of Approval: The History of the Comics Code.* Jackson: University Press of Mississippi.

Olwig, K. 2008. "Landscape, Monuments, and National Identity." In *Nations and Nationalism: A Global Historical Overview,* ed. G. Herb and D. Kaplan, 59–71. Santa Barbara, CA: ABC-CLIO.

Ó Tuathail, G. 1996. *Critical Geopolitics.* Minneapolis: University of Minnesota Press.

———. 2005. "The Frustrations of Geopolitics and the Pleasures of War: *Behind Enemy Lines* and American Geopolitical Culture." *Geopolitics* 10:356–377.

Paasi, A. 2003. "Territory." In *A Companion to Political Geography,* ed. J. Agnew, K. Mitchell, and G. Ó Tuathail, 109–122. Oxford: Blackwell.

Pease, D. 2009. *The New American Exceptionalism.* Minneapolis: University of Minnesota Press.

Peterson, B., and E. Gerstein. 2005. "Fighting and Flying: Archival Analysis of Threat, Authoritarianism, and the North American Comic Book." *Political Psychology* 26:887–904.

Peterson, V. 1992. *Gendered States: Feminist (Re)visions of International Relations Theory.* Boulder, CO: Lynne Rienner.

Pfaff, W. 2009. *The Irony of Manifest Destiny: The Tragedy of America's Foreign Policy.* New York: Walker.

Power, M., and A. Crampton. 2005. "Reel Geopolitics: Cinemato-graphing Political Space." *Geopolitics* 10:193–203.

Puar, J. 2007. *Terrorist Assemblages: Homonationalism in Queer Times.* Durham, NC: Duke University Press.

Raab, B., and J. Cassaday. 1999. "Faith." In *Union Jack #2,* ed. T. Brevoort and B. Harras, 1–32. New York: Marvel Comics.

Raab, B., and S. Larroca. 1997. "Dragon Moon Rising." In *Excalibur #109,* ed. M. Idelson, 1–22. New York: Marvel Comics.

Raento, P. 2006. "Communicating Geopolitics through Postage Stamps: The Case of Finland." *Geopolitics* 11:601–629.

Raento, P., and S. Brunn. 2000. "Picturing a Nation: Finland on Postage Stamps, 1917–2000." *National Identities* 10:49–75.

———. 2005. "Visualizing Finland: Postage Stamps as Political Messengers. *Geografiska Annaler, Series B* 87:145–164.

Rasmussen, C., and M. Brown. 2005. "The Body Politic as Spatial Metaphor." *Citizenship Studies* 9:469–584.

Reynolds, R. 1992. *Superheroes: A Modern Mythology.* Jackson: University Press of Mississippi.

Rieber, J. N., and J. Cassaday. 2002a. "Dust." In *Captain America vol. 4, #1,* ed. S. Moore, 1–32. New York: Marvel Comics.

———. 2002b. "One Nation." In *Captain America vol. 4, #2,* ed. S. Moore, 1–32. New York: Marvel Comics.

Ro, R. 2004. *Tales to Astonish: Jack Kirby, Stan Lee, and the American Comic Book Revolution.* New York: Bloomsbury.

Robinson, J., and J. Phillips. 1997. "Crossroads." In *Captain America vol. 2, #7,* ed. M. Heisler and M. Rockwitz, 1–22. New York: Marvel Comics.

Robinson, L. 2004. *Wonder Women: Feminisms and Superheroes.* New York: Routledge.

Romita, J. 1953. "Back from the Dead!" In *Young Men #24,* ed. S. Lee, 12–17. New York: Atlas Comics.

Said, E. 1983. "Opponents, Audiences, Constituencies and Community." In *Postmodern Culture,* ed. H. Foster, 135–159. London: Pluto.

Saldanha, A. 2008. "The Political Geography of Many Bodies." In *The SAGE Handbook of Political Geography,* ed. K. Cox, M. Low, and J. Robinson, 323–333. Los Angeles: Sage.

Sasson-Levy, O. 2003. "Feminism and Military Gender Practices: Israeli Women Soldiers in 'Masculine' Roles." *Sociological Inquiry* 73:440–465.

Schlereth, T. 1994. "Columbia, Columbus, and Columbianism." In *Discovering America: Essays on the Search for an Identity,* ed. D. Thelen and F. Hoxie, 103–134. Chicago: University of Illinois Press.

Schott, G. 2010. "From Fan Appropriation to Industry Re-appropriation: The Sexual Identity of Comic Superheroes." *Journal of Graphic Novels and Comics* 1:17–29.

Scott, A. B. 2006. "Superpower vs. Supernatural: Black Superheroes and the Quest for a Mutant Reality." *Journal of Visual Culture* 5:295–314.

Shetterly, W. 2011. E-mail interview with author.

Shetterly, W., and V. Stone. 1986. "The Making of a Hero." In *Captain Confederacy #1*, ed. W. Shetterly, 1–28. Minneapolis, MN: SteelDragon Press.

———. 1987. "Passages." In *Captain Confederacy #7*, ed. W. Shetterly, 1–20. Minneapolis, MN: SteelDragon Press.

———. 1991a. "Crossroad." In *Captain Confederacy vol. 2, #1*, ed. N. Yomtov, 1–28. New York: Epic Comics.

———. 1991b. "The Last Fair Deal Gone Down." In *Captain Confederacy vol. 2, #2*, ed. N. Yomtov, 1–28. New York: Epic Comics.

Shores, S. 1943. "The Curse of the Yellow Scourge." In *Captain America Comics #30*, ed. V. Fago, 28–33. New York: Timely Comics.

Shores, S., and V. Alascia. 1948. "The Singer Who Wanted to Fight!" In *Captain America Comics #67*, ed. S. Lee, 19–27. New York: Timely Comics.

Sim, D. 1973. "A Conversation with Adrian and Pat Dingle and Bill Thomas." *Now and Then Times* 1:27–29.

Simon, J., and J. Kirby. 1940. "Case #1: Meet Captain America." In *Captain America Comics #1*, ed. J. Simon, 1–8. New York: Timely Comics.

Singer, M. 2008. "Embodiments of the Real: The Counterlinguistic Turn in the Comic-book Novel." *Critique* 49:273–289.

*Sir Gawain and the Green Knight*. 2006. London: Penguin Classics.

Skidmore, M., and J. Skidmore. 1983. "More Than Mere Fantasy: Political Themes in Contemporary Comic Books." *Journal of Popular Culture* 17:83–92.

Smith, N. 2004. *American Empire: Roosevelt's Geographer and the Prelude to Globalization*. Berkeley: University of California Press.

———. 2005. *The Endgame of Globalization*. London: Routledge.

Smith, W. D. 1980. "Friedrich Ratzel and the Origins of Lebensraum." *German Studies Review* 3:51–68.

Spanos, W. 2008. *American Exceptionalism in the Age of Globalization: The Specter of Vietnam*. Albany: State University of New York Press.

Sparke, M. 2000. "Excavating the Future in Cascadia: Geoeconomics and the Imagined Geographies of a Cross Border Region." *BC Studies* 127:5–45.

———. 2005. *In the Space of Theory: Postfoundational Geographies of the Nation-state*. Minneapolis: University of Minnesota Press.

Stepan, N. 1991. *The Hour of Eugenics: Race, Gender, and Nation in Latin America*. Ithaca, NY: Cornell University Press.

Stern, R., and J. Byrne. 1981. "The Living Legend." In *Captain America #255*, ed. J. Salicrup, 1–22. New York: Marvel Comics.

Stevens, J. R. 2007. "The Ultimate Critique: Neoconservatism, Captain America and Marvel's *Ultimates*." Paper presented at the Midwest Popular Culture Association/ Midwest American Culture Association meeting, Kansas City, MO.

———. 2011. "'Let's Rap with Cap': Redefining American Patriotism through Popular Discourse and Letters." *Journal of Popular Culture* 44:606–632.

Sutliff, J. 2009. "The Ultimate American?" In *Captain America and the Struggle of the Superhero: Critical Essays*, ed. R. Weiner, 121–124. Jefferson, NC: McFarland.

Sylvester, C. 2002. *Feminist International Relations: An Unfinished Journey*. Cambridge: Cambridge University Press.

Tait, S. 2008. "Pornographies of Violence? Internet Spectatorship on Body Horror." *Critical Studies in Media Communication* 25:91–111.

Taylor, A. 2007. "'He's Gotta Be Strong, and He's Gotta Be Fast, and He's Gotta Be Larger Than Life': Investigating the Engendered Superhero Body." *Journal of Popular Culture* 40:344–360.

Taylor, P. 1996. "Embedded Statism and the Social Sciences: Opening Up to New Spaces." *Environment and Planning A* 28:1917–1995.

———. 1999. *Modernities: A Geohistorical Interpretation.* Minneapolis: University of Minnesota Press.

Terkel, S. 1997. *The Good War: An Oral History of World War II.* New York: New Press.

Thomas, Ronald. 2009. "Hero of the Military-Industrial Complex: Reading *Iron Man* through Burke's Dramatism." In *Heroes of Film, Comics and American Culture: Essays on Real and Fictional Defenders of Home*, ed. L. DeTora, 152–166. Jefferson, NC: McFarland.

Thomas, Roy, R. Buckler, and D. Ayers. 1975. "Red Skull in the Sunset." In *The Invaders #5*, ed. R. Thomas, 1–18. New York: Marvel Comics.

Thomas, Roy, D. Glut, A. Kupperberg, and D. Heck. 1979. "U-Man Comes to Town." In *The Invaders #38*, ed. R. Thomas, 1–31. New York: Marvel Comics.

Thomas, Roy, and F. Robbins. 1976. "The Blackout Murders of Baron Blood!" In *The Invaders #7*, ed. R. Thomas, 1–17. New York: Marvel Comics.

———. 1977. "The Scarab of the Nile." In *The Invaders #23*, ed. A. Goodwin, 1–32. New York: Marvel Comics.

———. 1978. "The Power and the Panzers." In *The Invaders #25*, ed. R. Thomas, 1–31. New York: Marvel Comics.

Thomas, Roy, F. Robbins, and F. Springer. 1977. "The Golem Walks Again." In *The Invaders #13*, ed. R. Thomas, 1–31. New York: Marvel Comics.

Tilly, C. 2002. *Stories, Identities, and Political Change.* Lanham, MD: Rowman and Littlefield.

Trushell, J. 2004. "American Dreams of Mutants: The X-Men; 'Pulp' Fiction, Science Fiction, and Superheroes." *Journal of Popular Culture* 38:149–168.

Tyner, J. 2004. "Territoriality, Social Justice and Gendered Revolutions in the Speeches of Malcolm X." *Transactions of the Institute of British Geographers* 29:330–343.

Vaughan, B., and S. Harris. 1999. "An Ending." In *Captain America: Sentinel of Liberty #7*, ed. M. Idelson, 13–22. New York: Marvel Comics.

Venezia, T. 2010. "Archives, Alan Moore and the Historio-graphic Novel." *International Journal of Comic Art* 12:183–199.

Verheiden, M., and C. Marrinan. 1992. "Lost in America, Part 3." In *The American: Lost in America*, ed. R. Stradley and J. Bricker, 1–24. Milwaukie, OR: Dark Horse Comics.

Verheiden, M., and G. Miehm. 1988. "The Reality, Part 1." In *The American #7*, ed. R. Stradley, 1–24. Milwaukie, OR: Dark Horse Comics.

Vincent, A. 1987. *Theories of the State.* Oxford: Blackwell.

Waid, M., and R. Garney. 1995. "Hope and Glory." In *Captain America #444*, ed. R. Macchio, 1–30. New York: Marvel Comics.

———. 1998a. "The Return of Steve Rogers, Captain America." In *Captain America vol. 3, #1*, ed. M. Idelson, 1–34. New York: Marvel Comics.

———. 1998b. "Credibility Gap." In *Captain America vol. 3, #5*, ed. M. Idelson, 1–23. New York: Marvel Comics.

Waid, M., and C. Hamner. 1999. "Flashpoint." In *Captain America: Sentinel of Liberty #8*, ed. B. Harras, 1–22. New York: Marvel Comics.

Waid, M., and A. Kubert. 1998. "The Growing Darkness." In *Captain America vol. 3, #10*, ed. M. Idelson, 1–22. New York: Marvel Comics.

Walker, R.B.J. 2010. *After the Globe, Before the World*. London: Routledge.

Warf, B. 2002. "The Way It Wasn't: Alternative Histories, Contingent Geographies." In *Lost in Space: Geographies of Science Fiction*, ed. R. Kitchin and J. Kneale, 17–38. London: Continuum.

Warner, J., and F. Robbins. 1975. "The Madness Maze!" In *Captain America and the Falcon #187*, ed. L. Wein, 1–31. New York: Marvel Comics.

Weber, C. 1999. *Faking It: U.S. Hegemony in a "Post-phallic" Era*. Minneapolis: University of Minnesota Press.

———. 2005. *Imagining America at War: Morality, Politics and Film*. London: Routledge.

Weiner, R. 2009. "Sixty-Five Years of Guilt over the Death of Bucky." In *Captain America and the Struggle of the Superhero: Critical Essays*, ed. R. Weiner, 90–103. Jefferson, NC: McFarland.

Weinstein, M. 2006. "Captain America, Tuskegee, Belmont, and Righteous Guinea Pigs: Considering Scientific Ethics through Official and Subaltern Perspectives." *Science and Education* 17:961–975.

Weitz, E. 2003. *A Century of Genocide: Utopias of Race and Nation*. Princeton, NJ: Princeton University Press.

Williams, A. 2011. "Reconceptualizing Spaces of the Air: Performing the Multiple Spatialities of UK Military Airspaces." *Transactions of the Institute of British Geographers* 36:253–267.

Williams, R. 2009. E-mail interview with author.

Williams, R., T. Hairsine, and T. Foreman. 2009. *Cla$$war: Series 1, collected edition*. London: Com.x.

Wolf-Meyer, M. 2003. "The World Ozymandias Made: Utopias in the Superhero Comic, Subculture, and the Conservation of Difference." *Journal of Popular Culture* 36: 497–517.

Wright, B. 2001. *Comic Book Nation: The Transformation of Youth Culture in America*. Baltimore: Johns Hopkins University Press.

# Index

**Jason Dittmer** is Reader in Human Geography at University College London. He is the author of *Popular Culture, Geopolitics, and Identity* and coeditor (with Tristan Sturm) of *Mapping the End Times: American Evangelical Geopolitics and Apocalyptic Visions.*